C# Threading Handbook

Tobin Titus
Fabio Claudio Ferracchiati
Tejaswi Redkar
Srinivasa Sivakumar

® Wrox Press Ltd.

C# Threading Handbook

© 2003 Wrox Press Ltd

First published March 2003

Some material first published in a different form in
Visual Basic .NET Threading Handbook (1-86100-713-2), June 2002

Published by Wrox Press Ltd,
Arden House, 1102 Warwick Road, Acocks Green,
Birmingham, B27 6BH
United Kingdom
Printed in the United States
ISBN 1-86100-829-5

Trademark Acknowledgments

Credits

Authors
Tobin Titus
Fabio Claudio Ferracchiati
Tejaswi Redkar
Srinivasa Sivakumar

Additional Material
Kourosh Ardestani
Sandra Gopikrishna
Andrew Polshaw

Commissioning Editors
Nick Manning
Andrew Polshaw

Technical Editors
James Hart
Nick Manning
Douglas Patterson

Project Manager
Beckie Stones

Managing Editor
Emma Batch

Technical Reviewers
Kourosh Ardestani
Richard Bonneau
Mark Horner
Craig McQueen
Saurabh Nandu
Erick Sgarbi
David Whitney

Publisher
Jan Kolasinski

Index
Michael Brinkman

Production Coordinator
Neil Lote

Proof Reader
Chris Smith

Cover
Natalie O'Donnell

About the Authors

Tobin Titus

Tobin has several years of experience in software development and in the consulting industry. He started working with BASIC in the 5th grade on an Atari 800XL computer. With the release of Visual Basic, Tobin moved to Windows programming and has been developing Windows and web-based solutions ever since. Tobin specializes in internet applications solutions with Visual Basic, Java, and now Microsoft .NET tools – VB.NET, C#, and ASP.NET. He is also authoring the BrainBench certification exam on Visual Basic .NET (www.brainbench.com). Currently, Tobin does work for some of the best companies in the world including his own – Dax Software and Consulting, LLC (www.daxsoftware.com).

Thanks go to everyone who has supported me in my career. To the staff at Bethel Christian High School in Pennsylvania and Bob Jones University in South Carolina, thank you for your unfailing faith and uncompromising positions. Thanks go to Carol, for putting up with my never-ending work schedule. Special thanks to my parents who sacrificed so much for our family. And a special loving memory to my Grandmother Helm who was always able to encourage me to do better with just a simple hug – and maybe a little taste of fudge!

Fabio Claudio Ferracchiati

Fabio Claudio Ferracchiati is a software developer and technical writer. In the early years of his ten-year career he worked with classical languages and 'old' Microsoft tools like Visual Basic and Visual C++. After five years he decided to dedicate his attention to the Internet and all the related technologies. In 1998 he started a parallel career writing technical articles for Italian and international magazines. He works in Rome for CPI Progetti Spa (http://www.cpiprogetti.it), where he develops Internet/Intranet solutions using Microsoft technologies. Fabio would like to thank Wrox for the chance to write this book.

> *Dedication to Danila: As in every book I write and will write, a special thank you goes to my unique love. You can't imagine how is important to have a woman like her near me in the happy and sad moments that life gives to us. I love you so much...*

Tejaswi Redkar

Tejaswi Redkar is a software evangelist. He holds a Master's degree in Engineering from San Jose State University, California. His areas of interest include designing scalable multi-tiered distributed applications and new generation embedded devices. Recently he filed a patent for his innovations in managing telemetry gateways. When he is not working he can be found eating exotic food.

> *I would like to thank Wrox Press for giving me the opportunity to express my ideas through articles. I would also like to thank my dear wife Arohi for continuing to motivate me.*

Srinivasa Sivakumar

Srinivasa Sivakumar is a software consultant, developer, and writer. He specializes in web and mobile technologies using Microsoft solutions. He currently works at Chicago for TransTech, LLC. He has co-authored various books, including *Professional ASP.NET Web Services, ASP.NET Mobile Controls – Tutorial Guide*, .NET Compact Framework, *Beginning ASP.NET 1.0 with VB.NET, Professional ASP.NET Security, The Complete Visual C# Programmer's Reference Guide*, and *.NET Compact Framework*. He has also written technical articles for *ASP Today, C# Today, .NET Developer*, and more. In his free time he likes to watch Tamil movies and listen to Tamil sound tracks (Especially ones sung by Mr. S.P Balasubramaniyam).

C#
Threading

Handbook

Table of
Contents

Table of Contents

C#

Threading

Handbook

Introduction

Introduction

Multithreading is what enables complex applications to appear to be performing numerous tasks at the same time. They may respond to user events, while at the same time accessing network resources, or the file system. Such concurrent applications are written in different ways depending on the platform and the operating system, giving varying control over this process. Visual Basic 6, for instance, gave you little or no control, and it would implement threading behind the scenes, so that when an event occurred, it would execute the appropriate handling code within a particular threading model, but the application programmer never needed to concern themself with it. Visual C++ developers had access to the full complexity of the Windows threading and process model, but with great power comes great responsibility: C++ programmers could easily create multithreaded monsters, and had to learn and use a range of complex tricks to ensure that the threads were kept under control.

The .NET Framework's managed coding environment has made available a full and powerful threading model that allows you to control exactly what runs in a thread, when the thread exits, and how much data it should have access to. However, just as the Common Language Runtime has taken responsibility for memory management out of the hands of programmers, it has also taken much of the responsibility for managing and cleaning up threads. So, in .NET we have a happy medium between the power of C++ and the simplicity of Visual Basic. That said, multithreaded applications introduce a whole range of programming problems that single-threaded programs never encounter.

This book will teach you how to take advantage of the threading capabilities provided by the .NET Framework, guiding you through the various features made available to you, while pointing out pitfalls for you to avoid.

When is threading used? Well, in fact, all programs execute in threads, so understanding how .NET and Windows execute threads will help you understand just what's going on inside your program at run time. Windows Forms applications use event-loop threads to handle user interface events. Separate forms execute on separate threads, so if you need to communicate between Windows Forms, you need to communicate between threads. ASP.NET pages execute inside the multi-threaded environment of IIS – separate requests for the same page may execute on different threads, and the same page may be executing on more than one thread simultaneously. When accessing shared resources from an ASP.NET page, you'll encounter threading issues.

As well as writing code that is executed in a multithreaded environment such as this, we often need to take control and actively create and control our own threads. Perhaps you need to create an application that never or rarely waits while processing some data, and is permanently available to respond to users and events. This can only happen if you build a multithreaded application. You can find many articles on the Web, and chapters in other books that tell you how to create a thread with the .NET Framework and how to perform some rudimentary operations; however, implementing the code is only half of the story. When you are using a multithreaded application, the type of operations that would normally block your application, such as file system operations, and so are ideal candidates for threading, are the kinds of operations that could produce synchronization or scalability issues, as more than one thread could be operating on the same file at the same time. This book, apart from teaching you how to create and manipulate threads, teaches you how to design your application so that you can avoid many of these issues by applying the appropriate kind of lock, and not blocking a thread while it waits for some other operation to complete.

Who Is This Book For?

This book is for C# developers who want to explore the full capabilities of the .NET platform. If you want to understand how C# code is executed inside the .NET Runtime, write code which is safe to execute in a multi-threaded system, and create and control threads in your own code, then this book will help you.

This book assumes you're already coding with C#, you're already familiar with the basic syntax, and you're regularly writing code that works. You should be familiar with your chosen development tools and know how to compile and run C# code.

What Will You Learn?

The book takes a top-down look at how exactly .NET executes C# code. We begin by describing what a Windows thread is, and how threads relate to .NET processes, application domains, and threads. We examine thread scheduling (how the operating system decides which thread to process next), then look at how we write .NET code to work with threads. Then we look at thread synchronization, so that we can safely allow multiple threads to access the same resources. We look at some typical architectures that multithreaded programs employ, in particular thread pooling. We also examine how to debug multithreaded code. We finish with a fully worked example showing how threading can help us build a scalable, high performance network server.

Chapter by chapter, here's what to expect:

❏ **Chapter 1 – Defining Threads**

This chapter explains what exactly a thread is, what role threads play in .NET, and how threads are created, executed, and terminated in the operating system.

❏ **Chapter 2 – Threading in .NET**

In the second chapter, we examine how the concepts explored in Chapter 1 are implemented in .NET. We see how C# code can create threads, access information about their state and lifecycle, and perform basic operations like sleeping, stopping, and interrupting.

❏ **Chapter 3 – Working with Threads**

This chapter explores in more depth how we can work with multiple threads in an application. We look at synchronization and locking, to ensure exclusive access to data by one thread at a time, and examine the danger of deadlock, and how to avoid it.

❏ **Chapter 4 – Threading Design Principles**

In this chapter, we look at some of the common patterns employed in multithreaded code – architectures that we can use confidently, knowing that if we implement them following these tried and tested principles, we should avoid the dangers of deadlocks.

❏ **Chapter 5 – Scaling Threaded Applications**

We can't go on creating threads forever – there is, with threads, a law of diminishing returns. Often, however, when we want to execute multiple simultaneous tasks on separate threads, we can achieve the effect without spawning more and more threads by employing a thread pool. This chapter examines .NET's own thread pool, and how to implement your own.

❏ **Chapter 6 – Debugging and Tracing Threads**

Multithreaded applications can be much more complex to debug. This chapter examines some of .NET's most useful debugging tools, and explains how to use them to debug multithreaded code.

❏ **Chapter 7 – Networking and Threading**

Networking operations can be slow in a single-threaded program. The application spends a lot of its time waiting for traffic to travel across the network, and during that time, it is doing nothing. Multithreading is therefore a common requirement in network applications, enabling them to get on with other activities while waiting for network traffic. In this chapter, we look at how threading can enable us to build a fast, scalable network server.

What Do You Need?

To make use of this book, you need to be able to compile and execute code written in C#. This means you will require either:

❑ The .NET Framework SDK obtainable from Microsoft's MSDN site (http://msdn.microsoft.com), in the Software Development Kits category. The download page at time of publication could be reached via the following URL:

http://msdn.microsoft.com/downloads/sample.asp?
url=/msdn-files/027/000/976/msdncompositedoc.xml

❑ A version of Visual Studio .NET that incorporates Visual C# .NET. The 2002 edition of the Visual C# .NET IDE is included with the following Microsoft products:

- Microsoft Visual C# .NET Standard

- Microsoft Visual Studio .NET Enterprise Architect

- Microsoft Visual Studio .NET Enterprise Developer

- Microsoft Visual Studio .NET Professional

The product homepage is at http://msdn.microsoft.com/vstudio/.

There are several .NET implementations for other platforms underway, and support for C# compilation on Linux, UNIX, and Windows is provided by the Mono project (http://www.go-mono.com/). Mono code does not have access to the full Microsoft .NET class library, but follows the same syntactic rules as Microsoft's C#. The threading model is not guaranteed to be the same as it is in .NET, but implementations of the classes and facilities described in this book are part of the Mono platform's goals, so the lessons described in this book should apply. However, the code in this book has not been tested with Mono.

C#

Threading

Handbook

1

1

Defining Threads

Threading is the ability of a development framework to spin off parts of an application into "threads", which run out of step with the rest of the program. In most programming languages, you have the equivalent of a Main() method, and each line is executed in sequence, with the next line executing only after the previous has completed. A thread is a special object that is part of the general multitasking abilities of an operating system and allows a part of the application to run independently from the execution of other objects, and so out of the general **execution sequence** of the application. In this chapter, we will also discuss the different types of multitasking.

Another concept is that of **free threading**, which is not new to most C++ or Java developers; we will define this term and further explain the support provided in C#. We will briefly compare this free-threading model to other models, such as Visual Basic 6.0's apartment-threading model. We won't dwell on the differences for too long since this isn't a history lesson and this book certainly isn't about Visual Basic 6.0. However, understanding what sets these models apart will help you to understand why free threading is so wonderful. This chapter's concepts are essential to your understanding of the remainder of this book, as you will learn:

- ❏ What a thread is, conceptually

- ❏ Some comparisons between various multitasking and threading models

- ❏ Where threads exist and how they are allocated processor time

- ❏ How threads are controlled and managed using interrupts and priorities

- ❏ The concept of application domains, and how they provide finer grained control on the security of your application than that provided in a simple process environment

By understanding many of the concepts of threading and how they are structured in .NET, you will be better placed to make programming decisions on how to implement these features in your applications, before learning the details of implementation as provided in the rest of the book.

Threading Defined

By the end of this section, you will understand the following:

❑   What multitasking is and what the different types of multitasking are

❑   What a process is

❑   What a thread is

❑   What a primary thread is

❑   What a secondary thread is

Multitasking

As you probably know, the term **multitasking** refers to an operating system's ability to run more than one application at a time. For instance, while this chapter is being written, Microsoft Outlook is open as well as two Microsoft Word windows, with the system tray showing further applications running in the background. When clicking back and forth between applications, it would appear that all of them are executing at the same time. The word "application" is a little vague here, though; what we really are referring to are processes. We will define the word "process" a little more clearly later in this chapter.

Classically speaking, multitasking actually exists in two different flavors. These days Windows uses only one style in threading, which we will discuss at length in this book. However, we will also look at the previous type of multitasking so we can understand the differences and advantages of the current method.

In earlier versions of Windows – such as Windows 3.x – and in some other operating systems, a program is allowed to execute until it **cooperates** by releasing its use of the processor to the other applications that are running. Because it is up to the application to cooperate with all other running programs, this type of multitasking is called cooperative multitasking. The downside to this type of multitasking is that if one program does not release execution, the other applications will be locked up. What is actually happening is that the running application hangs and the other applications are waiting in line. This is quite like a line at a bank. A teller takes one customer at a time. The customer more than likely will not move from the teller window until all their transactions are complete. Once finished, the teller can take the next person in line. It doesn't really matter how much time each person is going to spend at the window. Even if one person only wants to deposit a check, they must wait until the person in front of them who has five transactions has finished.

Thankfully, we shouldn't encounter this problem with current versions of Windows (2000 and XP) as the method of multitasking used is very different. An application is now allowed to execute for a short period before it is involuntarily interrupted by the operating system and another application is allowed to execute. This interrupted style of multitasking is called **pre-emptive multitasking**. Pre-emption is simply defined as interrupting an application to allow another application to execute. It's important to note that an application may not have finished its task, but the operating system is going to allow another application to have its time on the processor. The bank teller example above does not fit here. In the real world, this would be like the bank teller pausing one customer in the middle of their transaction to allow another customer to start working on their business. This doesn't mean that the next customer would finish their transaction either. The teller could continue to interrupt one customer after another – eventually resuming with the first customer. This is very much like how the human brain deals with social interaction and various other tasks. While pre-emption solves the problem of the processor becoming locked, it does have its own share of problems as well. As you know, some applications may share resources such as database connections and files. What happens if two applications are accessing the same resource at the same time? One program may change the data, then be interrupted, allowing another program to again change the data. Now two applications have changed the same data. Both applications assumed that they had exclusive access to the data. Let's look at the simple scenario illustrated in Figure 1.

Figure 1

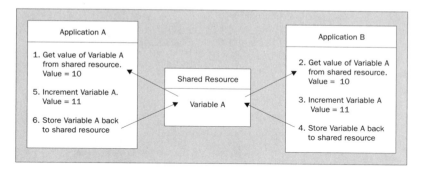

In Step 1, Application A obtains an integer value from a data store and places it in memory. That integer variable is set to 10. Application A is then pre-empted and forced to wait on Application B. Step 2 begins and Application B then obtains that same integer value of 10. In Step 3, Application B increments the value to 11. The variable is then stored to memory by Application B in Step 4. In Step 5, Application A increments this value as well. However, because they both obtained a reference to this value at 10, this value will still be 11 after Application A completes its increment routine. The desired result was for the value to be set to 12. Both applications had no idea that another application was accessing this resource, and now the value they were both attempting to increment has an incorrect value. What would happen if this were a reference counter or a ticket agency booking plane tickets?

The problems associated with pre-emptive multitasking are solved by synchronization, which is covered in Chapter 3.

Processes

When an application is launched, memory and any other resource for that application are allocated. The physical separation of this memory and resources is called a **process**. Of course, the application may launch more than one process. It's important to note that the words "application" and "process" are not synonymous. The memory allocated to the process is isolated from that of other processes and only that process is allowed to access it.

In Windows, you can see the currently running processes by accessing the Windows Task Manager. Right-clicking in an empty space in the taskbar and selecting Task Manager will load it up, and it will contain three tabs: Applications, Processes, and Performance. The Processes tab shows the name of the process, the process ID (PID), CPU usage, the processor time used by the process so far, and the amount of memory it is using. Applications and the processes appear on separate tabs, for a good reason. Applications may have one or more processes involved. Each process has its own separation of data, execution code, and system resources.

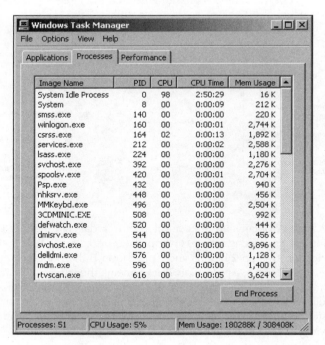

Threads

You will also notice that the Task Manager has summary information about process CPU utilization. This is because the process also has an execution sequence that is used by the computer's processor. This execution sequence is known as a **thread**. This thread is defined by the registers in use on the CPU, the stack used by the thread, and a container that keeps track of the thread's current state. The container mentioned in the last sentence is known as **Thread Local Storage**. The concepts of registers and stacks should be familiar to any of you used to dealing with low-level issues like memory allocation; however, all you need to know here is that a stack in the .NET Framework is an area of memory that can be used for fast access and either stores value types, or pointers to objects, method arguments, and other data that is local to each method call.

Single-Threaded Processes

As noted above, each process has at least one of these sequential execution orders, or threads. Creating a process includes starting the process running at a point in the instructions. This initial thread is known as the **primary** or **main thread**. The thread's actual execution sequence is determined by what you code in your application's methods. For instance, in a simple .NET Windows Forms application, the primary thread is started in the static `Main()` method placed in your project. It begins with a call to `Application.Run()`.

Now that we have an idea of what a process is and that it has at least one thread, let's look at a visual model of this relationship in Figure 2:

Figure 2

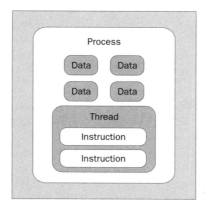

Looking at the diagram above, you'll notice that the thread is in the same isolation as the data. This is to demonstrate that the data you declare in this process can be accessed by the thread. The thread executes on the processor and uses the data within the process, as required. This all seems simple; we have a physically separated process that is isolated so no other process can modify the data. As far as this process is concerned, it is the only process running on the system. We don't need to know the details of other processes and their associated threads to make our process work.

> **To be more precise, the thread is really a pointer into the instruction stream portion of a process. The thread does not actually contain the instructions, but rather it indicates the current and future possible paths through the instructions determined by data and branching decisions.**

Time Slices

When we discussed multitasking, we stated that the operating system grants each application a period to execute before interrupting that application and allowing another one to execute. This is not entirely accurate. The processor actually grants time to the process. The period that the process can execute is known as a **time slice** or a **quantum**. The period of this time slice is unknown to the programmer and unpredictable to anything besides the operating system. Programmers should not consider this time slice as a constant in their applications. Each operating system and each processor may have a different time allocated.

Nevertheless, we did mention a potential problem with concurrency earlier, and we should consider how that would come into play if each process were physically isolated. This is where the challenge starts, and is really the focus of the remainder of this book. We mentioned that a process has to have at least one thread of execution – at least one. Our process may have more than one task that it needs to be doing at any one point in time. For instance, it may need to access a SQL Server database over a network, while also drawing the user interface.

Multithreaded Processes

As you probably already know, we can split up our process to share the time slice allotted to it. This happens by spawning additional threads of execution within the process. You may spawn an additional thread in order to do some background work, such as accessing a network or querying a database. Because these secondary threads are usually created to do some work, they are commonly known as **worker threads**. These threads share the process's memory space that is isolated from all the other processes on the system. The concept of spawning new threads within the same process is known as **free threading**.

The concept of free threading gives a significant advantage over the apartment-threading model – the threading model used in Visual Basic 6.0. With apartment threading, each process was granted its own copy of the global data needed to execute. Each thread spawned was spawned within its own process, so that threads could not share data in the process's memory. Let's look at these models side by side for comparison. Figure 3 demonstrates the apartment-threading concept, while Figure 4 demonstrates the free-threading concept. We won't spend a much time on this because we are not here to learn about Visual Basic 6.0, but it's important to describe these differences:

Figure 3

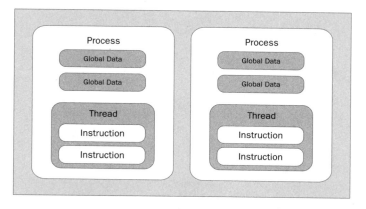

As you can see, each time you want to do some background work, it happens in its own process. This is therefore called running **out-of-process**. This model is vastly different from the free-threading model shown in Figure 4.

Figure 4

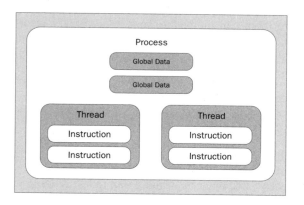

You can see that we can get the CPU to execute an additional thread using the same process's data. This is a significant advantage over single threaded apartments. We get the benefits of an additional thread as well as the ability to share the same data. It is very important to note, however, that only one thread is executing on the processor at a time. Each thread within that process is then granted a portion of that execution time to do its work. Let's go one more time to a diagram (Figure 5) to help illustrate how this works.

Figure 5

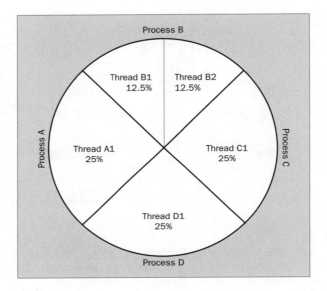

For the sake of this book, the examples and diagrams assume a single processor. However, there is an even greater benefit to multi-threading your applications if the computer has more than one processor. The operating system now has two places to send execution of the thread. In the bank example that we spoke of earlier, this would be similar to opening up another line with another teller. The operating system is responsible for determining which threads are executed on which processor. However, the .NET platform does provide the ability to control which CPU a process uses if the programmer so chooses. This is made possible with the `ProcessorAffinity` property of the `Process` class in the `System.Diagnostics` namespace. Bear in mind, however, that this is set at the process level and so all threads in that particular process will execute on the same processor.

The scheduling of these threads is vastly more complicated than demonstrated in the last diagram, but for our purposes, this model is sufficient for now. Since each thread is taking its turn to execute, we might be reminded of that frustrating wait in line at the bank teller. However, remember that these threads are interrupted after a brief period. At that point, another thread, perhaps one in the same process, or perhaps a thread in another process, is granted execution. Before we move on, let's look at the Task Manager again.

Launch the Task Manager and return to the Processes tab. Once open, go to the View | Select Columns menu. You will see a list of columns that you can display in the Task Manager. We are only concerned with one additional column at this point – the Thread Count option. Select this checkbox. You should see something like this:

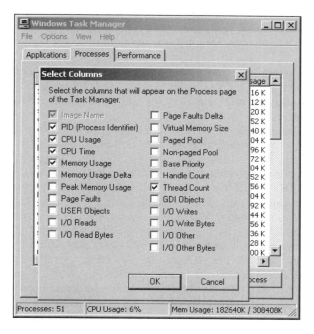

Once you click OK you will notice that several of your processes have more than one thread listed in the Thread Count column. This reinforces the idea that your program may have many threads for one just one process.

How Interrupts and Thread Local Storage Work

When one thread runs out of time in its allocated time slice, it doesn't just stop and wait its turn again. Each processor can only handle one task at a time, so the current thread has to get out of the way. However, before it jumps out of line again, it has to store the state information that will allow its execution to start again from the point it left earlier. If you remember, this is a function of Thread Local Storage (**TLS**). The TLS for this thread, as you may remember, contains the registers, stack pointers, scheduling information, address spaces in memory, and information about other resources in use. One of the registers stored in the TLS is a program counter that tells the thread which instruction to execute next.

Interrupts

Remember that we said that processes don't necessarily need to know about other processes on the same computer. If that were the case, how would the thread know that it's supposed to give way to anther process? This scheduling decision nightmare is handled by the operating system for the most part. Windows itself (which after all is just another program running on the processor) has a main thread, known as the system thread, which is responsible for the scheduling of all other threads.

Windows knows when it needs to make a decision about thread scheduling by using **interrupts**. We've used this word already, but now we are going to define exactly what an interrupt is. An interrupt is a mechanism that causes the normally sequential execution of CPU instructions to branch elsewhere in the computer memory without the knowledge of the execution program. Windows determines how long a thread has to execute and places an instruction in the current thread's execution sequence. This period can differ from system to system and even from thread to thread on the same system. Since this interrupt is obviously placed in the instruction set, it is known as a software interrupt. This should not be confused with hardware interrupts, which occur outside the specific instructions being executed. Once the interrupt is placed, Windows then allows the thread to execute. When the thread comes to the interrupt, Windows uses a special function known as an interrupt handler to store the thread's state in the TLS. The current program counter for that thread, which was stored before the interrupt was received, is then stored in that TLS. As you may remember, this program counter is simply the address of the currently executing instruction. Once the thread's execution has timed out, it is moved to the end of the thread queue for its given priority to wait its turn again. Look at Figure 6 for a diagram of this interruption process:

Figure 6

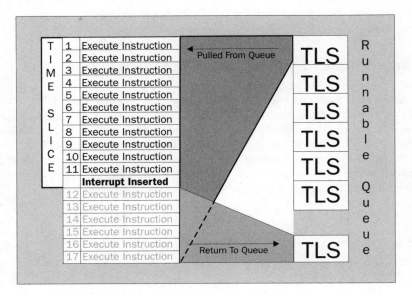

> **The TLS is not actually saved to the queue; it is stored in the memory of the process that contains the thread. A pointer to that memory is what is actually saved to the queue.**

This is, of course, fine if the thread isn't done yet or if the thread needs to continue executing. However, what happens if the thread decides that it doesn't need to use all of its execution time? The process in context switching (that is switching from the context of one thread to another) is slightly different initially, but the results are the same. A thread may decide that it needs to wait on a resource before it can execute again. Therefore, it may yield its execution time to another thread. This is the responsibility of the programmer as well as the operating system. The programmer signals the thread to yield. The thread then clears any interrupts that Windows may have already placed in its stack. A software interrupt is then simulated. The thread is stored in TLS and moved to the end of the queue just as before. We will not diagram this concept as it's quite easy to understand and very similar to the diagram opposite. The only thing to remember is that Windows may have already placed an interrupt on the thread's stack. This must be cleared before the thread is packed up; otherwise, when the thread is again executed, it may be interrupted prematurely. Of course, the details of this are abstracted from us. Programmers do not have to worry about clearing these interrupts themselves.

Thread Sleep and Clock Interrupts

As we stated, the program may have yielded execution to another thread so it can wait on some outside resource. However, the resources may not be available the next time the thread is brought back to execute. In fact, it may not be available the next 10 or 20 times a thread is executed. The programmer may wish to take this thread out of the execution queue for a long period so that the processor doesn't waste time switching from one thread to another just to realize it has to yield execution again. When a thread voluntarily takes itself out of the execution queue for a period, it is said to **sleep**. When a thread is put to sleep, it is again packed up into TLS, but this time, the TLS is not placed at the end of the running queue; it is placed on a separate sleep queue. In order for threads on a sleep queue to run again, they are marked to do so with a different kind of interrupt called a **clock interrupt**. When a thread is put into the sleep queue, a clock interrupt is scheduled for the time when this thread should be awakened. When a clock interrupt occurs that matches the time for a thread on the sleep queue, it is moved back to the runnable queue where it will again be scheduled for execution. Figure 7 illustrates this:

Figure 7

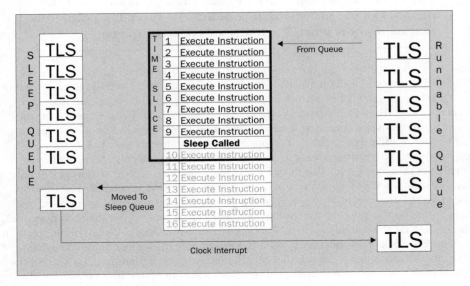

Thread Abort

We've seen a thread interrupted, and we've seen a thread sleep. However, like all other good things in life, threads must end. Threads can be stopped explicitly as a request during the execution of another thread. When a thread is ended in this way, it is called an **abort**. Threads also stop when they come to the end of their execution sequence. In any case, when a thread is ended, the TLS for that thread is de-allocated. The data in the process used by that thread does not go away, however, unless the process also ends. This is important because the process may have more than one thread accessing that data. Threads cannot be aborted from within themselves; a thread abort must be called from another thread.

Thread Priorities

We've seen how a thread can be interrupted so that another thread can execute. We have also seen how a thread may yield its execution time by either yielding that execution once, or by putting itself to sleep. We have also seen how a thread can end. The last thing we need to cover for the basic concept of threading is how threads prioritize themselves. Using the analogy of our own lives, we understand that some tasks we need to do take priority over other tasks. For instance, while there is a grueling deadline to meet with this book, the author also needs to eat. Eating may take priority over writing this book because of the need to eat. In addition, if this author stays up too late working on this book, rest deprivation may elevate the body's priority to sleep. Additional tasks may also be given by other people. However, those people cannot make that task the highest priority. Someone can emphasize that a task may be important, but it's ultimately up to the recipient of the task to determine what should be of extremely high importance, and what can wait.

The information above contains much theory and analogy; however, this very closely relates to our threading concept. Some threads just need to have a higher priority. Just as eating and sleeping are high priorities because they allow us to function, system tasks may have higher priorities because the computer needs them to function. Windows prioritizes threads on a scale of 0 to 31, with larger numbers meaning higher priorities.

A priority of 0 can only be set by the system and means the thread is idle. Priorities between 1 and 15 can be set by users of a Windows system. If a priority needs to be set higher than 15, it must be done by the administrator. We will discuss how an administrator does this later. Threads running in a priority between 16 and 31 are considered to be running real-time. When we refer to the term real-time, we mean that the priority is so high that they pre-empt threads in lower priorities. This pre-emption has the effect of making their execution more immediate. The types of items that might need to run in real-time mode are processes like device drivers, file systems, and input devices. Imagine what would happen if your keyboard and mouse input were not high priorities to the system! The default priority for user-level threads is 8.

One last thing to remember is that threads inherit the priority of the processes in which they reside. Let's diagram this for your future reference in Figure 8. We'll also use this diagram to break these numbers down even further.

Figure 8

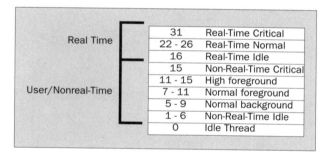

Real Time	31	Real-Time Critical
	22 - 26	Real-Time Normal
	16	Real-Time Idle
	15	Non-Real-Time Critical
	11 - 15	High foreground
User/Nonreal-Time	7 - 11	Normal foreground
	5 - 9	Normal background
	1 - 6	Non-Real-Time Idle
	0	Idle Thread

In some operating systems, such as Windows, as long as threads of a higher priority exist, threads in lower priority are not scheduled for execution. The processor will schedule all threads at the highest priority first. Each thread of that same priority level will take turns executing in a round-robin fashion. After all threads in the highest priority have completed, then the threads in the next highest level will be scheduled for execution. If a thread of a higher priority is available again, all threads in a lower priority are pre-empted and use of the processor is given to the higher priority thread.

Administrating Priorities

Based on what we know about priorities, it may be desirable to set certain process priorities higher so that any threads spawned from those processes will have a higher likelihood of being scheduled for execution. Windows provides several ways to set priorities of tasks administratively and programmatically. Right now, we will focus on setting priorities administratively. This can be done with tools such as the task manager, and two other tools called pview (installed with Visual Studio) and pviewer (installed with either a resource kit for Windows NT or directly with Windows XP Professional). You can also view the current priorities using the Windows Performance Monitor. We won't concentrate on all of these tools right now. We will briefly look at how to set the general priority of processes. If you remember, back when we first introduced processes, we launched the Task Manager to view all of the processes currently running on the system. What we didn't cover is the fact that we can elevate the priority of a particular process in that very same window.

Let's try changing a process's priority. First, open up an instance of an application such as Microsoft Excel. Now launch the Task Manager and go to the Processes tab again. Look at an instance of Excel running as a process. Right-click on EXCEL.EXE in the list and choose Set Priority from the menu. As you can see, you can change the priority class as you wish. It wouldn't make much sense to set the priority of Excel high, but the point is you could if you wanted to. Every process has a priority and the operating system isn't going to tell you what priorities you should and should not have. However, it will warn you that you may be about to do something with undesirable consequences; but the choice is still left up to you.

In the previous screenshot, you can see that one of the priorities has a mark next to it. This mark represents the current priority of the process. It should be noted that when you set a priority for one process, you are setting it for that one instance only. This means that all other currently running instances of that same application will retain their default process levels. Additionally, any future instances of the process that are launched will also have the default process level.

Thread Support in .NET and C#

Free threading is supported in the .NET Framework and is therefore available in all .NET languages, including C# and VB.NET. In this next section, we will look at how that support is provided and more of how threading is done as opposed to what it is. We will also cover some of the additional support provided to help further separate processes

By the end of this section, you will understand:

❑ What the `System.AppDomain` class is and what it can do for you

❑ How the .NET runtime monitors threads

System.AppDomain

When we explained processes earlier in this chapter, we established that they are a physical isolation of the memory and resources needed to maintain themselves. We later mentioned that a process has at least one thread. When Microsoft designed the .NET Framework, it added one more layer of isolation called an **application domain** or **AppDomain**. This application domain is not a physical isolation as a process is; it is a further logical isolation within the process. Since more than one application domain can exist within a single process, we receive some major advantages. In general, it is impossible for standard processes to access each other's data without using a proxy. Using a proxy incurs major overheads and coding can be complex. However, with the introduction of the application domain concept, we can now launch several applications within the same process. The same isolation provided by a process is also available with the application domain. Threads can execute across application domains without the overhead associated with inter-process communication. Another benefit of these additional in-process boundaries is that they provide type checking of the data they contain.

Microsoft encapsulated all of the functionality for these application domains into a class called `System.AppDomain`. Microsoft .NET assemblies have a very tight relationship with these application domains. Any time that an assembly is loaded in an application, it is loaded into an `AppDomain`. Unless otherwise specified, the assembly is loaded into the calling code's `AppDomain`. Application domains also have a direct relationship with threads; they can hold one or many threads, just like a process. However, the difference is that an application domain may be created within the process and without a new thread. This relationship could be modeled as shown in Figure 9.

Figure 9

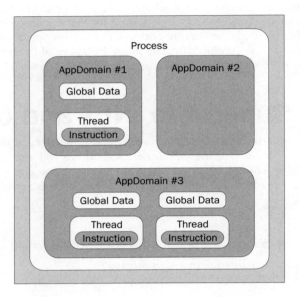

In .NET, the `AppDomain` and `Thread` classes cannot be inherited for security reasons.

Each application contains one or more `AppDomain`s. Each `AppDomain` can create and execute multiple threads. If you look at Figure 10, in Machine X there are two OS processes Y and Z running. The OS process Y has four running `AppDomain`s: A, B, C, and D. The OS process Z has two `AppDomain`s: A and B.

Figure 10

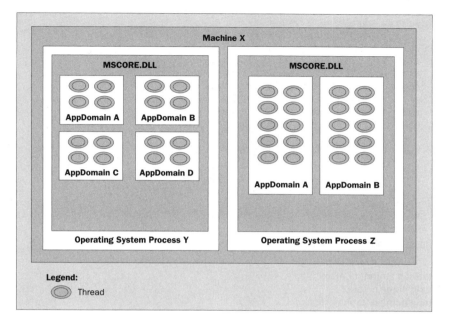

Setting AppDomain Data

You've heard the theory and seen the models; now let's get our hands on some real code. In the example below, we will be using the AppDomain to set data, retrieve data, and identify the thread that the AppDomain is executing. Create a new class file called appdomain.cs and enter the following code:

```
using System;

public class MyAppDomain
{
  public AppDomain Domain;
  public int ThreadId;

  public void SetDomainData(string vName ,string vValue)
  {
    Domain.SetData(vName, (object)vValue);
    ThreadId = AppDomain.GetCurrentThreadId();
  }

  public string GetDomainData(string name)
  {
    return (string)Domain.GetData(name);
  }
```

```
public static void Main()
{
  string DataName = "MyData";
  string DataValue = "Some Data to be stored";

  Console.WriteLine("Retrieving current domain");
  MyAppDomain Obj = new MyAppDomain();
  Obj.Domain = AppDomain.CurrentDomain;

  Console.WriteLine("Setting domain data");
  Obj.SetDomainData(DataName, DataValue);

  Console.WriteLine("Getting domain data");
  Console.WriteLine("The Data found for key '" + DataName
                  + "' is '" + Obj.GetDomainData(DataName)
                  + "' running on thread id: " + Obj.ThreadId);
}
}
```

Your output should look something like this:

```
Retrieving current domain
Setting domain data
Getting domain data
The Data found for key 'MyData' is 'Some Data to be stored' running on thread id: 1372
```

This is straightforward for even unseasoned C# developers. However, let's look at the code and determine exactly what is happening here. This is the first important piece of this class:

```
public void SetDomainData(string vName ,string vValue)
{
  Domain.SetData(vName, (object)vValue);
  ThreadId = AppDomain.GetCurrentThreadId();
}
```

This method takes parameters for the name of the data to be set, and the value. You'll notice that the SetData() method has done something a little different when it passes the parameters in. Here we cast the string value to an Object data type as the SetData() method takes an object as its second parameter. Since we are only using a string, and a string inherits from System.Object, we could just use the variable without casting it to an object. However, other data that you might want to store would not be as easily handled as this. We have done this conversion as a simple reminder of this fact. In the last part of this method, you will notice that we can obtain the currently executing ThreadId with a simple call to the GetCurrentThreadId property of our AppDomain object.

Let's move on to the next method:

```
public string GetDomainData(string name)
{
    return (string)Domain.GetData(name);
}
```

This method is very basic as well. We use the `GetData()` method of the `AppDomain` class to obtain data based on a key value. In this case, we are just passing the parameter from our `GetDomainData()` method to the `GetData()` method. We return the result of that method to the calling method.

Finally, let's look at the `Main()` method:

```
public static void Main()
{
    string DataName = "MyData";
    string DataValue = "Some Data to be stored";

    Console.WriteLine("Retrieving current domain");
    MyAppDomain Obj = new MyAppDomain();
    Obj.Domain = AppDomain.CurrentDomain;

    Console.WriteLine("Setting domain data");
    Obj.SetDomainData(DataName, DataValue);

    Console.WriteLine("Getting domain data");
    Console.WriteLine("The Data found for key '" + DataName
                    + "' is '" + Obj.GetDomainData(DataName)
                    + "' running on thread id: " + Obj.ThreadId);
}
```

We start by initializing the name and value pairs we want to store in our `AppDomain` and writing a line to the console to indicate our method has started execution. Next, we set the `Domain` field of our class with a reference to the currently executing `AppDomain` object (the one in which your `Main()` method is executing). Next we call our methods – passing both parameters to the `SetDomainData()` method:

```
Obj.SetDomainData(DataName, DataValue);
```

Moving on, we pass one parameter into `GetDomainData()` method to get the data we just set and insert it into our console output stream. We also output the `ThreadId` property of our class to see what our executing `ThreadId` was in the method we called.

Executing Code within a Specified AppDomain

Now let's look at how to create a new application domain and make some important observations about the behavior when creating threads within the newly created AppDomain. The following code is contained within create_appdomains.cs:

```csharp
using System;

public class CreateAppDomains
{
  public static void Main()
  {
    AppDomain DomainA;
    DomainA = AppDomain.CreateDomain("MyDomainA");
    string StringA = "DomainA Value";
    DomainA.SetData("DomainKey", StringA);

    CommonCallBack();

    CrossAppDomainDelegate delegateA =
        new CrossAppDomainDelegate(CommonCallBack);
    DomainA.DoCallBack(delegateA);
  }

  public static void CommonCallBack()
  {
    AppDomain Domain;
    Domain = AppDomain.CurrentDomain;

    Console.WriteLine("The Value '" + Domain.GetData("DomainKey") +
        "' was found in " + Domain.FriendlyName.ToString() +
        " running on thread id: " +
        AppDomain.GetCurrentThreadId().ToString());
  }
}
```

The output of this compiled class should look similar to this:

```
The Value " was found in create_appdomains.exe running on thread id: 1372
The Value 'DomainA Value' was found in MyDomainA running on thread id: 1372
```

You'll notice in this example we have created two application domains. To do this, we call the `CreateDomain()` static method of the `AppDomain` class. The parameter that the constructor takes is a friendly name for the `AppDomain` instance that we are creating. We will see that we can access the friendly name later by way of a read-only property. Here is the code that creates the `AppDomain` instance:

```csharp
AppDomain DomainA;
DomainA = AppDomain.CreateDomain("MyDomainA");
```

Next we call the SetData() method that we saw in the previous example. We won't redisplay the code here because we explained its use earlier. However, what we need to explain next is how we get code to execute in a given AppDomain. We do this with the DoCallBack() method of the AppDomain class. This method takes a CrossAppDomainDelegate as its parameter. In this case, we have created an instance of a CrossAppDomainDelegate passing the name of the method we wish to execute into the constructor:

```
CommonCallBack();

CrossAppDomainDelegate delegateA =
    new CrossAppDomainDelegate(CommonCallBack);
DomainA.DoCallBack(delegateA);
```

You'll notice that we call CommonCallBack() first. This is to execute our CommonCallBack() method within the context of the main AppDomain. You'll also notice from the output that the FriendlyName property of the main AppDomain is the executable's name.

Lastly, let's look at the CommonCallBack() method itself:

```
public static void CommonCallBack()
{
    AppDomain Domain;
    Domain = AppDomain.CurrentDomain;

    Console.WriteLine("The Value '" + Domain.GetData("DomainKey") +
        "' was found in " + Domain.FriendlyName.ToString() +
        " running on thread id: " +
        AppDomain.GetCurrentThreadId().ToString());
}
```

You'll notice that this is rather generic so it will work in no matter what instance we run it. We use the CurrentDomain property once again to obtain a reference to the domain that is executing the code. Then we use the FriendlyName property again to identify the AppDomain we are using.

Lastly, we call the GetCurrentThreadId() method again here. When you look at the output, you can see that we get the same thread ID no matter what AppDomain we are executing in. This is important to note because this not only means that an AppDomain can have zero or many threads, but also that a thread can execute across different domains.

27

Thread Management and the .NET Runtime

The .NET Framework provides more than just the ability for free-threaded processes and logical application domains. In fact, the .NET Framework supplies an object representation of processor threads. These object representations are instances of the System.Threading.Thread class. We will go into this in more depth in the next chapter. However, before we move on to the next chapter, we must understand how **unmanaged threads** work in relation to **managed threads**. That is to say, how unmanaged threads (threads created outside of the .NET world) relate to instances of the managed Thread class, which represent threads running inside the .NET CLR.

The .NET runtime monitors all threads that are created by .NET code. It also monitors all unmanaged threads that may execute managed code. Since managed code can be exposed by COM-callable wrappers, it is possible for unmanaged threads to wander into the .NET runtime.

When unmanaged code does execute in a managed thread, the runtime will check the TLS for the existence of a managed Thread object. If a managed thread is found, the runtime will use that thread. If a managed thread isn't found, it will create one and use it. It's very simple, but is necessary to note. We would still want to get an object representation of our thread no matter where it came from. If the runtime didn't manage and create the threads for these types of inbound calls, we wouldn't be able to identify the thread, or even control it, within the managed environment.

The last important note to make about thread management is that once an unmanaged call returns back to unmanaged code, the thread is no longer monitored by the runtime.

Summary

We have covered a wide range of topics in this chapter. We covered the basics of what multitasking is and how it is accomplished by the use of threads. We established that multitasking and free threading are not the same thing. We described processes and how they isolate data from other applications. We also described the function of threads in an operating system like Windows. You now know that Windows interrupts threads to grant execution time to other threads for a brief period. That brief period is called a time slice or quantum. We described the function of thread priorities and the different levels of these priorities, and that threads will inherit their parent process's priority by default.

We also described how the .NET runtime monitors threads created in the .NET environment and additionally any unmanaged threads that execute managed code. We described the support for threading in the .NET Framework. The System.AppDomain class provides an additional layer of logical data isolation on top of the physical process data isolation. We described how threads could cross easily from one AppDomain to another. Additionally, we saw how an AppDomain doesn't necessarily have its own thread as all processes do.

C#

Threading

Handbook

2

2

Threading in .NET

In Chapter 1 we described *what* threading is. We covered a lot of the common ground that many may be familiar with already. Knowing the *what* portion of threading is important. In this chapter, you will see how to implement some basic threading; however, it is of equal, if not greater importance, to understand **when** to use threading.

By the end of this chapter, you will understand:

- ❑ The System.Threading namespace
- ❑ What design issues there are in the use of threads
- ❑ What resources are used by threads
- ❑ What are good opportunities for threading
- ❑ What mistakes to avoid when using threads

System.Threading Namespace

We have already mentioned that threads in managed code are represented by a System.Threading.Thread class instance. In this section, we will discuss the System.Threading namespace in depth, as well as its contents. The classes available in the System.Threading namespace are listed in the following table.

Class	Description
`AutoResetEvent`	This event notifies one or more waiting threads that an event has occurred.
`Interlocked`	This class protects against errors by providing atomic operations for variables that are shared by multiple threads.
`ManualResetEvent`	This event occurs when notifying one or more waiting threads that an event has occurred.
`Monitor`	This class provides a mechanism that synchronizes access to objects.
`Mutex`	A synchronization primitive that grants exclusive access to a shared resource to only one thread. It can also be used for inter-process synchronization.
`ReaderWriterLock`	This class defines a lock that allows single-writer and multiple-reader semantics.
`RegisteredWaitHandle`	This class represents a handle that has been registered when calling the `RegisterWaitForSingleObject()` method.
`SynchronizationLockException`	This exception is thrown when a synchronized method is invoked from an unsynchronized block of code.
`Thread`	This class creates and controls a thread, sets its priority, and gets its status.
`ThreadAbortException`	This exception is thrown when a call is made to the `Abort()` method.
`ThreadExceptionEventArgs`	This class provides data for the `ThreadException` event.
`ThreadInterruptedException`	This exception is thrown when a thread is interrupted while it is in a waiting state.
`ThreadPool`	This class provides a pool of threads that can be used to post work items, process asynchronous I/O, wait on behalf of other threads, and process timers.
`ThreadStateException`	This is the exception that is thrown when a thread is in an invalid state for the method call.

Class	Description
Timeout	This class simply contains a constant integer used when we want to specify an infinite amount of time.
Timer	This class provides a mechanism for executing methods at specified intervals.
WaitHandle	This class encapsulates operating system-specific objects that wait for exclusive access to shared resources.

We won't use all of these classes in this section, but it's useful to understand what this namespace makes available to us. The other classes will be discussed in later chapters.

Thread Class

Right now, we are going to focus on the Thread class, since this class represents our processing threads. This class allows us to do everything, from managing a thread's priority, to reading its status.

Let's start by looking at a table of this class's public methods.

Public Method Name	Description
Abort()	This overloaded method raises a ThreadAbortException in the thread on which it is invoked, to begin the process of terminating the thread. Calling this method usually terminates the thread.
AllocateDataSlot()	This static method allocates an unnamed data slot on all the threads.
AllocateNamedDataSlot()	This static method allocates a named data slot on all threads.
FreeNamedDataSlot()	This static method frees a previously allocated named data slot.
GetData()	This static method retrieves the value from the specified slot on the current thread, within the current thread's current domain.
GetDomain()	This static method returns the current domain in which the current thread is running.

Table continued on following page

Public Method Name	Description
GetDomainID()	This static method returns a unique application domain identifier.
GetHashCode()	This method serves as a hash function for a particular type, suitable for use in hashing algorithms and data structures like a hash table.
GetNamedDataSlot()	This static method looks up a named data slot.
Interrupt()	This method interrupts a thread that is in the WaitSleepJoin thread state.
Join()	This overloaded method blocks the calling thread until a thread terminates.
ResetAbort()	This static method cancels an Abort() requested for the current thread.
Resume()	This method resumes a thread that has been suspended.
SetData()	This static method sets the data in the specified slot on the currently running thread, for that thread's current domain.
Sleep()	This static and overloaded method blocks the current thread for the specified number of milliseconds.
SpinWait()	This static method causes a thread to wait the number of times defined by the iterations parameter.
Start()	This method causes the operating system to change the state of the current instance to ThreadState.Running.
Suspend()	This method will either suspend the thread, or if the thread is already suspended, has no effect.

Now let's look at another table, this time containing its public properties.

Public Property Name	Description
ApartmentState	Sets or gets the apartment state of this thread.
CurrentContext	This static property gets the current context in which the thread is executing.
CurrentCulture	Sets or gets the culture for the current thread.
CurrentPrincipal	This static property sets or gets the thread's current principal. It is used for role-based security.
CurrentThread	This static property gets the currently running thread.

Public Property Name	Description
CurrentUICulture	Used at run time, this property sets or gets the current culture used by the Resource Manager to look up culture-specific resources.
IsAlive	Gets a value that indicates the execution status of the current thread.
IsBackground	Sets or gets a value that indicates whether a thread is a background thread or not.
IsThreadPoolThread	Gets a value indicating whether a thread is part of a thread pool.
Name	Sets or gets the name of the thread.
Priority	Sets or gets a value that indicates the scheduling priority of a thread.
ThreadState	Gets a value that contains the states of the current thread.

Again, we won't use all of these properties and methods in this chapter. We've seen these class members, but it does us little good until we can at least create a thread – or a reference to one. So let's get our feet wet with a simple C# threading example.

Creating a Thread

We are going to use a simple example here. This isn't a good example of why you should use a new thread but it strips off all of the complexities that will be covered later. Create a new console application with a file called simple_thread.cs and place the following code in it:

```
using System;
using System.Threading;

public class SimpleThread
{
  public void SimpleMethod()
  {
    int i = 5;
    int x = 10;
    int result = i * x;
    Console.WriteLine("This code calculated the value " +
                  result.ToString() + " from thread ID: " +
                  AppDomain.GetCurrentThreadId().ToString());

  }

  public static void Main()
  {
```

```
    // Calling the method from our current thread
    SimpleThread simpleThread = new SimpleThread();
    simpleThread.SimpleMethod();

    // Calling the method on a new thread
    ThreadStart ts = new ThreadStart(simpleThread.SimpleMethod);
    Thread t = new Thread(ts);
    t.Start();
    Console.ReadLine();
  }
}
```

Now save, compile, and execute the file. Your output should look something like this:

```
This code calculated the value 50 from thread id: 1400
This code calculated the value 50 from thread id: 1040
```

Let's walk through this simple example and make sure we understand what is happening here. As we have already established, the threading functionality is encapsulated in the System.Threading namespace. As such, we must first import this namespace into our project. Once the namespace is imported, we want to create a method that can be executed on the main (primary) thread and on our new worker thread. We use SimpleMethod() in our example:

```
    public void SimpleMethod()
    {
      int i = 5;
      int x = 10;
      int result = i * x;
      Console.WriteLine("This code calculated the value " +
                        result.ToString() + " from thread ID: " +
                        AppDomain.GetCurrentThreadId().ToString());
    }
```

As you can see, we are using the AppDomain class that we introduced in Chapter 1 to find out what thread we are running on. This method, whenever it is executed, simply does a sum, and prints the result, along with a report of which thread the calculation was performed on.

Our program's entry point is the Main() method. The first thing we do inside this method is execute our SimpleMethod() method. This calls the method on the same thread as that on which the Main() method is running. The next part is important: we get our first look at creating a thread. Before we can create a thread in C#, we must first create a ThreadStart delegate instance. A delegate is really an object-oriented type-safe function pointer. Since we are going to tell a thread what function to execute, we are essentially passing a function pointer to the thread's constructor. This is demonstrated in our application as follows:

```
    ThreadStart ts = new ThreadStart(simpleThread.SimpleMethod);
```

One thing to notice is that the method name is not accompanied by parentheses; it simply takes the method's name. Once we have created our `ThreadStart` delegate, we can then create our `Thread` for execution. The only constructor for a `Thread` takes an instance of the `ThreadStart` delegate. We again demonstrated this in our code with the following line:

```
Thread t = new Thread(ts);
```

We are declaring a variable called t as a new `Thread`. The `Thread` class constructor takes the `ThreadStart` delegate as its sole parameter.

On our next line we call the `Start()` method of the `Thread` object. This starts off a new execution thread, which begins by invoking the `ThreadStart` delegate we passed into the constructor, which in turn invokes the method. We follow this up with `Console.ReadLine()` so the program will wait on your key input before exiting our main thread:

```
t.Start();
Console.ReadLine();
```

When the method is executed this second time, we can see that the code is indeed executing on a different thread.

OK, so we've created a thread, but that doesn't really provide any insight into the power of threads. The fact that we are displaying different thread IDs doesn't really do much – we haven't executed more than one thing at once yet. To see how we can use this same threading code in a more realistic application, we are going to create another program that simulates a long process executing in the background while another process executes in the foreground. Create a new console application and place this code in a new file called do_something_thread.cs:

```csharp
using System;
using System.Threading;

public class DoSomethingThread
{
  static void WorkerMethod()
  {
    for(int i = 1; i < 1000; i++)
    {
      Console.WriteLine("Worker Thread: " + i.ToString());
    }
  }

  static void Main()
  {
    ThreadStart ts = new ThreadStart(WorkerMethod);
    Thread t = new Thread(ts);
    t.Start();
```

```
    for(int i = 1; i < 1000; i++)
    {
      Console.WriteLine("Primary Thread: " + i.ToString());
    }

    Console.ReadLine();
  }
}
```

Your output may be somewhat different every time. The thread execution will be switched at different points in the loop every time. But your concatenated results will look something like this:

```
Primary Thread: 1
Primary Thread: 2
Primary Thread: 3
. . .
Worker Thread: 743
Worker Thread: 744
Worker Thread: 745
. . .
Primary Thread: 1000
```

We won't walk through this code because it doesn't introduce any new coding techniques. However, as we can see, execution time is shared between the two threads. Neither thread is completely blocked until the other finishes. Instead, each thread is given a small amount of time to execute. After one thread has run out of execution time, the next thread begins executing in its time slice. Both threads continue to alternate until execution is completed. Actually, there are more than just our two threads that are alternating and sharing time slices. We aren't just switching between the two threads in our application. In reality, we are sharing our execution time with many other threads currently running on our computer.

ThreadStart and Execution Branching

Take a look, once again, at the ThreadStart delegate we mentioned earlier. We can do some interesting work with these delegates. Let's examine a quick example in a real-world scenario. Suppose that you want to perform some background routine when a user launches an application. Depending on who is launching the application, you want to perform different routines. For instance, let's say that when an administrator logs into an application, you want to run a background process that will gather report data and format it. That background process will alert the administrator when the report is available. You probably wouldn't want to perform the same reporting function for an ordinary user as you would for an administrator. This is where the object-oriented nature of ThreadStart is useful.

Let's look at some example code. We aren't going to code the exact scenario described
above, but we will show you how you can branch based on a certain criteria defined
in a `ThreadStart`. Create a new console application and place the following code in
a file called `ThreadStartBranching.cs`:

```csharp
using System;
using System.Threading;

public class ThreadStartBranching
{
  enum UserClass
  {
    ClassAdmin,
    ClassUser
  }

  static void AdminMethod()
  {
    Console.WriteLine("Admin Method");
  }

  static void UserMethod()
  {
    Console.WriteLine("User Method");
  }

  static void ExecuteFor(UserClass uc)
  {
    ThreadStart ts;
    ThreadStart tsAdmin = new ThreadStart(AdminMethod);
    ThreadStart tsUser = new ThreadStart(UserMethod);

    if(uc == UserClass.ClassAdmin)
      ts = tsAdmin;
    else
      ts = tsUser;

    Thread t = new Thread(ts);
    t.Start();
  }

  static void Main()
  {
    // execute in the context of an admin user
    ExecuteFor(UserClass.ClassAdmin);

    // execute in the context of a regular user
    ExecuteFor(UserClass.ClassUser);

    Console.ReadLine();
  }
}
```

The output from the code is quite simple:

```
Admin Method
User Method
```

We will detail some of the important points to observe here. First, you will notice that we created an enumeration of the types of user that may be executing code:

```
enum UserClass
{
   ClassAdmin,
   ClassUser
}
```

The next thing you'll notice is that we created two methods: `AdminMethod()` and `UserMethod()`. These would theoretically execute a long series of instructions that would be completely different for the two different user types. In our case, we just want to identify that they have run so we write them out to the console:

```
static void AdminMethod()
{
   Console.WriteLine("Admin Method");
}

static void UserMethod()
{
   Console.WriteLine("User Method");
}
```

The next thing you'll notice is that within the `ExecuteFor()` method we declared a variable called `ts` as a `ThreadStart` class, but didn't create an instance with the `New` keyword. We then created two new `ThreadStart` objects that point to the different methods created above:

```
ThreadStart ts;
ThreadStart tsAdmin = new ThreadStart(AdminMethod);
ThreadStart tsUser = new ThreadStart(UserMethod);
```

So, now we have two new `ThreadStart` objects and a variable that can hold an instance of a `ThreadStart`. Then we branch our code with an `If` statement and set our empty `ts` variable to the instance of the `ThreadStart` that coincides with our business rule:

```
if(uc == UserClass.ClassAdmin)
   ts = tsAdmin;
else
   ts = tsUser;
```

Lastly, we pass the dynamically assigned `ThreadStart` delegate to our `Thread` constructor to create a thread, and begin its execution:

```
Thread t = new Thread(ts);
t.Start();
```

Thread Properties and Methods

As we showed in the beginning of this chapter, there are many properties and methods of the `Thread` class. We promised that controlling the execution of threads was made much simpler with the `System.Threading` namespace. So far, all we have done is create threads and start them.

Let's look at two more members of the `Thread` class; the `Sleep()` method and the `IsAlive` property. In Chapter 1 we said that a thread may go to sleep for a time until it is clock-interrupted. Putting a thread to sleep is as simple as calling the static `Sleep()` method. We also stated that we could determine a thread's state. In the following example we are going to use the `IsAlive` property to determine if a thread has completed its executions, and the `Sleep()` method to pause the execution of a thread. Look at the following code, `thread_sleep.cs`, where we will make use of both of these members:

```
using System;
using System.Threading;

public class ThreadState
{
    static void WorkerFunction()
    {
        string ThreadState;

        for(int i = 1; i < 50000; i++)
        {
            if(i % 5000 == 0)
            {
                ThreadState = Thread.CurrentThread.ThreadState.ToString();
                Console.WriteLine("Worker: " + ThreadState);
            }
        }
        Console.WriteLine("Worker Function Complete");
    }

    static void Main()
    {
        string ThreadState;
        Thread t = new Thread(new ThreadStart(WorkerFunction));
        t.Start();
```

```
    while(t.IsAlive)
    {
      Console.WriteLine("Still waiting. I'm going back to sleep.");
      Thread.Sleep(200);
    }

    ThreadState = t.ThreadState.ToString();
    Console.WriteLine("He's finally done! Thread state is: "
                      + ThreadState);
    Console.ReadLine();
  }
}
```

Your output should look similar to the following (try experimenting with the values in the for loop and passed to the sleep() method to see different results):

```
Still waiting. I'm going back to sleep.
Worker: Running
Worker: Running
Worker: Running
Worker: Running
Worker: Running
Worker: Running
Worker: Running
Worker: Running
Worker: Running
Worker: Running
Worker Function Complete
He's finally done! Thread state is: Stopped
```

Let's look at the Main() method where we have used our new concepts First, we create a thread and pass it the method we want to execute as a delegate:

```
Thread t = new Thread(new ThreadStart(WorkerFunction));
t.Start();
```

Notice that instead of creating a variable to hold our ThreadStart class, we simply created one on the fly and passed it as the parameter of our Thread constructor. As usual, our Main() method continues to execute alongside our new thread as the processor switches between them. Then we use the IsAlive property of our newly created thread to see if it is still executing. We will continue to test this variable. While the worker thread is alive, the main thread will continue to sleep for 200 milliseconds, wake up the thread, and test if our worker thread is still alive again:

```
while(t.IsAlive)
{
  Console.WriteLine("Still waiting. I'm going back to sleep.");
  Thread.CurrentThread.Sleep(200);
}
```

Next we want to look at the `ThreadState` property that we have used twice in our code. The `ThreadState` property is actually a property that returns an enumerated type. The enumeration tells you exactly what state the thread is in. We can either test this property with an `if` statement as we did in our last example or use the `ToString()` method on the property and write out its state in text form:

```
ThreadState = t.ThreadState.ToString();
Console.WriteLine("He's finally done! Thread state is: "
        + ThreadState);
```

The rest of this code is standard and doesn't need to be reviewed. There are some important things to note. The first is that we tell one thread to sleep for a specified period so that we yield execution to our other threads. We do that with the `Thread` object's `Sleep()` method – passing in the length of time in milliseconds that we want to the thread to sleep. In addition, we can test our threads to see if they have finished executing by using the `IsAlive` property. Lastly, we can use the `ThreadState` property of our thread instances to determine their exact thread state.

Thread Priorities

The thread priority determines the relative priority of the threads against each other. The `ThreadPriority` enumeration defines the possible values for setting a thread's priority. The available values are:

❑   Highest

❑   AboveNormal

❑   Normal

❑   BelowNormal

❑   Lowest

When a thread is created by the runtime and it has not been assigned any priority then it will initially have the `Normal` priority. However, this can be changed using the `ThreadPriority` enumeration. Before seeing an example for the thread priority, let's see what a thread priority looks like. Let's create a simple threading example that just displays the name, state, and the priority information about the current thread, `thread_priority.cs`:

```
using System;
using System.Threading;

public class ThreadPriority
{
  public static Thread worker;
  static void Main()
  {
```

```
      Console.WriteLine("Entering void Main()");
      worker = new Thread(new ThreadStart(FindPriority));
      // Let's give a name to the thread
      worker.Name = "FindPriority() Thread";
      worker.Start();
      Console.WriteLine("Exiting void Main()");
   }

   public static void FindPriority()
   {
      Console.WriteLine("Name: " + worker.Name);
      Console.WriteLine("State: " + worker.ThreadState.ToString());
      Console.WriteLine("Priority: " + worker.Priority.ToString());
   }
}
```

There is a simple method called FindPriority() that displays the name, state, and priority information of the current thread, which produces output like the following:

```
Entering the void Main()
Exiting the void Main()
Name: FindPriority() Thread
State: Running
Priority: Normal
```

We know the worker thread is running with a Normal priority. Let's add a new thread, and call our reporting method with a different priority. Here's thread_priority2.cs:

```
using System;
using System.Threading;

public class ThreadPriority2
{
   public static Thread worker;
   public static Thread worker2;

   static void Main()
   {
      Console.WriteLine("Entering void Main()");
      worker = new Thread(new ThreadStart(FindPriority));
      worker2 = new Thread(new ThreadStart(FindPriority));

      // Let's give a name to the thread
      worker.Name = "FindPriority() Thread";
      worker2.Name = "FindPriority() Thread 2";

      // Give the new thread object the highest priority
      worker2.Priority = System.Threading.ThreadPriority.Highest;

      worker.Start();
      worker2.Start();
```

```
      Console.WriteLine("Exiting void Main()");
      Console.ReadLine();
    }

    static public void FindPriority()
    {
      Console.WriteLine("Name: " + worker.Name);
      Console.WriteLine("State: " + worker.ThreadState.ToString());
      Console.WriteLine("Priority: " + worker.Priority.ToString());
    }

  }
```

The output from `thread_priority2.cs` will be something like the following:

```
Entering void Main()
Name: FindPriority() Thread2
State: Running
Priority: Highest
Exiting void Main()
Name: FindPriority() Thread
State: Running
Priority: Normal
```

Threads are scheduled for execution based on the priority set using the `Priority` property. Every operating system will execute a thread priority differently and the operating system could change the priority of the thread.

> *There is no way that our application can restrict the operating system from changing the priority of the thread that was assigned by the developer, since the OS is the master of all threads and it knows when and how to schedule them. For example, the priority of the thread could be dynamically changed by the OS due to several factors, such as system events like user input that has higher priority, or lack of memory that will trigger the garbage-collection process.*

Timers and Callbacks

We've seen some simple examples of threading. What we haven't covered at all is the issue of synchronization, although we will cover that in much greater detail in the next chapter. As threads run out of sequence from the rest of the application code, we cannot be certain that actions affecting a particular shared resource that occur in one thread will be completed before code in another thread wants to access that same shared resource. There are various methods of dealing with these issues, but here we will cover one simple way; the use of timers. Using a timer, we can specify that a method is executed at a specific regular interval, and this method could check that the required actions have been completed before continuing. This is a very simple model, but can apply to a variety of situations.

Timers are made up of two objects, a `TimerCallback` and a `Timer`. The `TimerCallback` delegate defines the method to be called at a specified interval, whereas the `Timer` is the timer itself. The `TimerCallback` associates a specific method with the timer. The `Timer`'s constructor (which is overloaded) requires four arguments. The first is the `TimerCallback` specified earlier. The second is an object that can be used to transmit state across to the method specified. The last two arguments are the period after which to start periodic method calls, and the interval between subsequent `TimerCallback` method calls. They can be entered as integers or longs representing numbers of milliseconds, but as you will see below, an alternative is to use the `System.TimeSpan` object with which you can specify the intervals in ticks, milliseconds, seconds, minutes, hours, or days.

The easiest way to show how this works is by demonstration, so below we will detail an application that fires two threads. The second thread will not perform its operations until the first has completed its operations; `thread_timer.cs`:

```
using System;
using System.Threading;
using System.Text;

public class TimerExample
{
   private string message;
   private static Timer tmr;
   private static bool complete;
```

Everything is straightforward above. We declare `tmr` as static and class-wide as it will be defined in the `Main()` method:

```
public static void Main()
{
   TimerExample obj = new TimerExample();
   Thread t = new Thread(new ThreadStart(obj.GenerateText));
   t.Start();

   TimerCallback tmrCallBack = new TimerCallback(obj.GetText);
   tmr = new Timer(tmrCallBack, null, TimeSpan.Zero,
                   TimeSpan.FromSeconds(2));
```

Here we fire up a new thread that will execute on the `GenerateText()` method, which iterates through a `for` loop to generate a string and store it in the class-wide `message` field:

```
   do
   {
     if( complete )
        break;
   } while(true);
   Console.WriteLine("Exiting Main...");
   Console.ReadLine();
}
```

The above loop just freezes the `Main()` loop until the `complete` field is `true`. In a GUI different methods could be used, as the `Application.Run()` method puts the application in a perpetual loop anyway:

```
public void GenerateText()
{

    StringBuilder sb = new StringBuilder();

    for(int i = 1; i < 200; i++)
    {
        sb.Append(sb.Length, "This is Line ");
        sb.Append(sb.Length, i.ToString());
        sb.Append(sb.Length, System.Environment.NewLine);
    }

    message = sb.ToString();
}
```

Above is the first method used, which just generates 200 lines of text using a `StringBuilder` object, and then stores them in the `message` field.

```
public void GetText(object state)
{
    if(message == null)
        return;
    Console.WriteLine("Message is :");
    Console.WriteLine(message);
    tmr.Dispose();
    complete = true;
}
} // class
```

The last method used in this class is fired every two seconds by the timer. If `message` hasn't been set yet, then it exits; otherwise it outputs a message and then disposes of the timer. This stops the timer from continuing to count. This should be performed as soon as the timer is no longer necessary.

The output from `thread_timer.cs` will be as follows:

```
Message is :
This is Line 1
This is Line 2

...

This is Line 199
This is Line 200

Exiting Main...
```

47

Spinning Threads with Threads

We've seen in code how to spawn a thread from the void Main(). In a similar way, we can also spawn multiple threads within a thread. For example, let's say we have a Car class that has a public method called StartTheEngine(). The StartTheEngine() method calls another three private methods called CheckTheBattery(), CheckForFuel(), and CheckTheEngine(). Since each of these tasks, checking the battery, fuel, and engine, can happen simultaneously, we can run each of these methods in a different thread. Here is how the Car class is implemented in thread_spinning.cs:

```csharp
using System;
using System.Threading;

class Car
{
    public void StartTheEngine()
    {
        Console.WriteLine("Starting the engine!");
        //Declare three new threads
        Thread batt = new Thread(new ThreadStart(CheckTheBattery));
        Thread fuel = new Thread(new ThreadStart(CheckForFuel));
        Thread eng = new Thread(new ThreadStart(CheckTheEngine));

        batt.Start();
        fuel.Start();
        eng.Start();

        for(int i = 1; i < 100000000; i++)
        {
            // some real executing code here
        }
        Console.WriteLine("Engine is ready!");
    }

    private void CheckTheBattery()
    {
        Console.WriteLine("Checking the Battery!");
        for(int i = 1; i < 100000000; i++)
        {
            // some real executing code here
        }
        Console.WriteLine("Finished checking the Battery!");
    }

    private void CheckForFuel()
    {
        Console.WriteLine("Checking for Fuel!");
        for(int i = 1; i < 100000000; i++)
        {
            // some real executing code here
        }
```

```
      Console.WriteLine("Fuel is available!");
   }

   private void CheckTheEngine()
   {
      Console.WriteLine("Checking the engine!");
      for(int i = 1; i < 100000000; i++)
      {
         // some real executing code here
      }
      Console.WriteLine("Finished checking the engine!");
   }
}
```

In the `StartTheEngine()` method, we create three threads and then start each of them one by one. Let's add an entry point to our class so we can see some results of our code:

```
public static void Main()
{
   Console.WriteLine("Entering void Main!");
   int j ;
   Car myCar = new Car();
   Thread worker = new Thread(new ThreadStart(myCar.StartTheEngine));
   worker.Start();
   for(int i = 1; i < 100000000; i++)
   {
      //
   }
   Console.WriteLine("Exiting void Main!");
   Console.ReadLine();
}
```

In the `void Main()` method we simply create one more thread and execute the `StartTheEngine()` method in that thread, as illustrated in Figure 1.

Figure 1.

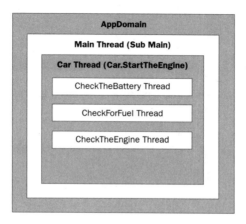

The output should look something like the following:

```
Entering void Main!
Exiting void Main!
Starting the engine!
Checking the Battery!
Checking for Fuel!
Checking the engine!
Finished checking the Battery!
Fuel is available!
Finished checking the engine!
Engine is ready!
```

As you can see, each of these methods works in it's own thread and is executed in its own time-sliced slot.

Spinning Threads with Threads with Threads

We can split the Car class into separate classes and we could build two more methods in a new Engine class called check1() and check2(). Then the Engine class will execute the check1() and check2() methods in its own thread as shown in Figure 2.

Figure 2.

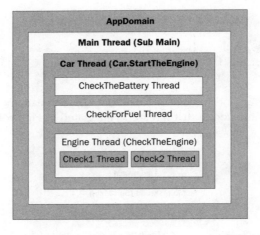

We'll remove the CheckTheEngine() method from the Car class and create one more class called Engine; see thread_spinning2.cs:

```
using System;
using System.Threading;

class Engine
{
```

```
    public void CheckTheEngine()
    {
        Thread chck1 = new Thread(new ThreadStart(Check1));
        Thread chck2 = new Thread(new ThreadStart(Check2));

        chck1.Start();
        chck2.Start();
        Console.WriteLine("Checking the engine!");
        for(int i = 1; i < 100000000; i++)
        {
            // some real executing code here
        }
        Console.WriteLine("Finished checking the engine!");
    }

    private void Check1()
    {
        Console.WriteLine("Starting the engine check!!");
        for(int i = 1; i < 100000000; i++)
        {
            // some real executing code here
        }
        Console.WriteLine("Finished engine check1!");
    }

    private void Check2()
    {
        Console.WriteLine("Starting the engine check2!");
        for(int i = 1; i < 100000000; i++)
        {
            // some real executing code here
        }
        Console.WriteLine("Finished engine check2!");
    }
}
```

The Engine class has the public method CheckTheEngine() that creates two more threads and calls the check1() and check2() methods. Here is how the results may look:

```
Entering void Main!
Exiting void Main!
Starting the engine!
Checking the Battery!
Checking for Fuel!
Checking the engine!
Starting the engine check!!
Starting the engine check2!
Finished checking the Battery!
Fuel is available!
Engine is ready!
Finished engine check1!
Finished checking the engine!
Finished engine check2!
```

As you can see, spawning threads from within threads is very easy. However, you may be interested in knowing the disadvantages: as the number of active threads goes up, the performance degrades.

Performance Considerations

The more threads you create, the more work the system has to do to maintain the thread contexts and CPU instructions. The Processes tab of the Windows Task Manager will tell you how many processes and threads are currently running. However, these will be OS processes and they're not equivalent to the AppDomains. You can also look at the running threads while debugging a given .NET application by using the threads window.

If we want to know how many threads are running inside the CLR then you have to use the Windows Performance Monitor tool and add a couple of CLR-specific performance categories. The CLR exposes a performance counter category called .NET CLR LocksAndThreads and we can use this category to get more information about the CLR-managed threads. Let's run the Performance Monitor and add the counters shown in the following table from the .NET CLR LocksAndThreads category.

Performance Counter	Description
# of current logical Threads	This counter displays the number of current managed threads in the application and includes both the running and stopped threads.
# of current physical Threads	This counter displays the number of OS threads created and owned by the CLR. This counter may not map one to one with managed threads.
# of total recognized threads	This counter displays the number of current threads recognized by the CLR.
Current Queue Length	This counter displays number of threads that are waiting to acquire locks in the managed application.
Total # of Contentions	This counter displays the number of failures when the managed applications try to acquire locks.

Here is how the values looks for our thread_spinning2 application:

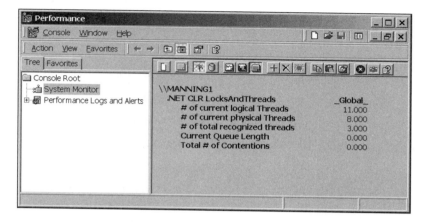

Here is a comprehensive overview of the ".NET CLR LocksAndThreads" performance counter information.

- ❑ The counter # of current local Threads specifies that 11 managed threads are created and owned by the CLR

> **Since we've added the counter instance "_Global_", we see all the threads created by the CLR.**

- ❑ The counter # of current physical Threads specifies that 8 OS threads are created and owned by the CLR

- ❑ The counter # of total recognized Threads specifies that 3 OS threads are recognized by the CLR and they're created by the Thread object

- ❑ The counter Total # of Contentions specifies that the runtime did not fail when it tried to acquire managed locks. Managed lock fails are bad for the execution of code

Lifecycle of Threads

When a thread is scheduled for execution it can go through several states, including unstarted, alive, sleeping, etc. The Thread class contains methods that allow you to start, stop, resume, abort, suspend, and join (wait for) a thread. We can find the current state of the thread using its ThreadState property, which will be one of the values specified in the ThreadState enumeration:

- ❑ Aborted – The thread is in the stopped state, but did not necessarily complete execution

53

- ❏ AbortRequested – The Abort() method has been called but the thread has not yet received the System.Threading.ThreadAbortexception that will try to terminate it – the thread is not stopped but soon will be.

- ❏ Background – The thread is being executed in the background

- ❏ Running – The thread has started and is not blocked

- ❏ Stopped – The thread has completed all its instructions, and stopped

- ❏ StopRequested – The thread is being requested to stop

- ❏ Suspended – The thread has been suspended

- ❏ SuspendRequested – The thread is being requested to suspend

- ❏ Unstarted – The Start() method has not yet been called on the thread

- ❏ WaitSleepJoin – The thread has been blocked by a call to Wait(), Sleep(), or Join()

Figure 3 shows the lifecycle of a thread.

Figure 3.

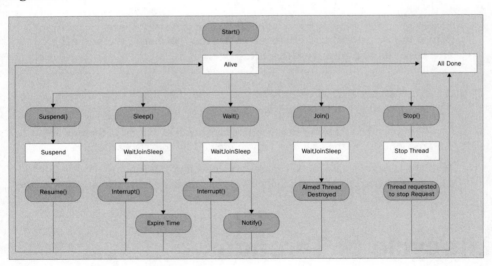

In this section, we'll explore the lifecycle of threads.

Putting a Thread to Sleep

When we create a new thread we have to call the `Start()` method of the `Thread` object to schedule that thread. At this time, the CLR will allocate a time slice to the address of the method passed to the constructor of the `Thread` object. Once the thread is in the `Running` state, it can go back to either the `Sleep` or `Abort` states when the OS is processing the other threads. We can use the `Sleep()` method of the `Thread` class to put a thread to sleep. The `Sleep()` method is really useful if you are waiting for a resource and you want to retry for it. For example, let's say your application cannot proceed due to unavailability of a resource that it is trying to access. You may want your application to retry to access the resource after few milliseconds, in which case the `Sleep()` method is a good way to put the thread to sleep for a specified time before the application retries to access the resource.

The overloaded `Sleep()` method is available in two flavors. The first overload takes an integer as the parameter that will suspended the thread for number of milliseconds specified. For example, if you pass `100` to the parameter the thread will be suspended for 100 milliseconds. This will place the thread into the `WaitSleepJoin` state. Let's see an example for this, `thread_sleep2.cs`:

```csharp
using System;
using System.Threading;

public class ThreadSleep
{
    public static Thread worker;
    public static Thread worker2;

    public static void Main()
    {
        Console.WriteLine("Entering the void Main!");

        worker = new Thread(new ThreadStart(Counter));
        worker2 = new Thread(new ThreadStart(Counter2));

        // Make the worker2 object as highest priority
        worker2.Priority = System.Threading.ThreadPriority.Highest;

        worker.Start();
        worker2.Start();

        Console.WriteLine("Exiting the void Main!");
    }

    public static void Counter()
    {
        Console.WriteLine("Entering Counter");
        for(int i = 1; i < 50; i++)
        {
            Console.Write(i + " ");
```

```
        if(i == 10)
            Thread.Sleep(1000);
    }
    Console.WriteLine();
    Console.WriteLine("Exiting Counter");
}

public static void Counter2()
{
    Console.WriteLine("Entering Counter2");
    for(int i = 51; i < 100; i++)
    {
        Console.Write(i + " ");
        if( i == 70 )
            Thread.Sleep(5000);
    }
    Console.WriteLine();
    Console.WriteLine("Exiting Counter2");
}
}
```

The Counter() method counts numbers from 1 to 50 and when it reaches 10 it sleeps for 1000 milliseconds. The Counter2() method counts from 51 to 100 and when it reaches 70 it sleeps for 5000 milliseconds. Here is how the output might look:

```
Entering the void Main!
Entering Counter2
51 52 53 54 55 56 57 58 59 60 61 62 63 64 65 66 67 68 69 70 Exiting
the void Main!
Entering Counter
1 2 3 4 5 6 7 8 9 10 11 12 13 14 15 16 17 18 19 20 21 22 23 24 25 26
27 28 29 30 31 32 33 34 35 36 37 38 39 40 41 42 43 44 45 46 47 48 49
50
Exiting Counter
71 72 73 74 75 76 77 78 79 80 81 82 83 84 85 86 87 88 89 90 91 92 93
94 95 96 97 98 99 100
Exiting Counter2
```

The second overload takes a TimeSpan as parameter and, based on the TimeSpan value, the current thread will be suspended. The TimeSpan is a structure defined in the System namespace. The TimeSpan structure has a few useful properties that return the time interval based on clock ticking. We can use public methods such as FromSeconds() and FromMinutes() to specify the sleep duration. Here is an example, thread_sleep3.cs:

```
public static void Counter()
{
    ...
    for(i = 1; i < 50; i++)
    {
```

```
            Console.Write(i + " ");
            if(i == 10)
               Thread.Sleep(System.TimeSpan.FromSeconds(1))
      }
      ...
   }

   public static void Counter2()
   {
      ...
      for(int i = 51; i < 100; i++)
      {
          Console.Write(i + " ");
          if( i == 70 )
             Thread.Sleep(5000);
      }
      ...
   }
```

The output will be similar to that of thread_sleep2.

Interrupting a Thread

When a thread is put to sleep, the thread goes to the WaitSleepJoin state. If the
thread is in the sleeping state the only way to wake the thread, before its timeout
expires, is using the Interrupt() method. The Interrupt() method will place the
thread back in the scheduling queue. Let's see an example for this,
thread_interrupt.cs:

```
using System;
using System.Threading;

public class Interrupt
{
   public static Thread sleeper;
   public static Thread worker;

   public static void Main()
   {
      Console.WriteLine("Entering the void Main!");

      sleeper = new Thread(new ThreadStart(SleepingThread));
      worker = new Thread(new ThreadStart(AwakeTheThread));

      sleeper.Start();
      worker.Start();

      Console.WriteLine("Exiting the void Main!");
   }
```

```
public static void SleepingThread()
{
   for(int i = 1; i < 50; i++)
   {
      Console.Write(i + " ");
      if(i == 10 || i == 20 || i == 30)
      {
         Console.WriteLine("Going to sleep at: " + i);
         Thread.Sleep(20);
      }
   }
}

public static void AwakeTheThread()
{
   for(int i = 51; i < 100; i++)
   {
      Console.Write(i + " ");
      if(sleeper.ThreadState ==
         System.Threading.ThreadState.WaitSleepJoin)
      {
         Console.WriteLine("Interrupting the sleeping thread");
         sleeper.Interrupt();
      }
   }
}
}
```

In the above example, the first thread (sleeper) is put to sleep when the counter reaches 10, 20, and 30. The second thread (worker) checks if the first thread is asleep. If so, it interrupts the first thread and places it back in the scheduler. The Interrupt() method is the best way to bring the sleeping thread back to life and you can use this functionality if the waiting for the resource is over and you want the thread to become alive. The output will look similar to the following:

```
Entering the Sub Main!
Exiting the Sub Main!
51 52 53 54 55 56 57 58 59 60 61 62 63 64 65 66 67 68 69 70 71 72 73
74 75 76 77 78 79 80 81 82 83 84 85 86 87 88 89 90 91 92 93 94 95 96
97 98 99 100 1 2 3 4 5 6 7 8 9 10 Going to sleep at: 10
11 12 13 14 15 16 17 18 19 20 Going to sleep at: 20
21 22 23 24 25 26 27 28 29 30 Going to sleep at: 30
31 32 33 34 35 36 37 38 39 40 41 42 43 44 45 46 47 48 49 50
```

Pausing and Resuming Threads

The Suspend() and Resume() methods of the Thread class can be used to suspend and resume the thread. The Suspend() method will suspend the current thread indefinitely until another thread wakes it up. When we call the Suspend() method, the thread will be place in the SuspendRequested or Suspended state.

Let's see an example for this. We'll create a new C# application that generates prime numbers in a new thread. This application will also have options to pause and resume the prime number generation thread. To make this happen let's create a new C# WinForms project called `PrimeNumbers` and build a UI like this in `Form1`.

We have a `ListBox` and three command buttons in the UI. The `ListBox` is used to display the prime numbers and three command buttons are used to start, pause, and resume the thread. Initially we've disabled the pause and the resume buttons, since they can't be used until the thread is started. Let's see what the code is going to look like. We've declared a class-level `Thread` object that is going to generated prime numbers.

```
using System;
using System.Drawing;
using System.Collections;
using System.ComponentModel;
using System.Windows.Forms;
using System.Threading;

namespace Chapter_02
{
  public class Form1 : System.Windows.Forms.Form
  {
    // private thread variable
    private Thread primeNumberThread;
```

Double-click on the Start command button and add the following code.

```
private void cmdStart_Click(object sender, System.EventArgs e)
{
  // Let's create a new thread
  primeNumberThread = new Thread(
    new ThreadStart(GeneratePrimeNumbers));

  // Let's give a name for the thread
  primeNumberThread.Name = "Prime Numbers Example";

  primeNumberThread.Priority = ThreadPriority.BelowNormal;

  // Enable the Pause Button
  cmdPause.Enabled = true;
  // Disable the Start button
  cmdStart.Enabled = false;

  // Let's start the thread
  primeNumberThread.Start();
}
```

All the Start button does is create a new Thread object with the ThreadStart
delegate of the GeneratePrimeNumbers() method and assign the name Prime
Number Example to the thread. Then it enables the Pause button and disables the Start
button. Then it starts the prime number generating thread using the Start method of
the Thread class.

Let's double-click on the Pause button and add the following code.

```
private void cmdPause_Click(object sender, System.EventArgs e)
{
  try
  {
  try
  {
    // If current state of thread is Running,
    // then pause the Thread
    if (primeNumberThread.ThreadState ==
      System.Threading.ThreadState.Running)
    {

      //Pause the Thread
      primeNumberThread.Suspend();

      //Disable the Pause button
      cmdPause.Enabled = false;

      //Enable the resume button
      cmdResume.Enabled = true;
    }
  }
  catch(ThreadStateException Ex)
```

```
            {
                MessageBox.Show(Ex.ToString(), "Exception",
                    MessageBoxButtons.OK, MessageBoxIcon.Error,
                    MessageBoxDefaultButton.Button1);
            }
        }
```

The Pause button checks if the thread is in the Running state. If it is in the Running state, it pauses the thread by calling the Suspend method of the Thread object. Then it enables the Resume button and disables the Pause button. Since the Suspend method can raise the ThreadStateException exception, we're wrapping the code with in a try...catch block.

Double-click on the Resume button and add the following code.

```
        private void cmdResume_Click(object sender, System.EventArgs e)
        {
            if(primeNumberThread.ThreadState ==
                System.Threading.ThreadState.Suspended ||
                primeNumberThread.ThreadState ==
                System.Threading.ThreadState.SuspendRequested)
            {
                try
                {
                    // Resume the thread
                    primeNumberThread.Resume();

                    // Disable the resume button
                    cmdResume.Enabled = false;

                    // Enable the Pause button
                    cmdPause.Enabled = true;
                }
                catch(ThreadStateException Ex)
                {
                    MessageBox.Show(Ex.ToString(), "Exception",
                        MessageBoxButtons.OK, MessageBoxIcon.Error,
                        MessageBoxDefaultButton.Button1);
                }
            }
        }
```

The Resume button checks if the state of the thread is Suspended or SuspendRequested before resuming the thread. If the state of the thread is either Suspended or SuspendRequested then it resumes the thread and disables the Resume button and enables the Pause button.

Well, so far our business logic is ready. Let's see the code that generates the prime numbers. Since our main aim is to use multithreading and not prime number generation, I'm not going to go deep into the code. The GeneratePrimeNumbers() method generates the first 255 prime numbers starting from 3. When the method finds a prime number it'll add the new prime number to an array as well as to the listbox. The first prime number, 2, will be automatically added to the listbox. Finally, the method will enable the Start button and disable the Pause button.

```
public void GeneratePrimeNumbers()
{
    long lngCounter;
    long lngNumber;
    long lngDivideByCounter;
    bool blnIsPrime;
    long[] PrimeArray = new long[256];

    // initialize variables
    lngNumber = 3;
    lngCounter = 2;

    // We know that the first prime is 2. Therefore,
    // let's add it to the list and start from 3
    PrimeArray[1] = 2;
    lstPrime.Items.Add(2);

    while(lngCounter < 256)
    {
        blnIsPrime = true;

        // Try dividing this number by any already found prime
        // which is smaller then the root of this number.
        for(lngDivideByCounter = 1; PrimeArray[lngDivideByCounter]
            * PrimeArray[lngDivideByCounter] <= lngNumber;
            lngDivideByCounter++)
        {
            if(lngNumber % PrimeArray[lngDivideByCounter] == 0)
            {
                // This is not a prime number
                blnIsPrime = false;
                // Exit the loop
                break;
            }
        }

        // If this is a prime number then display it
        if(blnIsPrime)
        {
            // Guess we found a new prime.
            PrimeArray[lngCounter] = lngNumber;
            // Increase prime found count.
            lngCounter++;
            lstPrime.Items.Add(lngNumber);
```

```
    // Let's put the thread to sleep for 100 milliseconds.
    // This will simulate the time lag and we'll get time
    // to pause and resume the thread
    Thread.Sleep(100);
  }

  // Increment number by two
  lngNumber += 2;
}
// Once the thread is finished execution enable the start
// and disable the pause button
cmdStart.Enabled = true;
cmdPause.Enabled = false;
}
```

Well everything is ready now. Let's run the code and see how our application looks.

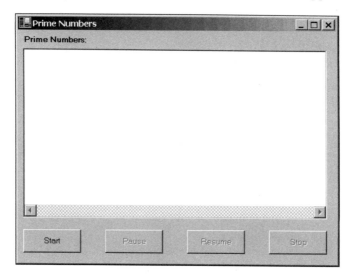

Well, everything looks good now and the code is apparently working fine. But there is a huge flaw in our code. When the GeneratePrimeNumbers() method finds a prime number it adds the prime number back to the listbox control. It may not look like a problem for you if this code is running in a synchronized execution manner where both the prime number generation code and the user interface are running on the same thread. But in our example, the UI is running in a different thread from the GeneratePrimeNumbers() method. Therefore, when we go between threads to write data this could cause some unexpected behaviors in our application.

The best way to address this problem is using delegates. We can declare a delegate and we can use the delegate to inform the UI thread to update the listbox control itself. In this way, we're not crossing the threading boundaries and the application stability is not compromised.

Let's see how we can implement this operation. Let's add one more public delegate called UpdateData:

```
public  delegate void UpdateData(string returnVal);
```

Let's modify the GeneratePrimeNumbers() method a little bit to call the delegate from it. We've added a new string array with the initial value as 2, since the first prime number is 2. Then we've declared a new object of the type UpdateData as a delegate and we've passed the address of the UpdateUI method. Then we've used the this.Invoke method with the delegate object and the string array to inform the user interface to update itself. We've done the same when we found a prime number.

Form1 is represented as this in this context.

```
public void GeneratePrimeNumbers()
{
   long lngCounter;
   long lngNumber;
   long lngDivideByCounter;
   bool blnIsPrime;
   long[] PrimeArray = new long[255];
   string[] args = new string[] {"2"};
   UpdateData UIDel = new UpdateData(UpdateUI);


   ...
   this.Invoke(UIDel, args);

   while(lngCounter <= 255)
   {
      ...
      // If this is a prime number then display it
      if(blnIsPrime)
      {
         // Guess we found a new prime.
         PrimeArray[lngCounter] = lngNumber;
         // Increase prime found count.
         lngCounter++;

         args[0] = lngNumber.ToString();
         this.Invoke(UIDel, args);
         ...
      }
      ...
   }
   ...
}
```

The UpdateUI() method simply accepts the value that needs to be added to the listbox in its parameter and adds the value to the listbox. Since the UpdateUI method runs in the UI thread there are no cross-boundary thread updates and the stability of our application is not compromised:

```
void UpdateUI(string result )
{
  lstPrime.Items.Add(result);
}
```

Destroying Threads

The Abort() method can be used to destroy the current thread. The Abort() method would be very useful, if you want to terminate the thread for whatever reason, such as the thread is taking too much time to execute or the user has changed their mind by selecting cancel. You might want this behavior in a search process that takes a long time. A search may continue running but the user may have seen the results they wish to see and discontinue the thread that is carrying on the search routine. When Abort() is called against a thread, the ThreadAbortException exception will be raised. If it isn't caught in any code in the thread, then the thread will terminate. Think twice before writing generic exception handling code inside methods that will be accessed in a multithreaded context, since a catch (Exception e) will also catch ThreadAbortExceptions – from which you probably don't want to recover. As we'll see, ThreadAbortException isn't so easily stopped, and your program flow may not continue as you expect it to.

Let's see an example for this. We're going to create a new project called Destroying and we'll copy the code from the previous prime number generation code into the new Form1.cs class. Let's add one more Stop button to the UI like this.

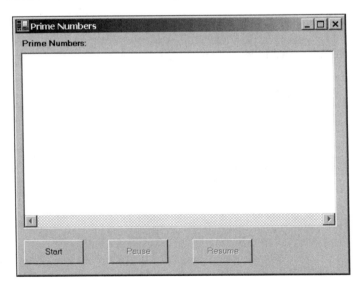

Let's add the following code into the Stop button.

```
private void cmdStop_Click(object sender, System.EventArgs e)
{
  // Enable the Start button and disable all others
  cmdStop.Enabled   = false;
  cmdPause.Enabled  = false;
  cmdResume.Enabled = false;
  cmdStart.Enabled  = true;
  // Destroy the thread
  primeNumberThread.Abort();
}
```

This example is very similar to the previous example. The only difference is that we're using the Abort() method to destroy the thread when the user clicks on the Stop button. Then we're enabling the Start button and disabling all other buttons. You might also note that the ThreadAbortException is a special exception. Like all other exceptions it can be caught. However, once the catch block has completed, the exception will automatically be raised again. When the exception is raised, the runtime executes all the finally blocks before killing the thread.

Joining Threads

The Join() method blocks a given thread until the currently running thread is terminated. When we call the Join() method against a given thread instance, the thread will be placed in the WaitSleepJoin state. This method is very useful, if one thread is dependent upon another thread. By simply joining two threads we are saying that the thread that is running when the Join() method is called will enter the WaitSleepJoin state and not return to the Running state until the thread upon which the Join() method was called completes its tasks. This may sound a bit confusing, but let's see an example for this in the following code sample, thread_joining.cs:

```
using System;
using System.Threading;
namespace Chapter_02
{
  public class JoiningThread
  {
    public static Thread SecondThread;
    public static Thread FirstThread;
    static void First()
    {
      for(int i = 1; i <= 250; i++)
        Console.Write(i + " ");
    }

    static void Second()
    {
      FirstThread.Join();
```

```
      for(int i = 251; i <= 500; i++)
        Console.Write(i + " ");
    }

    public static void Main()
    {
      FirstThread  = new Thread(new ThreadStart(First));
      SecondThread = new Thread(new ThreadStart(Second));

      FirstThread.Start();
      SecondThread.Start();
    }
  }
}
```

In this simple example, the aim is to output numbers to the console sequentially, starting at 1 and finishing at 500. The `First()` method will output the first 250 numbers and the `Second()` method will produce those from 251 to 500. Without the `FirstThread.Join()` line in the `Second()` method, execution would switch back and forth between the two methods and our output would be scrambled (try commenting out the line and running the example again). By calling the `FirstThread.Join()` method within the `Second()` method, the execution of the `Second()` method is paused until the execution of whatever is in `FirstThread` (the `First()` method) has completed.

The `Join()` method is overloaded; it can accept either an integer or a `TimeSpan` as a single parameter and returns a Boolean. The effect of calling one of the overloaded versions of this method is that the thread will be blocked until either the other thread completes or the time period elapses, whichever occurs first. The return value will be `true` if the thread has completed and `false` if it has not.

Why Not Thread Everything?

We've seen several very useful benefits to threading; we can have several processes running at once, and several threads running within those processes. So, with all these benefits, why don't we just use new threads for all of our methods? Wouldn't that just make everything run fast? Not really. As a matter of fact, we will see in this section that quite the opposite can happen if we overuse threading.

Multithreaded applications require resources. Threads require memory to store the thread-local storage container. As you can imagine, the number of threads used is limited by the amount of memory available. Memory is fairly inexpensive these days so many computers have large amounts of memory. However, you should not assume that this is the case. If you are running your application on an unknown hardware configuration, you cannot assume that your application will have enough memory. Additionally, you cannot assume that your process will be the only one spawning threads and consuming system resources. Just because a machine has a lot of memory, doesn't mean it's all for your application.

You will also discover that each thread also incurs additional processor overhead. Creating too many threads in your applications will limit the amount of time that your thread has to execute. Therefore, your processor could potentially spend more time switching between threads as opposed to actually executing the instructions that the threads contain. If your application is creating more threads, your application will gain more execution time than all the other processes with fewer threads.

To make this concept easier to understand, take the parallel example you'll find down at your local grocery store. Two cashiers are scanning groceries for their customers. However, there is only one bagger, who takes turns switching between the two cashiers. The bagger is rather efficient at jumping back and forth between the two registers and bagging the groceries because they don't pile up any faster than the bagger can bag the groceries. However, if two more cashiers open up lanes, it will become apparent that the bagger will spend more time jumping back and forth between the registers than they spend actually bagging groceries. Eventually, the store will need to get another bagger. In the case of threading, think of the cashiers as applications – or threads, and the bagger as a processor. The processor has to switch between threads. As the "threads" increase, the grocery store has to add another "processor" to be sure that the customers get the attention they need.

The phrase "too many threads" is a rather generic term – and rightly so. What constitutes "too many" on one system could be fine on another. Since hardware configurations largely dictate the number of threads available on a system, "too many" is an unquantifiable variable without specific configuration details and lots of testing.

It is for these reasons that Microsoft recommends that you use as few threads as possible in your applications. This limits the amount of resources required by the operating system.

Threading Opportunities

So, now I may have you wondering why we would thread at all if it could potentially have a negative impact on our application. The idea is that you will learn there is a time and place for threading. Learning which circumstances represent good opportunities to spawn a new thread is the key to making good design decisions. There are two distinct opportunities for which to consider spawning a new thread. In this section, we will discuss what those opportunities are.

Background Processes

The first opportunity to spawn a new thread occurs when your application needs to run a large process in the background while still keeping its user interface active and usable. We have all run into times when an application just didn't seem to respond because we had told it to query data or process a large piece of information. Take, for example, the case of professional graphics packages that are required to render graphics into a specific file format. In early versions of some products, asking the application to render a large graphic would result in the application becoming unresponsive until the rendering process had finished. You'd often have to finish working with the application, then set it to render overnight – coming back in the morning to see if the results were what you expected – because sitting and waiting in front of the computer for an hour was just not viable. This problem presents an ideal time to set a background thread to do your computer-intensive processing while leaving your user interface to run on the main application thread.

Let's take a look at an example of a background process that needs to spawn a new thread. This example demonstrates searching for files. When the search routine finds a file matching the pattern specified, it adds a new item to the `ListBox`.

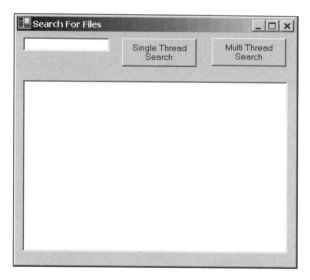

The code below will demonstrate that this method does indeed need its own thread:

```
using System.Threading;
using System.IO;
public class Threaded_Search : System.Windows.Forms.Form
{
    string search;
    int fileCount;
```

```
private void cmdSingle_Click(object sender, System.EventArgs e)
{
  Search();
}

public void Search()
{
  search = TextBox1.Text;
  ListBox1.Items.Clear();
  fileCount = 0;
  SearchDirectory(@"C:\winnt");
}

public void SearchDirectory(string Path)
{
  // Search the directory
  DirectoryInfo di = new DirectoryInfo(Path);
  FileInfo[] f = di.GetFiles(search);

  ListBox1.BeginUpdate();

  foreach(FileInfo myFile in f)
    ListBox1.Items.Add(myFile.FullName);

  ListBox1.EndUpdate();

  // Search its sub directories
  DirectoryInfo[] d = di.GetDirectories();

  foreach(DirectoryInfo myDir in d)
    SearchDirectory(myDir.FullName);
}
}
```

Go ahead and compile this example and run it. Type a search term in the search textbox, such as *.*, click the Single Thread Search button, and observe our problem. As you will see, we are searching for files and trying to update the user interface every time we find a file with our search criteria. However, because both the user interface and the search code are running on the same thread, we don't see the updates until the search code has completely finished its processing. Additionally, we cannot resize our form while the search is processing.

This rather long piece of code is actually a very simple demonstration. Let's see if we can correct this problem with a simple change. In the Button2_Click routine, add the following code to call the Search() method with the use of a new thread:

```
private void cmdMulti_Click(object sender, System.EventArgs e)
{
  Thread t = new Thread(new ThreadStart(Search));
  t.Start();
}
```

Now recompile and run the program again. This time, type in the same search term and click the Multi Thread Search button. You can see that there is quite a difference. This time our results are displayed immediately. This is because Windows is now switching execution back and forth between the user interface and the search thread. The processor is now given a time slice to update the interface to reflect the changes in the ListBox. You will also notice that we can now resize our form while it is searching.

There are other background processes that may cause our interface to be unresponsive. We might want to do some intense processing, such as searching, sorting, formatting, parsing, and filtering a large number of records in a database. This would be another opportunity to consider using a new thread. You may also want to spawn a new thread if you want to run a routine that is constantly logging information. The user interface won't necessarily be unresponsive in this instance, but it may appear slow or sluggish if this type of routine isn't on its own thread.

Accessing External Resources

The second circumstance in which you might want to consider spawning a new thread occurs when you are accessing resources that are not local to your system. This might be a database process or a network file share somewhere on your network. In such cases, network performance could adversely affect your application performance.

Let's take the following example. We are going to connect to a database in this example. Let's assume that network performance is poor and may cause this application to be slow. Let's also assume that company policy dictates that no applications can be installed on the database server:

```
using System.Threading;
using System.IO;
using System.Data;
using System.Data.SqlClient;

namespace Chapter_02
{
  public class Threaded_Resource : System.Windows.Forms.Form
  {
    public void Button1_Click(object sender , System.EventArgs e)
    {
      QueryData();
    }

    public void QueryData()
    {
      SqlDataReader objReader;
      SqlConnection objConn;
      SqlCommand objCommand;
      int intEmployeeID;
      string strFirstName;
      string strTitle;
      int intReportsTo;
```

```
        objConn = new SqlConnection("server=RemoteServer;" +
            "UID=RemoteUser;PWD=Password;database=northwind");
        objCommand = new SqlCommand("SELECT EmployeeID, FirstName, " +
            "Title, ReportsTo FROM Employees", objConn);
        objConn.Open();
        objReader = objCommand.ExecuteReader(
            CommandBehavior.CloseConnection );

        while (objReader.Read())
        {
          intEmployeeID = objReader.GetInt32(0);
          strFirstName = objReader.GetString(1);
          strTitle = objReader.GetString(2);
          if(objReader.IsDBNull(3))
            intReportsTo = 0;
          else
            intReportsTo = objReader.GetInt32(3);

          listBox1.Items.Add(intEmployeeID.ToString() + " " +
              strFirstName + " " + strTitle + " " +
              intReportsTo.ToString());
        }
        objReader.Close();
        objConn.Close();
      }

      public static void Main()
      {
        Application.Run(new Threaded_Resource());
      }
    }
}
```

As you can see in this example, all we are doing is querying a remote database. The data returned will not be excessive, but you will notice that the user interface freezes while it takes time to get the data and update the listbox. We can again correct this by simply spawning a new thread and executing our database code within that thread. Let's add a second button and use the following code:

```
    private void button2_Click(object sender, System.EventArgs e)
    {
      Thread t = new Thread(new ThreadStart(QueryData));
      t.Start();
    }
```

Now when we run the code, we get a result similar to our last example. We can resize the form while the query runs. The interface is responsive throughout the entire query process.

Of course, I want to reiterate that this doesn't necessarily mean you should spawn a new thread every time you connect to a database. However, analyze your options to find out if you can move the database or the application so they reside on the same server. Also, make sure that this component isn't going to be continuously called from various client applications. Doing so would spawn additional threads for every call and consume more resources than you intended. There are ways to reuse objects and their threads without using a new thread every time your object is called. These issues will be covered in Chapters 3 and 5.

Threading Traps

We've seen the two main situations where it can be a good idea to use threading in your applications. However, there are some circumstances in which spawning a new thread would be a bad idea. Obviously, this isn't going to be a complete listing of inappropriate times to create new threads, but it is meant to give you an idea of what constitutes a bad threading decision. There are two main areas we'll look at here: the first is an instance where execution order is extremely important, and the second is a mistake seen quite often in code – creating new threads in a loop.

Execution Order Revisited

Recall the example do_something_thread.cs from earlier in the chapter where we created some code demonstrating the fact that execution randomly jumped from one thread to the other. It looked as if one thread would execute and show 10 lines in the console, then the next thread would show 15, and then return back to the original thread to execute 8. A common mistake in deciding whether to use threads or not is to assume that you know exactly how much code is going to execute in the thread's given time slice.

Here's an example that demonstrates this problem. It looks as if the thread t1 will finish first because it starts first, but that's a big mistake. Create a console application called ExecutionOrder and set its startup object to Main(). Build and run this example a few times – you'll get differing results:

```
using System;
using System.Threading;

namespace Chapter_02
{
  public class ExecutionOrder
  {
    static Thread t1;
    static Thread t2;

    public static void WriteFinished(string threadName)
    {
```

```
      switch(threadName)
      {
        case "T1":
          Console.WriteLine();
          Console.WriteLine("T1 Finished");
          break;
        case "T2":
          Console.WriteLine();
          Console.WriteLine("T2 Finished");
          break;
      }
    }

    public static void Main()
    {
      t1 = new Thread(new ThreadStart(Increment));
      t2 = new Thread(new ThreadStart(Increment));
      t1.Name = "T1";
      t2.Name = "T2";

      t1.Start();
      t2.Start();
      Console.ReadLine();
    }

    public static void Increment()
    {
      for(long i = 1; i <=1000000; i++)
      {
        if(i % 100000 == 0 )
          Console.Write(" {" + Thread.CurrentThread.Name + "}");
      }
      WriteFinished(Thread.CurrentThread.Name);
    }
  }
}
```

Sometimes t1 will finish then t2 will execute some more code and then finish.
Sometimes t2 will finish completely and then t1 will execute to completion. The point
is that you can't count on the threads completing in the order they were started. Later
in this book we will discuss how you can synchronize threads to execute in a specified
order. However, it's important to note synchronization doesn't happen by default.

This isn't the only problem associated with execution order. Take the next piece of
example code where we show that data can be adversely affected by unsynchronized
threads, ExecutionOrder2:

```
using System;
using System.Threading;
```

```
public class ExecutionOrder2
{
  static Thread t1;
  static Thread t2;
  static int iIncr;

  public static void WriteFinished(string threadName)
  {
    switch(threadName)
    {
      case "T1":
        Console.WriteLine();
        Console.WriteLine("T1 Finished: iIncr = " + iIncr.ToString);
        break;
      case "T2":
        Console.WriteLine();
        Console.WriteLine("T2 Finished: iIncr = " + iIncr.ToString);
        break;
    }
  }

  public static void Main()
  {
    iIncr = 0;
    t1 = new Thread(new ThreadStart(Increment));
    t2 = new Thread(new ThreadStart(Increment));
    t1.Name = "T1";
    t2.Name = "T2";
    t1.Start();
    t2.Start();
    Console.Read();
  }

  public static void Increment()
  {
    for(long i = 1; i <= 1000000; i++)
    {
      if(i % 100000 = 0)
        Console.WriteLine(" {" + Thread.CurrentThread.Name + "} " +
            iIncr.ToString());
    }
    iIncr++;
    WriteFinished(Thread.CurrentThread.Name);
  }
}
```

This is a very similar class to `ExecutionOrder`. This time, however, we created a
shared incrementing counter called `iIncr`. We tell the application to increment the
variable before moving on to the `WriteFinished()` method. If we execute this
application a few times, you will notice that the value of the incrementing counter will
change at different times. Keep in mind again that we will show you how to
synchronize these threads later on. These two examples should act as warnings that
threads do not execute in the order that you want by default. However, in these cases,
you can use synchronization tactics such as using the `Join()` method we discussed
earlier. Thread synchronization will be covered more in depth later in this book.

Threads in a Loop

One other common mistake made when someone discovers the joys of threading is
that they create and use them within a loop. There follows a code example that
demonstrates this, which is often implemented by programmers who are new to the
threading concept. It is a common concept used by developers or system
administrators to send notifications when an event occurs. The idea is not bad, but its
implementation using a thread in the loop can cause many problems.

> **Please be aware that running this code may well disable your
> system. Don't run it unless you don't mind rebooting your
> machine to reclaim the resources the program will waste.**

```csharp
using System;
using System.Threading;
using System.Web.Mail;
using System.Collections;

public class LoopingThreads
{
    public delegate void SendMail(string oMessageTo);

    private class MyMail
    {
        public string EmailTo;
        public string EmailFrom;
        public string EmailSubject;
        public string EmailBody;
        public SendMail SendThisEmail;      // Delegate instance

        public void Send()
        {
            System.Web.Mail.MailMessage oMail =
                new System.Web.Mail.MailMessage();
            oMail.To   = EmailTo;
            oMail.From = EmailFrom;
            oMail.Body = EmailBody;
```

```
            oMail.Subject = EmailSubject;
            oMail.BodyFormat = MailFormat.Text;
            SmtpMail.Send(oMail);
            SendThisEmail(EmailTo);
        }
    }

    public static Thread CreateEmail(SendMail oSendEmail,
        string EmailTo , string EmailFrom ,
        string EmailBody , string EmailSubject )
    {
        MyMail oMail = new MyMail();
        oMail.EmailFrom = EmailFrom;
        oMail.EmailBody = EmailBody;
        oMail.EmailSubject = EmailSubject;
        oMail.EmailTo = EmailTo;
        oMail.SendThisEmail = oSendEmail;

        Thread t = new Thread(new ThreadStart(oMail.Send));
        return t;
    }
}

class Mailer
{
    public static void MailMethod(string oString)
    {
        Console.WriteLine("Sending Email: " + oString);
    }
}

public class DoMail
{
    static ArrayList al = new ArrayList();

    public static void Main()
    {
        for(int i = 1; i <= 1000; i++)
        {
            al.Add(i.ToString() + "@someplace.com");
        }
        SendAllEmail();
    }

    public static void SendAllEmail()
    {
        int loopTo = al.Count - 1;
        for(int i = 0; i <= loopTo; i++)
        {
            Thread t = LoopingThreads.CreateEmail(
                new LoopingThreads.SendMail(Mailer.MailMethod),
                (string)al[i],
                "johndoe@somewhere.com",
```

```
                  "Threading in a loop", "Mail Example");
         t.Start();
         t.Join(Timeout.Infinite);
      }
   }
}
```

The code may be a little more complex than you thought because it also demonstrates how to use a delegate and a lengthy set of classes to call a thread with parameters. This is necessary because **threads can only create an entry on a method that has no parameters.** As such, it is the duty of the programmer to create proxy methods that create the parameters for another method and return a thread object (we'll see more of this in later chapters). The calling method can then use the reference to the returned Thread to start execution.

Let's concentrate on the SendAllEmail method. This is where we loop through the ArrayList and send our parameters to the proxy method. We start a new thread for each and every e-mail we want to send:

```
public static void SendAllEmail()
{
   int loopTo = al.Count - 1;
   for(int i = 0; i <= loopTo; i++)
   {
      Thread t = LoopingThreads.CreateEmail(
          new LoopingThreads.SendMail(Mailer.MailMethod),
          (string)al[i],
          "johndoe@somewhere.com",
          "Threading in a loop", "Mail Example");
      t.Start();
      t.Join(Timeout.Infinite);
   }
}
```

At first glance, this sounds like a good idea. Why not send e-mail on another thread? It takes a long time to process sometimes doesn't it? This is true, but the problem is that we are now tying up the processor's execution time by switching between the threads. By the time this process is done, the time slice allocated to each thread is mainly spent unpacking and packing the thread local storage. Very little time is spent executing the instructions in the thread. The system may even lock up completely leaving poor John without any mail from us. What may make more sense is to create a single thread and execute the SendAllEmail method on that thread. Additionally, you could use a thread pool with a fixed number of threads. In this instance, when one thread in the pool has completed, it will spawn the next thread and send another e-mail.

One common programming practice is to place work into a queue to be processed by a service. For instance, a bank may place an XML-based file in a network directory to be picked up by a service running on another server. The service would scan the directory for new files and process them one at a time. If more than one file is placed in the directory at a time, the service would process them one by one. In a typical environment, new files would be placed in this directory infrequently. Based on this information, at first glance, this might seem like a good time to start a new thread when a file is found. You would be right, but think about what would happen if the service that processes these files was stopped. What happens if a network problem prevents the service from accessing the directory for a long period of time? The files would pile up in the directory. When the service finally started again, or was allowed access to the directory once again, each file would essentially spawn a new thread on the service. Anyone who has used this model can tell you that this situation can bring a server to its knees.

The file model is just one example. Another similar model may be to use Microsoft BizTalk Server or Microsoft Message Queue with a service that processes items in a queue. All of these implementations have the same basic structure. The actual implementation isn't the important thing to note here. The point to walk away with is that if your work is being placed into a queue and you feel that multithreading is the answer, you might want to consider using thread pooling.

Summary

In this chapter we introduced the `System.Threading` namespace and examined the `Thread` class in detail. We also discussed some basic ideas to help you hone your decision making skills when it comes to multithreading your applications. You must always keep in mind the fact that threads require resources. Before you consume those resources, analyze what affect their use will have on the system and how you can minimize that overhead. You should consider creating a thread if you are accessing outside resources such as a network share or remote databases. You should also consider spawning a new thread when you plan to execute a lengthy process such as printing, I/O operations, or background data processing.

Whatever your situation, keep the number of your threads to a minimum. You will reduce the overhead on your processor, increase the amount of time that your time slice uses to process instructions within your thread, and reduce the amount of memory required by your application.

C#

Threading

Handbook

3

3

Working with Threads

In the previous chapters, we discussed how threads play an important role in developing multi-user applications. We used threads to solve some significant problems, like giving multiple users or clients access to the same resource at the same time. However, in the learning process we ignored one issue that we now need to address: what would happen to the resource if one user changes the state of the resource and at the same time another user wants to change the state of the same resource?

Let's take the example of an ATM. Mr. X and his wife Mrs. X both decide to empty their joint checking account by withdrawing $1,000 from an ATM. Unfortunately they forget to decide who will actually do the job. So, ironically, Mr. X and Mrs. X both access the checking account from different ATMs, at exactly the same time. If two users access the same account at the same time, and if the application is not thread-safe, it may possible that both the ATMs detect that there is enough amount in the checking account and dispense $1,000 to each of their users. The two users are causing two servier-side threads to access the account database at the same time. In an ideal scenario, when one user is trying to update their account, nobody else should have access to that account at that instance. In short, the access to that account should be locked when the user accesses it for updating any information regarding that account.

> **The .NET Framework provides specific mechanisms to deal with such problems. The phenomenon of allowing only one thread to access a resource at any point of time is called Synchronization. Synchronization is a feature available to developers for creating thread-safe access to critical resources.**

Why Worry About Synchronization?

There are two main reasons why any .NET developer needs to keep synchronization in mind when designing a multithreaded application:

❑ To avoid **race conditions**

❑ To ensure **threadsafety**

Since the .NET Framework has built-in support for threading, there is a possibility that any class you develop may eventually be used in a multithreaded application. You don't need to (and shouldn't) design every class to be thread-safe, because thread safety doesn't come for free. But you should at least *think* about thread safety every time you design a .NET class. The costs of thread safety and guidelines concerning when to make classes thread-safe are discussed later in the chapter. You need not worry about multithreaded access to local variables, method parameters, and return values, because these variables reside on the stack and are inherently thread-safe. But instance and class variables will only be thread-safe if you design your class appropriately.

Before we examine the nuts and bolts of synchronization, let's consider in detail the ATM example that we discussed at the beginning of the chapter. Figure 1 depicts with more clarity the ATM scenario where Mr. X and Mrs. X are both trying to withdraw the last $1,000 from the same account at the same time. Such a condition, where one thread accesses a resource and leaves it in an invalid state while at the same time another thread uses the object when in an invalid state to produce undesirable results, is called a *race condition*. To avoid the race condition, we need to make the `Withdraw()` method *thread-safe* so that only one thread can access the method at any point of time.

Figure 1

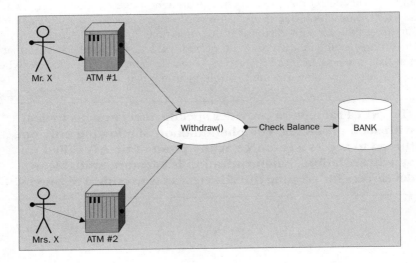

There are at least three ways to make an object thread-safe:

❑ Synchronize critical sections within the code

❑ Make the object immutable

❑ Use a thread-safe wrapper

Synchronize Critical Sections

To avoid undesirable effects caused by multiple threads updating a resource at the same time, we need to restrict access to that resource such that only one thread can update the resource at any point of time, or in other words, make the resource thread-safe. The most straightforward way to make an object or an instance variable thread-safe is to identify and synchronize its critical sections. A critical section is a piece of code in the program that may be accessed by multiple threads at the same time to update the state of the object. For example, in the above scenario where Mr. X and Mrs. X are both trying to access the same Withdraw() method at the same time, the Withdraw() method becomes the critical section and needs to be thread-safe. The easiest way to do this is to synchronize the method Withdraw() so that only one thread (either Mr. X or Mrs. X) can enter it at any one time. A process that cannot be interrupted during its execution is said to be **Atomic**. An atom (in the classical meaning of the word) is an indivisible unit, and atomic processes are units of code that execute as one complete unit – as if they were a single processor instruction. By making the Withdraw() method atomic, we ensure that it is not possible for another thread to change the balance of the same account until the first thread has finished changing the state of the account (emptying in our case). The following code listing is a pseudo-code representation of a non-thread-safe Account class:

```
public class Account
{
  public ApprovedOrNot Withdraw (Amount)
  {
    1.  Make sure that the user has enough cash (Check the Balance)
    2.  Update the Account with the new balance
    3.  Send approval to the ATM
  }
}
```

This next listing represents a thread-safe pseudo-code version of the Account class:

```
public class Account
{
  public ApprovedOrNot Withdraw (Amount)
  {
    lock this section (access for only one thread)
    {
      1.  Check the Account Balance
```

```
        2.   Update the Account with the new balance
        3.   Send approval to the ATM
      }
    }
  }
```

In the first listing, two or more threads can enter the critical section at the same time so there is a possibility that both the threads check the balance at the same time, with both the threads receiving the balance ($1,000) of the account. Due to this, there is a possibility that the ATM might dispense the $1,000 amount to both the users, thus causing the account to go overdrawn unexpectedly.

However, in the second listing, only one thread is allowed access to the critical section at any one time. Assuming that Mr. X's thread gets the first slice of time, Mr. X's thread will enter the `Withdraw()` method just before Mrs X's. So, when Mr. X's thread begins to execute the `Withdraw()` method, Mrs. X's thread is not allowed access to the critical section and has to wait until Mr. X's thread leaves the section. As a result, Mr. X's thread checks the balance of the account, updates the account with the new balance, which is $0 in this case, and then returns the approval Boolean value (`true` in this case) to the ATM for dispensing the cash. Until the cash is dispensed, no other thread has access to the critical section of Mr. and Mrs. X's `Account` object. After Mr. X receives the cash, Mrs. X's thread enters the critical section of the `Withdraw()` method. Now, when the method checks for the account balance, the returned amount is $0 and, as a result, the method returns a Boolean value of `false` indicating insufficient balance and the ATM denies the withdrawal.

Making the Account Object Immutable

An alternative way to make an object thread-safe is to make the object immutable. An immutable object is one whose state can't be changed once the object has been created. This can be achieved by not allowing any thread to modify the state of the `Account` object once it is created. In this approach, we separate out the critical sections that read the instance variables from those that write to instance variables. The critical sections that only read the instance variables are left as they are, whereas the critical sections that change the instance variables of the object are changed so that, instead of changing the state of the current object, a new object is created that embodies the new state, and a reference to that new object is returned. In this approach, we don't need to lock the critical section because no methods (only the constructor) of an immutable object actually writes to the object's instance variables, thus, an immutable object is by definition thread-safe.

Using a Thread-Safe Wrapper

The third approach to making an object thread-safe is to write a wrapper class over the object that will be thread-safe rather than making the object itself thread-safe. The object will remain unchanged and the new wrapper class will contain synchronized sections of thread-safe code. The following listing is a wrapper class over the Account object:

```
public class AccountWrapper
{
  private Account _a;

  public AccountWrapper (Account a)
  {
    this._a = a;
  }

  public bool Withdraw(double amount)
  {
    lock(_a)
    {
      return this._a.Withdraw(amount);
    }
  }
}
```

The AccountWrapper class acts as a thread-safe wrapper of the Account class. The Account instance is declared as a private instance variable of the AccountWrapper class so that no other object or thread can access the Account variable. In this approach, the Account object does not have any thread-safe features, since all the thread-safety is provided by the AccountWrapper class.

This approach is typically useful when you are dealing with a third-party library and the classes in that library are not designed for thread safety. For example, let's assume that the bank already has an Account class that it used for developing software for its mainframe system and, for the sake of consistency, wants to use the same Account class for writing the ATM software. From the documentation of the Account class that the bank has provided us, it is clear that the Account class is not thread-safe. Also, we are not given access to the Account source code for security reasons. In such a case, we would have to adopt the thread-safe wrapper approach where we develop the thread-safe AccountWrapper class as an extension to the Account class. Wrappers are used to add synchronization to non-thread-safe resources. All the synchronization logic will be in the wrapper class and keeping the non-thread-safe class intact.

.NET Synchronization Support

The .NET Framework provides a few classes in the `System.Threading`, `System.EnterpriseServices`, and `System.Runtime.Compiler` namespaces that allow the programmer to develop thread-safe code. The table below briefly describes some of the synchronization classes in the .NET Framework.

Class	Description
Monitor	`Monitor` objects are used to lock the critical sections of code so that one and only one thread has access to those critical sections at any point of time. They help ensure the *atomicity* of critical sections of code.
Mutex	`Mutex` objects are similar to `Monitor` objects with the exception that they grant exclusive access to a resource shared across processes to only one thread. The `Mutex` overloaded constructor can be used to specify `Mutex` ownership and name.
AutoResetEvent, ManualResetEvent	`AutoResetEvent` and `ManualResetEvent` are used to notify one or more waiting threads that an event has occurred. Both these classes are `NotInheritable`.
Interlocked	The `Interlocked` class has the `CompareExchange()`, `Decrement()`, `Exchange()`, and `Increment()` methods that provide a simple mechanism for synchronizing access to a variable that is shared by multiple threads.
SynchronizationAttribute	`SynchronizationAttribute` ensures that only one thread at a time can access an object. This synchronization process is automatic and does not need any kind of explicit locking of critical sections.
MethodImplAttribute	This attribute notifies the compiler on how the method should be implemented.

The MethodImplAttribute Class

The System.Runtime.CompilerServices namespace, as its name suggests, contains attributes that affect the runtime behaviour of the CLR (Common Language Runtime). MethodImplAttribute is one such attribute that notifies the CLR on how the method is implemented. One of the MethodImplAttribute constructors accepts the MethodImplOptions enumeration as a parameter. The MethodImplOptions enumeration has a field named Synchronized that specifies that only one thread is allowed to access this method at any point of time. This is similar to the lock keyword that we used in the previous example. The listing below of MI.cs shows how you can use this attribute to synchronize a method:

```csharp
using System;
using System.Runtime.CompilerServices;
using System.Threading;

namespace MethodImpl
{
  class MI
  {
    //This attribute locks the method for use
    //by one and only one thread at a time.
    [MethodImpl(MethodImplOptions.Synchronized)]
    public void doSomeWorkSync()
    {
      Console.WriteLine("doSomeWorkSync()" +
                  "--Lock held by Thread " +
                  Thread.CurrentThread.GetHashCode());

      //When a thread sleeps, it still holds the lock
      Thread.Sleep(5 * 1000);
      Console.WriteLine("doSomeWorkSync()" +
                  "--Lock released by Thread " +
                  Thread.CurrentThread.GetHashCode());
    }

    //This is a non synchronized method
    public void doSomeWorkNoSync()
    {
      Console.WriteLine("doSomeWorkNoSync()" +
                  "--Entered Thread is " +
                  Thread.CurrentThread.GetHashCode());
      Thread.Sleep(5 * 1000);
      Console.WriteLine("doSomeWorkNoSync()" +
                  "--Leaving Thread is " +
                  Thread.CurrentThread.GetHashCode());
    }

    [STAThread]
    static void Main(string[] args)
    {
```

```
        MI m = new MI();

        //Delegate for Non-Synchronous operation
        ThreadStart tsNoSyncDelegate =
            new ThreadStart(m.doSomeWorkNoSync);

        //Delegate for Synchronous operation
        ThreadStart tsSyncDelegate =
            new ThreadStart(m.doSomeWorkSync);

        Thread t1 = new Thread(tsNoSyncDelegate);
        Thread t2 = new Thread(tsNoSyncDelegate);

        t1.Start();
        t2.Start();

        Thread t3 = new Thread(tsSyncDelegate);
        Thread t4 = new Thread(tsSyncDelegate);

        t3.Start();
        t4.Start();
    }
  }
}
```

The output from the above listing will be similar to the following (output might vary from computer to computer as Thread IDs might differ):

```
doSomeWorkNoSync()--Entered Thread is 2
doSomeWorkNoSync()--Entered Thread is 3
doSomeWorkSync()--Lock held by Thread 4
doSomeWorkNoSync()--Leaving Thread is 2
doSomeWorkNoSync()--Leaving Thread is 3
doSomeWorkSync()--Lock released by Thread 4
doSomeWorkSync()--Lock held by Thread 5
doSomeWorkSync()--Lock released by Thread 5
```

In the above listing, the MI class has two methods: doSomeWorkSync() and doSomeWorkNoSync(). The MethodImpl attribute has been applied to the doSomeWorkSync() method to synchronize it, whereas doSomeWorkNoSync() is kept as it is so that multiple threads can access the method at the same time. In the Main() method, threads t1 and t2 access the non-synchronized method and threads t3 and t4 access the synchronized method. In both the methods, the Thread.Sleep() method is added to give sufficient time for another competing thread to enter the method while the first thread is still in the method. The expected behavior of the program should be such that threads t1 and t2 can simultaneously enter the doSomeWorkNoSync() method, whereas only one of the threads (either t3 or t4) will be allowed to enter the doSomeWorkSync() method. If t1 and t2 have the same priority, which thread will get the preference is totally at random; the .NET Framework does not guarantee the order in which the threads will be executed.

If you look at the output carefully, you will find that thread 2 (t1) and thread 3 (t2) entered the method doSomeWorkNoSync() at the same time, whereas, once thread 4 (t3) acquired the lock on the method doSomeWorkSync(), thread 5 (t4) was not allowed to enter the method until thread 4 (t3) released the lock on that method.

.NET Synchronization Strategies

The Common Language Infrastructure provides three strategies to synchronize access to instance and static methods and instance fields, namely:

❑   Synchronized contexts

❑   Synchronized code regions

❑   Manual synchronization

Synchronization Context

A context is a set of properties or usage rules that are common to a collection of objects with related run-time execution. The context properties that can be added include policies regarding synchronization, thread affinity, and transactions. In short, a context groups together like-minded objects. In this strategy, we use the SynchronizationAttribute class to enable simple, automatic synchronization for ContextBoundObject objects. Objects that reside in a context and are bound to the context rules are called context-bound objects. .NET automatically associates a synchronization lock with the object, locking it before every method call and releasing the lock (to allow other competing threads to access the object) when the method returns. This is a huge productivity gain, because thread synchronization and concurrency management are among the most difficult tasks that a developer encounters.

The SynchronizationAttribute class is useful to programmers who do not have experience of dealing with synchronization manually because it covers the instance variables, instance methods, and instance fields of the class to which this attribute is applied. It does not, however, handle synchronization of static fields and methods. It also does not help if you have to synchronize specific code blocks; synchronizing the entire object is the price you have to pay for ease of use. SynchronizationAttribute is very handy when programming with System.EnterpriseServices where objects belonging to a context (for example a transaction) are grouped together by the COM+ runtime.

Going back to our Account example, we can make our pseudo-code Account class thread-safe by using the SynchronizationAttribute. The listing below shows an example of synchronizing the Account class using the SynchronizationAttribute:

```
[SynchronizationAttribute(SynchronizationOption.Required)]
public class Account : ContextBoundObject
```

```
{
    public ApprovedOrNot Withdraw (Amount)
    {
    1.  Check the Account Balance
    2.  Update the Account with the new balance
    3.  Send approval to the ATM
    }
}
```

The SynchronizationAtttribute class has two constructors; a no-argument constructor and a constructor that takes in the SynchronizationOption enumeration as its only parameter. When using the default (no-argument) constructor, the SynchronizationOption is by default SynchronizationOption.Required. The other supported options are Disabled, NotSupported, RequiresNew, and Supported. The table below describes these options.

Synchronization Option	Description
Disabled	The synchronization requirements of the object are ignored, which means that the object is never thread-safe
NotSupported	The component is created without any governing synchronization, that is, the object cannot participate in any synchronization, regardless of the status of the caller
Required	Ensures that all the objects that are created are synchronized
RequiresNew	The component always participates in a new synchronization irrespective of the caller
Supported	Objects with this option participate in synchronization only if it exists (dependent on the caller)

Synchronized Code Regions

The second synchronization strategy concerns the synchronization of specific code regions. These specific code regions are critical pieces of code in methods that either change the state of the object or update another resource (for example a database, file). In this section we will look at the Monitor and ReaderWriterLock classes.

Monitors

Monitors are used to synchronize sections of code by acquiring a lock with the Monitor.Enter() method and then releasing that lock using the Monitor.Exit() method. The concept of a lock is normally used to explain the Monitor class. One thread gets a lock, while others wait until the lock is released. Once the lock is acquired on a code region, you can use the following methods within the Monitor.Enter() and Monitor.Exit() block:

❑   `Wait()` – This method releases the lock on an object and blocks the current thread until it reacquires the lock

❑   `Pulse()` – This method notifies a thread that is waiting in a queue that there has been a change in the object's state

❑   `PulseAll()` – This method notifies all threads that are waiting in a queue that there has been a change in the object's state

The Enter() and Exit() Methods

It is important to note that the `Monitor` methods are `static` and can be called on the `Monitor` class itself rather than an instance of that class. In the .NET Framework, each object has a lock associated with it that can be obtained and released so that only one thread at any time can access the object's instance variables and methods. Similarly, each object in the .NET Framework also provides a mechanism that allows it to be in a waiting state. Just like the lock mechanism, the main reason for this mechanism is to aid communication between threads. The need for such mechanism arises when one thread enters the critical section of an object and needs a certain condition to exist and assumes that another thread will create that condition from the same critical section.

The trick is now that only one thread is allowed in any critical section at any point of time, and when the first thread enters the critical section, no other thread can. So, how will the second thread create a condition in the critical section when the first thread is already in it? For example, if thread A has to get some data from the database and another thread B has to wait until all the data is received and then process the data, thread B calls the `Wait()` method and waits for thread A to notify it when the data arrives. When the data does arrive, A calls the `Pulse()` method, which notifies B so that B can process the data. This is achieved by the "Wait and Pulse" mechanism. The first thread enters the critical section and executes the `Wait()` method. The `Wait()` method releases the lock prior to waiting and the second thread is now allowed to enter the critical section, changes the required condition, and calls the `Pulse()` method to notify the waiting thread that the condition has been reached and it can now continue its execution. The first thread then reacquires the lock prior to returning from the `Monitor.Wait()` method and continues execution from the point where it called `Monitor.Wait()`.

No two threads can ever enter the `Enter()` method simultaneously. It is analogous to an ATM machine where only one person is allowed to operate at any point of time and no one else can get their chance until after the first person leaves. You can see that the names `Enter` and `Exit` have been chosen very aptly. Figure 2 illustrates the `Monitor` functionality.

Figure 2

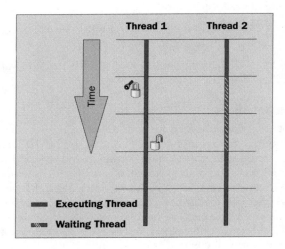

Let's see an example of using the `Enter()` and `Exit()` methods, `MonitorEnterExit.cs`:

```csharp
using System;
using System.Threading;

namespace MonitorEnterExit
{
  public class EnterExit
  {
    private int result = 0;

    public EnterExit()
    {
    }

    public void NonCriticalSection()
    {
      Console.WriteLine("Entered Thread " +
                        Thread.CurrentThread.GetHashCode());

      for(int i = 1; i <= 5; i++)
      {
        Console.WriteLine("Result = " + result++ + "  ThreadID "
                          + Thread.CurrentThread.GetHashCode());
        Thread.Sleep(1000);
      }

      Console.WriteLine("Exiting Thread " +
                        Thread.CurrentThread.GetHashCode());
    }
```

```
public void CriticalSection()
{
  //Enter the Critical Section
  Monitor.Enter(this);

  Console.WriteLine("Entered Thread " +
                  Thread.CurrentThread.GetHashCode());

  for(int i = 1; i <= 5 ; i++)
  {
    Console.WriteLine("Result = " + result++ + "  ThreadID " +
                  Thread.CurrentThread.GetHashCode());
    Thread.Sleep(1000);
  }

  Console.WriteLine("Exiting Thread " +
                  Thread.CurrentThread.GetHashCode());

  //Exit the Critical Section
  Monitor.Exit(this);
}

public static void  Main(String[] args)
{
  EnterExit e = new EnterExit( );

  if(args.Length > 0)
  {
    Thread nt1 =
        new Thread(new ThreadStart(e.NonCriticalSection));
    nt1.Start( );

    Thread nt2 =
        new Thread(new ThreadStart(e.NonCriticalSection));
    nt2.Start( );
  }
  else
  {
    Thread ct1 = new Thread(new ThreadStart(e.CriticalSection));
    ct1.Start( );

    Thread ct2 = new Thread(new ThreadStart(e.CriticalSection));
    ct2.Start( );
  }
 }
}
}
```

When you run the application without providing an input parameter you will get the output from the CriticalSection() method as follows:

```
Entered Thread 2
Result = 0   ThreadID 2
Result = 1   ThreadID 2
Result = 2   ThreadID 2
Result = 3   ThreadID 2
Result = 4   ThreadID 2
Exiting Thread 2
Entered Thread 3
Result = 5   ThreadID 3
Result = 6   ThreadID 3
Result = 7   ThreadID 3
Result = 8   ThreadID 3
Result = 9   ThreadID 3
Exiting Thread 3
```

Conversely, when you provide an input parameter, the corresponding output will be from the NonCriticalSection() method:

```
Entered Thread 2
Result = 0   ThreadID 2
Entered Thread 3
Result = 1   ThreadID 3
Result = 2   ThreadID 2
Result = 3   ThreadID 3
Result = 4   ThreadID 2
Result = 5   ThreadID 3
Result = 6   ThreadID 2
Result = 7   ThreadID 3
Result = 8   ThreadID 2
Result = 9   ThreadID 3
Exiting Thread 2
Exiting Thread 3
```

In the above example, we declare an EnterExit class with a global result variable and two methods: NonCriticalSection() and CriticalSection(). In the NonCriticalSection() section we don't specify any monitors to lock the section, while in the CriticalSection() method we lock the critical section using a monitor. Both the methods modify the value of result.

The critical section is defined as the code block between the Monitor.Enter(this) and Monitor.Exit(this) lines. The this parameter indicates that the lock should be held on the current object in consideration. It is always confusing to decide on which object to pass into the Enter() method as a parameter. When you need to lock the object so that no other thread can access the object under consideration, pass a this pointer as the parameter. For example, in the AccountWrapper example previously discussed, we passed the Account object to the Monitor, rather than a this pointer of the AccountWrapper object. This was because our intention was to lock the Account object and not the AccountWrapper object. We don't want multiple threads to access the Account object, but we don't mind multiple threads accessing AccountWrapper object.

In the `Main()` method, we run the appropriate methods based on the arguments provided. If no argument is supplied, we use the `CriticalSection()` method and, if any argument is supplied, we use the `NonCriticalSection()` method. In both the cases, we have two threads accessing the methods, started from the `Main()` method, at the same time and changing the `result` variable. Though they are declared sequentially, the `For` loop and the sleep time will ensure that the threads will try to compete for resources.

Comparing the outputs of the critical and non-critical sections makes the concept of critical sections clear. If you observe the output from the `NonCriticalSection()` method, both the threads `nt1` and `nt2` are changing the `result` variable at the same time, thus resulting in a mixed output. This is because there are no locks in the `NonCriticalSection()` method and thus the method is not thread-safe. Multiple threads can access the method and so the global variable at the same time. On the other hand, if you observe the output from the `CriticalSection()` method, it is clear that until the thread `ct1` exits the critical section, no other thread (`ct2` in this case) is allowed access to the critical section.

The Wait() and Pulse() Mechanism

The `Wait()` and `Pulse()` mechanism is used for interaction between threads. When a `Wait()` method is issued on an object, the thread that is accessing that object waits until it gets a signal to wake up. The `Pulse()` and `PulseAll()` are used for signaling to waiting thread(s). The following listing is an example of how the `Wait()` and `Pulse()` methods work, `WaitAndPulse.cs`:

> **The `Wait()` and `Pulse()` methods can be called only within the `Enter()` and `Exit()` code block.**

```
using System;
using System.Threading;

namespace WaitAndPulse
{
  public class LockMe
  {
  }

  public class WaitPulse1
  {
    private int result = 0;
    private LockMe _lM;

    public WaitPulse1()
    {
    }
```

```
      public WaitPulse1(LockMe l)
      {
        this._lM = l;
      }

      public void CriticalSection()
      {
        Monitor.Enter(this._lM);
        //Enter the Critical Section

        Console.WriteLine("WaitPulse1:Entered Thread " +
                         Thread.CurrentThread.GetHashCode());

        for(int i = 1; i <= 5; i++)
        {
          Monitor.Wait(this._lM);
          Console.WriteLine("WaitPulse1:WokeUp");
          Console.WriteLine("WaitPulse1:Result = " + result++ +
                         "  ThreadID " +
                         Thread.CurrentThread.GetHashCode());
          Monitor.Pulse(this._lM);
        }

        Console.WriteLine("WaitPulse1:Exiting Thread " +
                         Thread.CurrentThread.GetHashCode());

        //Exit the Critical Section
        Monitor.Exit(this._lM);
      }
    }

    public class WaitPulse2
    {
      private int result = 0;
      internal LockMe _lM;

      public WaitPulse2()
      {
      }

      public WaitPulse2(LockMe l)
      {
        this._lM = l;
      }

      public void CriticalSection()
      {
        Monitor.Enter(this._lM);
        //Enter the Critical Section

        Console.WriteLine("WaitPulse2:Entered Thread " +
                         Thread.CurrentThread.GetHashCode());
```

```
        for(int i = 1; i <= 5; i++)
        {
          Monitor.Pulse(this._lM);
          Console.WriteLine("WaitPulse2:Result = " + result++ +
                            " ThreadID " +
                            Thread.CurrentThread.GetHashCode());
          Monitor.Wait(this._lM);
          Console.WriteLine("WaitPulse2:WokeUp");
        }

        Console.WriteLine("WaitPulse2:Exiting Thread " +
                          Thread.CurrentThread.GetHashCode());

        //Exit the Critical Section
        Monitor.Exit(this._lM);
      }
    }

    public class ClassForMain
    {
      public static void  Main(String[] args)
      {
        LockMe l = new LockMe();

        WaitPulse1 e1 = new WaitPulse1(l);
        WaitPulse2 e2 = new WaitPulse2(l);

        Thread t1 = new Thread(new ThreadStart(e1.CriticalSection));
        t1.Start( );

        Thread t2 = new Thread(new ThreadStart(e2.CriticalSection));
        t2.Start( );

        //Wait till the user enters something
        Console.ReadLine();
      }
    }
}
```

The output from WaitAndPulse is:

```
WaitPulse1:Entered Thread 2
WaitPulse2:Entered Thread 3
WaitPulse2:Result = 0 ThreadID 3
WaitPulse1:WokeUp
WaitPulse1:Result = 0  ThreadID 2
WaitPulse2:WokeUp
WaitPulse2:Result = 1 ThreadID 3
WaitPulse1:WokeUp
WaitPulse1:Result = 1  ThreadID 2
WaitPulse2:WokeUp
WaitPulse2:Result = 2 ThreadID 3
```

```
WaitPulse1:WokeUp
WaitPulse1:Result = 2   ThreadID 2
WaitPulse2:WokeUp
WaitPulse2:Result = 3 ThreadID 3
WaitPulse1:WokeUp
WaitPulse1:Result = 3   ThreadID 2
WaitPulse2:WokeUp
WaitPulse2:Result = 4 ThreadID 3
WaitPulse1:WokeUp
WaitPulse1:Result = 4   ThreadID 2
WaitPulse1:Exiting Thread 2
WaitPulse2:WokeUp
WaitPulse2:Exiting Thread 3
WaitPulse1: Exiting Thread 2
WaitPulse2: WokeUp
WaitPulse2: Exiting Thread 3
```

In the Main() method, we create a LockMe object called 1. Then we create two objects of type WaitPulse1 and WaitPulse2, and pass them as delegates so that the threads can call the CriticalSection() method of both the objects. Note that the LockMe object instance in WaitPulse1 is the same as the LockMe object instance in WaitPulse2, as the object has been passed by reference to their respective constructors. After initializing the objects, we create two threads, t1 and t2, and pass them the two CriticalSection() methods respectively.

Assuming that WaitPulse1.CriticalSection() gets called first, then thread t1 enters the critical section of the method with a lock on the LockMe object and then executes Monitor.Wait() in the for loop. By executing Monitor.Wait(), it is waiting for a run-time notification (Monitor.Pulse()) from another thread to be woken up. We lock the LockMe object because we want only one thread to access the shared LockMe instance at any point of time.

Note that when the thread executes the Monitor.Wait() method, it releases the lock on the LockMe object temporarily, so that other threads can access it. After thread t1 goes into the waiting state, thread t2 is free to access the LockMe object. Even though the LockMe object is a separate object (WaitPulse1 and WaitPulse2), they both refer to the same object reference. Thread t2 acquires the lock on the LockMe object and enters the WaitPulse2.CriticalSection() method. As soon as it enters the for loop, it sends a run-time notification (Monitor.Pulse()) to the thread that is waiting on the LockMe object (t1 in this case) and goes off to the waiting state. As a result, t1 wakes up and acquires the lock on the LockMe object. Thread t1 then accesses the result variable and sends a run-time notification to the thread waiting on the LockMe object (thread t2 in this case). This cycle continues until the for loop ends.

If you compare the description above with the output of the program, the concept will be crystal clear. It is important to note that every Enter() method should be accompanied by an Exit() method or else the program will never quit.

The `Enter()` method takes an object as a parameter. If the object parameter is `null`, a method variable, or an object of a value type like an integer an exception will be thrown.

The TryEnter() Method

The `TryEnter()` method of the `Monitor` class is similar to the `Enter()` method in that it tries to acquire an exclusive lock on an object. However, it does not block like the `Enter()` method. If the thread enters successfully then the `TryEnter()` method will return `true`.

Two of the three overloads of `TryEnter()` take a timeout parameter representing the amount of time to wait for the lock. Let's see an example of how to use `TryEnter()`, `MonitorTryEnter.cs`:

```
using System;
using System.Threading;

namespace MonitorTryEnter
{
  public class TryEnter
  {
    public TryEnter()
    {
    }

    public void CriticalSection()
    {
      bool b = Monitor.TryEnter(this, 1000);
      Console.WriteLine("Thread " +
                        Thread.CurrentThread.GetHashCode() +
                        " TryEnter Value " + b);

      for (int i = 1; i <= 3; i++)
      {
        Thread.Sleep(1000);
        Console.WriteLine(i + " " +
                          Thread.CurrentThread.GetHashCode() + " ");
      }

      Monitor.Exit(this);
    }

    public static void Main()
    {
      TryEnter a = new TryEnter();
      Thread t1 = new Thread(new ThreadStart(a.CriticalSection));
      Thread t2 = new Thread(new ThreadStart(a.CriticalSection));
      t1.Start();
      t2.Start();
    }
  }
}
```

One possible output from `MonitorTryEnter` is:

```
Thread 2 TryEnter Value True
Thread 3 TryEnter Value False
1 2
1 3
2 2
2 3
3 2
3 3
```

`TryEnter()` is useful in situations where contention is likely to occur and you don't want to put the thread sleep for an unspecified period of time. A good example of this is dialing in to an ISP. Assume there are two applications A and B that both want to dial in to an ISP using the same modem. There is only one modem connection available and once the connection is established, we do not know how much time the connected application will stay connected. Suppose application A dials the ISP first and after some time application B wants to dial; there is no point in application B waiting indefinitely, as we don't know how long application A will remain connected. In this case, application B could use `TryEnter()` to determine whether the modem is already locked by anyother application (A in this case), rather than waiting indefinitely using the `Enter()` method.

The lock Statement

The `lock` keyword can be used as an alternative to the methods of the `Monitor` class. The following two blocks of code are equivalent:

```
Monitor.Enter(x)
   ...
Monitor.Exit(x)
```

```
lock(this)
{
   ...
}
```

The following example, `Locking.cs`, uses the `lock` keyword instead of the explicit `Monitor` methods:

```
using System;
using System.Threading;

namespace Lock
{
  public class LockWord
  {
    private int result = 0;
```

```
public void CriticalSection()
{
  lock(this)
  {
    //Enter the Critical Section
    Console.WriteLine("Entered Thread " +
                    Thread.CurrentThread.GetHashCode());

    for(int i = 1; i <= 5; i++)
    {
      Console.WriteLine("Result = " + result++ + "  ThreadID " +
                    Thread.CurrentThread.GetHashCode());
      Thread.Sleep(1000);
    }

    Console.WriteLine("Exiting Thread " +
                    Thread.CurrentThread.GetHashCode());
  }
}

public static void  Main()
{
  LockWord e = new LockWord();

  Thread t1 = new Thread(new ThreadStart(e.CriticalSection));
  t1.Start();

  Thread t2 = new Thread(new ThreadStart(e.CriticalSection));
  t2.Start();
}
}
}
```

The output from Locking.cs will be the same as for MonitorEnterExit (when a parameter has been supplied):

```
Entered Thread 2
Result = 0   ThreadID 2
Result = 1   ThreadID 2
Result = 2   ThreadID 2
Result = 3   ThreadID 2
Result = 4   ThreadID 2
Exiting Thread 2
Entered Thread 3
Result = 5   ThreadID 3
Result = 6   ThreadID 3
Result = 7   ThreadID 3
Result = 8   ThreadID 3
Result = 9   ThreadID 3
Exiting Thread 3
```

The ReaderWriterLock Class

A ReaderWriterLock defines the lock that implements single-writer and multiple-reader semantics. This class is popularly used in file operations where the file can be read by multiple threads but can be updated by one and only one thread. The four main methods in the ReaderWriterLock class are:

❑ AcquireReaderLock(): This overloaded method acquires a reader lock, using either an integer or a TimeSpan for the timeout value. The timeout can be an invaluable tool used to detect deadlocks.

❑ AcquireWriterLock(): This overloaded method acquires a writer lock, using either an integer or a TimeSpan for the timeout value.

❑ ReleaseReaderLock(): Releases the reader lock.

❑ ReleaseWriterLock(): Releases the writer lock.

> **Using the ReaderWriterLock class, any number of threads can safely read data concurrently. Only when threads are updating is data locked. Reader threads can acquire a lock only if there are no writers holding the lock. Writer threads can acquire lock only if there are no readers or writers holding the lock.**

The following listing, ReadWriteLock.cs, demonstrates the use of the ReaderWriterLock() lock:

```csharp
using System;
using System.Threading;

namespace ReadWriteLock
{
  public class ReadWrite
  {
    private ReaderWriterLock rwl;
    private int x;
    private int y;

    public ReadWrite()
    {
      rwl = new ReaderWriterLock();
    }

    public void ReadInts(ref int a, ref int b)
    {
      rwl.AcquireReaderLock(Timeout.Infinite);
```

FOR _____

Urgent ☐

DATE _____ TIME _____ A.M.
P.M.

While You Were Out

M _____

OF _____

PHONE _____
AREA CODE   NUMBER   EXTENSION

TELEPHONED		PLEASE CALL	
CAME TO SEE YOU		WILL CALL AGAIN	
RETURNED YOUR CALL		WANTS TO SEE YOU	

MESSAGE _____

_____

_____

_____

_____

_____

_____

adams

SIGNED

9711

```
    try
    {
      a = this.x;
      b = this.y;
    }
    finally
    {
      rwl.ReleaseReaderLock();
    }
  }

  public void WriteInts(int a, int b)
  {
    rwl.AcquireWriterLock(Timeout.Infinite);

    try
    {
      this.x = a;
      this.y = b;
      Console.WriteLine("x = " + this.x + " y = " + this.y +
                        " ThreadID = " +
                        Thread.CurrentThread.GetHashCode());
    }
    finally
    {
      rwl.ReleaseWriterLock();
    }
  }
}

public class RWApp
{
  private ReadWrite rw = new ReadWrite();

  public static void Main(String[] args)
  {
    RWApp e = new RWApp();

    //Writer Threads
    Thread wt1 = new Thread(new ThreadStart(e.Write));
    wt1.Start();
    Thread wt2 = new Thread(new ThreadStart(e.Write));
    wt2.Start();

    //Reader Threads
    Thread rt1 = new Thread(new ThreadStart(e.Read));
    rt1.Start();
    Thread rt2 = new Thread(new ThreadStart(e.Read));
    rt2.Start();
  }
```

```
    private void Write()
    {
      int a = 10;
      int b = 11;
      Console.WriteLine("********  Write *********");

      for (int i = 0; i < 5; i++)
      {
        this.rw.WriteInts(a++, b++);
        Thread.Sleep(1000);
      }
    }

    private void Read()
    {
      int a = 10;
      int b = 11;

      Console.WriteLine("********  Read *********");
      for (int i = 0; i < 5; i++)
      {
        this.rw.ReadInts(ref a, ref b);
        Console.WriteLine("For i = " + i + " a = " + a + " b = " + b +
                          " ThreadID = " +
                          Thread.CurrentThread.GetHashCode());
        Thread.Sleep(1000);
      }
    }
  }
}
```

An example output from ReadWriteLock could be as follows:

```
********  Read *********
For i = 0 a = 0 b = 0 ThreadID = 5
********  Read *********
For i = 0 a = 0 b = 0 ThreadID = 4
********  Write *********
x = 10 y = 11 ThreadID = 3
********  Write *********
x = 10 y = 11 ThreadID = 2
For i = 1 a = 10 b = 11 ThreadID = 4
x = 11 y = 12 ThreadID = 3
x = 11 y = 12 ThreadID = 2
For i = 1 a = 11 b = 12 ThreadID = 5
For i = 2 a = 11 b = 12 ThreadID = 4
x = 12 y = 13 ThreadID = 3
x = 12 y = 13 ThreadID = 2
For i = 2 a = 12 b = 13 ThreadID = 5
For i = 3 a = 12 b = 13 ThreadID = 4
x = 13 y = 14 ThreadID = 3
x = 13 y = 14 ThreadID = 2
```

```
For i = 3 a = 13 b = 14 ThreadID = 5
For i = 4 a = 13 b = 14 ThreadID = 4
x = 14 y = 15 ThreadID = 3
x = 14 y = 15 ThreadID = 2
For i = 4 a = 14 b = 15 ThreadID = 5
```

In the above listing, threads wt1 and wt2 are writer threads that acquire writer locks in the WriteInts() method and threads rt1 and rt2 are reader threads that acquire reader locks in the ReadInts() method. In the WriteInts() method, the instance variables x and y are changed to the new values a and b respectively. When thread wt1 or wt2 acquires a writer lock by calling AcquireWriterLock(), no other thread (including the reader threads rt1 and rt2) is allowed access to the object until the thread releases the lock by calling the ReleaseWriterLock() method. This behavior is similar to that of Monitors. In the ReadInts() method, threads rt1 and rt2 acquire reader locks by calling the AcquireReaderLock() method. In the ReadInts() method, both the threads rt1 and rt2 can be given concurrent access to the instance variables x and y. Until the reader threads release their reader locks, neither of the writer threads (wt1 and wt2) is given access to the object. Only reader threads can have concurrent access to the object after acquiring the reader lock.

Monitors might be "too safe" for threads that plan only to read the data rather than modify it. Monitors also have a performance hit associated with them and, for read-only type access, this performance hit is not necessary. The ReaderWriterLock class offers an elegant solution to dealing with read-and-write access to data by allowing any number of concurrent threads to read the data. It locks the data only when threads are updating the data. Reader threads can acquire a lock if and only if there are no writer threads holding the lock. Writer threads can acquire the lock if and only if there are no reader or writer threads holding the lock. Thus, the ReaderWriterLock behaves in the same way as a critical section. ReaderWriterLock also supports a timeout value that can be very useful in detecting deadlocks.

Manual Synchronization

The third synchronization strategy concerns manual techniques and the .NET Framework provides a classic suite of techniques. They give the programmer the ability to create and manage multithreaded applications using a low-level threading API analogous to the WIN32 Threading API.

The table overleaf shows some of the classes in the System.Threading namespace that can be used for Manual Synchronization.

Class	Description
AutoResetEvent	The AutoResetEvent class is used to make a thread wait until some event puts it in the signaled state by calling the Set() method. A signaled state indicates that there are no threads waiting. The AutoResetEvent is automatically reset to non-signaled by the system after a single waiting thread has been released. If no threads are waiting, the event object's state remains signaled. The AutoResetEvent corresponds to a Win32 CreateEvent call, specifying false for the bManualReset argument.
ManualResetEvent	The ManualResetEvent class is also used to make a thread wait until some event puts it in the signaled state by calling Set() method. The state of a ManualResetEvent object remains signaled until it is set explicitly to the non-signaled state by the Reset() method. The ManualResetEvent corresponds to a Win32 CreateEvent call, specifying true for the bManualReset argument.
Mutex	A Mutex lock provides cross-process as well as cross-thread synchronization. The state of the Mutex is signaled if no thread owns it. The Mutex class doesn't have all of the wait-and-pulse functionality of the Monitor class, but it does offer the creation of named mutexes (using the overloaded constructor) that can be used between processes. The benefit of using a Mutex over a Monitor is that a Mutex can be used across processes whereas a Monitor cannot.
Interlocked	The Interlocked class provides methods for atomic, non-blocking integer updates that are shared between multiple threads. The threads of different processes can use this mechanism if the variable is in shared memory.

The ManualResetEvent Class

A ManualResetEvent object can possess only one of the two states; signaled (true) or non-signaled (false). The ManualResetEvent class inherits from the WaitHandle class and the ManualResetEvent constructor takes in a parameter that affirms the initial state of the object. The Set() and Reset() methods return a Boolean value indicating whether the change has taken place successfully or not.

The following listing, NETThreadEvents.cs, shows the use of the ManualResetEvent class with a non-signaled state. First we create an object called mansig and give it a value of false. The WaitOne() method will wait until the mansig turns into true or the time value expires. Since the time duration elapsed while waiting, and the value of mansig was not set to true, it stopped blocking and returned with a value of false:

```
using System;
using System.Threading;

namespace NETThreadEvents
{
  public class NonSignaledManual
  {
    public static void Main()
    {
      ManualResetEvent mansig;
      mansig = new ManualResetEvent(false) ;
      Console.WriteLine("ManualResetEvent Before WaitOne " );
      bool b = mansig.WaitOne(1000,false);
      Console.WriteLine("ManualResetEvent After WaitOne " + b);
    }
  }
}
```

The output from NETThreadEvents with a value of false is:

```
ManualResetEvent Before WaitOne
ManualResetEvent After WaitOne False
```

In NETThreadEvents.cs, we construct a ManualResetEvent object with a value of false. The Boolean value false sets the initial state of the ManualResetEvent object to non-signaled. Then we call the WaitOne() method of the base class WaitHandle. The WaitOne() method takes two parameters. The first one is the number of milliseconds for which we want the thread to wait at the WaitOne() method; the thread therefore waits for one second before quitting. The second parameter is the exitContext. If you are already in the synchronization domain for the context and want to exit the synchronization context or if you want to reacquire the synchronization context, you should set this parameter to true.

The program blocks for one second at the WaitOne() method and then quits because of the timeout. The state of the ManualResetEvent is still false, thus the Boolean b returned by WaitOne() is false. Now let's figure out what will happen if we set the state of ManualResetEvent to signaled (true) when we create it:

```
using System;
using System.Threading;
```

```
namespace NETThreadEvents
{
  public class NonSignaledManual
  {
    public static void Main()
    {
      ManualResetEvent mansig;
      mansig = new ManualResetEvent(true);
      Console.WriteLine("ManualResetEvent Before WaitOne ");
      bool b = mansig.WaitOne(1000,false);
      Console.WriteLine("ManualResetEvent After WaitOne " + b);
      Console.ReadLine();
    }
  }
}
```

The output from NETThreadEvents with a value of true is:

```
ManualResetEvent Before WaitOne
ManualResetEvent After WaitOne True
```

By changing initial state of the ManualResetEvent to signaled, the thread does not wait at the WaitOne() method even though we specified the timeout value of 1,000 milliseconds. When the ManualResetEvent was non-signaled in the previous sample, the thread waited for the state to change to signaled, but it timed out after 1,000 milliseconds. The state is already signaled, so the thread has no reason to wait on the WaitOne() method. To change the state of the ManualResetEvent to non-signaled, we have to call the Reset() method of ManualResetEvent, and to change the state to signaled, we have to call the Set() method.

The following listing, ManualReset.cs, shows the usage of the Reset() method, and the next, ManualSet.cs, shows the usage of the Set() method:

```
using System;
using System.Threading;

namespace ManualReset
{
  class Reset
  {
    [STAThread]
    static void Main()
    {
      ManualResetEvent manRE;
      manRE = new ManualResetEvent(true);
      bool state = manRE.WaitOne(1000,true);
      Console.WriteLine("ManualResetEvent After first WaitOne " +
                        state);
```

```
          //Change the state to non-signaled
          manRE.Reset();
          state = manRE.WaitOne(5000,true);
          Console.WriteLine("ManualResetEvent After second WaitOne " +
                      state);
      }
    }
  }
```

The output from ManualReset is:

```
ManualResetEvent After first WaitOne True
ManualResetEvent After second WaitOne False
```

In ManualReset, we set the state of the ManualResetEvent object to signaled (True) in its constructor. As a result, the thread does not does not wait at the first WaitOne() method and returns true. Then we reset the state of the ManualResetEvent object to non-signaled (false), so we see that the thread has to wait for five seconds until it times out.

In ManualSet.cs we use the Set() method:

```
using System;
using System.Threading;

namespace ManualSet
{
  class Set
  {
    [STAThread]
    static void Main(string[] args)
    {
      ManualResetEvent manRE;
      manRE = new ManualResetEvent(false);
      Console.WriteLine("Before WaitOne");
      bool state = manRE.WaitOne(5000,true);
      Console.WriteLine("ManualResetEvent After first WaitOne " +
                  state);

      //Change the state to signaled
      manRE.Set();
      state = manRE.WaitOne(5000,true);
      Console.WriteLine("ManualResetEvent After second WaitOne " +
                  state);
    }
  }
}
```

The output from ManualSet is:

```
Before WaitOne
ManualResetEvent After first WaitOne False
ManualResetEvent After second WaitOne True
```

In `ManualSet`, we set the initial state of the `ManualResetEvent` object to non-signaled (`false`). As a result, the thread has to wait on the first `WaitOne()` method. Then we set the state to signaled using the `Set()` method, and the thread refuses to wait on the second `WaitOne()` method, and quits.

Just as the `WaitOne()` method waits for a single event object to become signaled, the `WaitAll()` method waits for all the event objects to become `true` or signaled, or it will stay there until the timeout occurs and the `WaitAny()` method waits for any of the event objects to become `true` or signaled.

The AutoResetEvent Class

The `AutoResetEvent` class works in a similar way to the `ManualResetEvent` class. It waits for the timeout to take place or the event to be signaled and then notifies the waiting threads about the event. One important difference between `ManualResetEvent` and `AutoResetEvent` is that `AutoResetEvent` changes state at the `WaitOne()` method. The following listing shows the usage of the `AutoResetEvent` class:

```
using System;
using System.Threading;

namespace AutoReset
{
  class Auto
  {
    [STAThread]
    static void Main()
    {
      AutoResetEvent aRE;
      aRE = new AutoResetEvent(true);
      Console.WriteLine("Before First WaitOne ");
      bool state = aRE.WaitOne(1000,true);
      Console.WriteLine("After First WaitOne " + state);
      state = aRE.WaitOne(5000,true);
      Console.WriteLine("After Second WaitOne " + state);
    }
  }
}
```

The output from `AutoReset` is the same as that from the `ManualReset` example shown earlier:

```
Before First WaitOne
After First WaitOne True
After Second WaitOne False
```

110

In AutoReset, the differences between the AutoResetEvent and ManualResetEvent are clear. The state of the event object changes from signaled to non-signaled at the first WaitOne(), and then it changes state again from non-signaled to signaled at the second WaitOne() method. As a result, the thread does not wait at the first WaitOne() method and has to wait at the second WaitOne() method until the time expires.

The Mutex Class

Like the ManualResetEvent and the AutoResetEvent classes, the Mutex class is also derived from the WaitHandle class. It is very similar to the Monitor class with the exception that it can be used for *interprocess* synchronization. Let's look at an example, WroxMutex.cs:

```
using System;
using System.Threading;

namespace WroxMutex
{
  class NETMutex
  {
    static Mutex myMutex;

    public static void Main()
    {
      myMutex = new Mutex(true, "WROX");
      NETMutex nm = new NETMutex();
      Thread t = new Thread(new ThreadStart(nm.Run));
      t.Start();
      Console.WriteLine("Thread Sleep for 5 sec");
      Thread.Sleep(5000);
      Console.WriteLine("Thread Woke Up");
      myMutex.ReleaseMutex();
      Console.WriteLine("Before WaitOne");
      myMutex.WaitOne();
      Console.WriteLine("Lock owned by Main Thread");
    }

    public void Run()
    {
      Console.WriteLine("In Run");
      myMutex.WaitOne();
      Console.WriteLine("Thread sleeping for 10 secs");
      Thread.Sleep(10000);
      Console.WriteLine("End of Run() method");
    }
  }
}
```

The output from WroxMutex is:

```
Thread will sleep for 5 seconds
In Run method
Thread Woke Up
Thread will sleep for 10 seconds
Before WaitOne
End of Run method
Lock owned by Main Thread
```

In `WroxMutex`, we construct a `Mutex` with a Boolean value indicating that the calling thread should have initial ownership of the `Mutex`, and a string that is the name of the `Mutex`. We then create a thread, which calls the `Run()` method. The `Mutex` is still owned by the main thread. In the `Run()` method, the thread `t` has to wait until the main thread releases the ownership of the `Mutex`. Thus, the thread `t` waits at the `WaitOne()` method call in the `Run()` method. After sleeping for five seconds, the main thread releases the `Mutex` lock. Thread `t` then gets the ownership of the `Mutex` lock and then goes off for a sleep. Now, the `Main()` method will not be able to acquire the ownership of the `Mutex` until the thread `t` releases the ownership or aborts. In this case, thread `t` times out and dies, so the ownership of the `Mutex` is transferred back to the main thread.

The Interlocked Class

`Interlocked` synchronizes access to an integer variable that is being shared by a number of threads. The operation is carried out in an *atomic* manner. Let's see an example, `WroxInterlocked.cs`:

```
using System;
using System.Threading;

namespace WroxInterlocked
{
  class WinterLocked
  {
    public ManualResetEvent a = new ManualResetEvent(false);
    private int i = 5;

    public void Run(object s)
    {
      Interlocked.Increment(ref i);
      Console.WriteLine("{0} {1}",
                        Thread.CurrentThread.GetHashCode(), i);
    }
  }

  public class MainApp
  {
    public static void  Main()
    {
      ManualResetEvent mR = new ManualResetEvent(false);
      WinterLocked wL = new WinterLocked();
```

```
        for(int i = 1; i <= 10; i++)
        {
            ThreadPool.QueueUserWorkItem(new WaitCallback(wL.Run), 1);
        }
        mR.WaitOne(10000, true);
    }
  }
}
```

The output for `WroxInterLocked` is:

```
Thread ID = 2 Count = 1
Thread ID = 2 Count = 2
Thread ID = 2 Count = 3
Thread ID = 2 Count = 4
Thread ID = 2 Count = 5
Thread ID = 2 Count = 6
Thread ID = 2 Count = 7
Thread ID = 2 Count = 8
Thread ID = 2 Count = 9
Thread ID = 2 Count = 10
```

`WroxInterLocked` shows the use of the `Interlocked` class. We increment the value of the global variable `i` in an atomic manner. Like the `Increment()` method, there is also a `Decrement()` method that reduces the value of a variable by one. In the same manner, the `Exchange()` method changes the value of two variables passed to it as `ByRef` parameters.

Static Variables and Methods and Synchronization

Variables and methods that are `static` are affected differently from instance variables and methods in a synchronization lock. `static` variables are class variables, whereas variables that belong to an object are object or instance variables. In other words, there will be only one instance of a `static` variable and a `static` method will be shared by multiple objects of the same class and every object of the same class has its own set of instance variables and methods. So, if you synchronize a `static` variable or a `static` method, the lock is applied on the *entire class*. As a result, no other object will be allowed to use the `static` variables of the class.

The ThreadStaticAttribute Class

`ThreadStaticAttribute` is used on a `static` variable to create a separate variable for each thread executing it, rather than sharing (default behavior) the `static` variable across threads. This means that a `static` variable with the `ThreadStaticAttribute` is not shared across different threads accessing it. Each thread accessing it will have a separate copy of the same variable. If one thread modifies the variable, another thread accessing it will not be able to see the changes. This behavior is contrary to the default behavior of `static` variables. In short, `ThreadStaticAttribute` gives us the best of both worlds (`static` and instance).

The following listing shows the use of ThreadStaticAttribute (WroxShared.cs):

```csharp
using System;
using System.Threading;

namespace WroxStatic
{
  class ThreadStatic
  {
    [System.ThreadStaticAttribute()]
    public static int x = 1;
    public static int y = 1;

    public void Run()
    {
      for (int i = 1; i <= 10; i++)
      {
        Thread t2 = Thread.CurrentThread;
        x++;
        y++;
        Console.WriteLine("i = " + i +
                    " ThreadID = " + t2.GetHashCode() +
                    " x(static attribute)= " + x +
                    " y = " + y);
        Thread.Sleep(1000);
      }
    }
  }

  public class MainApp
  {
    public static void Main()
    {
      ThreadStatic tS = new ThreadStatic();
      Thread t1 = new Thread(new ThreadStart(tS.Run));
      Thread t2 = new Thread(new ThreadStart(tS.Run));
      t1.Start();
      t2.Start();
    }
  }
}
```

The output from WroxStatic is:

```
i = 1 ThreadID = 2 x(static attribute)= 1 y = 2
i = 1 ThreadID = 3 x(static attribute)= 1 y = 3
i = 2 ThreadID = 2 x(static attribute)= 2 y = 4
i = 2 ThreadID = 3 x(static attribute)= 2 y = 5
i = 3 ThreadID = 2 x(static attribute)= 3 y = 6
i = 3 ThreadID = 3 x(static attribute)= 3 y = 7
i = 4 ThreadID = 2 x(static attribute)= 4 y = 8
i = 4 ThreadID = 3 x(static attribute)= 4 y = 9
```

```
i = 5  ThreadID = 2  x(static attribute)= 5  y = 10
i = 5  ThreadID = 3  x(static attribute)= 5  y = 11
i = 6  ThreadID = 2  x(static attribute)= 6  y = 12
i = 6  ThreadID = 3  x(static attribute)= 6  y = 13
i = 7  ThreadID = 2  x(static attribute)= 7  y = 14
i = 7  ThreadID = 3  x(static attribute)= 7  y = 15
i = 8  ThreadID = 2  x(static attribute)= 8  y = 16
i = 8  ThreadID = 3  x(static attribute)= 8  y = 17
i = 9  ThreadID = 2  x(static attribute)= 9  y = 18
i = 9  ThreadID = 3  x(static attribute)= 9  y = 19
i = 10 ThreadID = 2  x(static attribute)= 10 y = 20
i = 10 ThreadID = 3  x(static attribute)= 10 y = 21
```

We all know a static variable is a class variable and its value remains the same across multiple objects of the class. ThreadStaticAttribute allows each thread accessing a static variable to have its own copy. In WroxStatic, variable x has ThreadStaticAttribute applied to it. As a result, each of the threads t1 and t2 will have a separate copy of the static variable x and changes made to x by thread t1 will not be visible to thread t2. On the other hand, changes made to the variable y by thread t1 will be visible to thread t2. If you observe the output of the program, variable x is incremented separately for threads t1 and t2.

> **The difference between a static variable with a ThreadStaticAttribute and an instance variable is that the static variable does not require an object to access it, whereas an exception will be thrown if you try to access an instance variable without creating the instance of an object.**

Synchronization and Performance

Synchronization carries the overhead of the time required to acquire the synchronization lock. As a result, the performance is always poorer than the non-thread-safe version. As multiple threads might be trying to access objects at the same time to acquire the synchronization lock, the performance of the entire application might be affected inadvertently. This is a tradeoff a developer must be aware of when designing larger applications. The important part is that these thread contentions are not visible until a thorough stress test is performed. Stress testing is extremely important in designing large-scale multithreaded applications. The developer has to balance these factors:

❑ To be safe, synchronize as much as possible. This makes the program slower, at worst no better than its single-threaded version.

❑ For performance, synchronize as little as possible.

> **Multithreaded design is a continual tradeoff between these two factors.**

Beware of Deadlocks

Though essential for thread safety, synchronization, if not used properly, can cause deadlocks. As such, it is very important to understand what deadlocks are and how to avoid them. Deadlocks occur when two or more threads are waiting for two or more locks to be freed and the circumstances in the program logic are such that the locks will never be freed. Figure 3 illustrates a typical deadlock scenario.

Figure 3

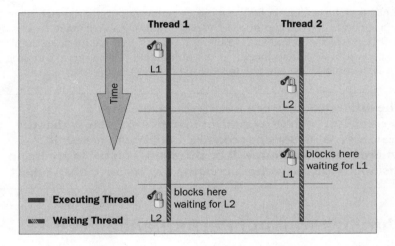

In the figure, Thread 1 acquires lock L1 on an object by entering its critical section. In this critical section, Thread 1 is supposed to acquire lock L2. Thread 2 acquires lock L2 and is supposed to acquire lock L1. So, now Thread 1 cannot acquire lock L2 because Thread 2 owns it and Thread 2 cannot acquire lock L1 because Thread 1 owns it. As a result, both the threads enter into an infinite wait or deadlock.

One of the best ways to prevent the potential for deadlock is to avoid acquiring more than one lock at a time, which is often practicable. However, if that is not possible, you need a strategy that ensures you acquire multiple locks in a consistent, defined order. Depending on each program design, the synchronization strategies to avoid deadlocks may vary. There is no standard strategy that can be applied to avoid all deadlocks. Most of the time, deadlocks are not detected until the application is deployed on a full-scale basis. We can consider ourselves lucky if we are able to detect deadlocks in our program during the testing phase.

A critical, but often overlooked element of any locking strategy is documentation. Unfortunately, even in cases where a good synchronization strategy is designed to avoid deadlocks, much less effort is made in documenting it. At the minimum, every method should have documentation associated with it that specifies the locks that it acquires and describes the critical sections within that method.

Let's take a look at an example, `Deadlock.cs`:

```
using System;
using System.Threading;

namespace DeadLock
{
  class DL
  {
    int field_1 = 0;
    private object lock_1 = new int[1];
    int field_2 = 0;
    private object lock_2 = new int[1];

    public void First(int val)
    {
      lock(lock_1)
        {
          Console.WriteLine("First:Acquired lock_1:" +
                            Thread.CurrentThread.GetHashCode() +
                            " Now Sleeping");

          //Try commenting Thread.Sleep()
          Thread.Sleep(1000);
          Console.WriteLine("First:Acquired lock_1:" +
                            Thread.CurrentThread.GetHashCode() +
                            " Now wants lock_2");

          lock(lock_2)
          {
            Console.WriteLine("First:Acquired lock_2:" +
                              Thread.CurrentThread.GetHashCode());
            field_1 = val;
            field_2 = val;
          }
        }
    }

    public void Second(int val)
    {
      lock(lock_2)
      {
        Console.WriteLine("Second:Acquired lock_2:" +
                          Thread.CurrentThread.GetHashCode());

        lock(lock_1)
```

```
                {
                    Console.WriteLine("Second:Acquired lock_1:" +
                                        Thread.CurrentThread.GetHashCode());
                    field_1 = val;
                    field_2 = val;
                }
            }
        }
    }

    public class MainApp
    {
        DL d = new DL();

        public static void Main()
        {
            MainApp m = new MainApp();
            Thread t1 = new Thread(new ThreadStart(m.Run1));
            t1.Start();
            Thread t2 = new Thread(new ThreadStart(m.Run2));
            t2.Start();
        }

        public void Run1()
        {
            this.d.First(10);
        }

        public void Run2()
        {
            this.d.Second(10);
        }
    }
}
```

The output from DeadLock is:

```
First:Acquired lock_1:2 Now Sleeping
Second:Acquired lock_2:3
First:Acquired lock_1:2 Now wants lock_2
```

In DeadLock, thread t1 calls the First() method, acquires lock_1, and goes to sleep for one second. In the meantime, thread t2 calls the Second() method and acquires lock_2. Then it tries to acquire lock_1 in the same method. But lock_1 is owned by thread t1, so thread t2 has to wait until thread t1 releases lock_1. When thread t1 wakes up, it tries to acquire lock_2. Now lock_2 is owned by thread t2 and thread t1 cannot acquire it until thread t2 releases lock_2. This results in a deadlock and a hung program. Commenting out the Thread.Sleep() line from the method First() does not result in deadlock, at least temporarily, because, thread t1 acquires lock_2 before thread t2. But, in real-world scenarios, instead of Thread.Sleep(), we might connect to a database resulting in thread t2 acquiring lock_2 before thread t1, and it will result in a deadlock. The example shows how important it is to carve out a good locking scheme in any multithreaded application. A good locking scheme may incorporate the acquisition of lock by all the threads in a well defined manner. In the case of the example above, thread t2 should not acquire lock_2 until it is release by thread t2 or thread t2 should not acquire lock_1 until thread t1 releases it. These decisions depend on specific application scenarios and cannot be generalized in any way. Testing of the locking scheme is equally important, because deadlocks usually occur in deployed systems due to lack of stress and functional testing.

End-to-End Examples

In this section of the chapter we will take a look at two larger examples. First, we'll take a look at creating thread-safe wrappers and then move on to a database connection pool.

Writing Your Own Thread-Safe Wrappers

The general idea of writing our own wrapper comes from the fact that you may not want to make every class in our library thread-safe, as synchronization has performance penalties associated with it. You would like to give the application developer a choice of whether to use a synchronized class or not. As the application developer would neither like to take the risk of a deadlock nor want to pay the performance penalty of using a thread-safe class in a single-threaded environment, they might prefer to have a choice of having a built-in synchronized wrapper for the same class in the library rather than writing a specific one. Collection classes like ArrayList and Hashtable in the System.Collections namespace already have this feature. You can decide whether you want to use a thread-safe Hashtable or not during initialization of the Hashtable. You can initialize a thread-safe Hashtable by calling the shared Synchronized() method of the Hashtable class as shown below:

```
Hashtable h;
h = Hashtable.Synchronized(new Hashtable());
```

It would be good to give the application developer such a choice. In this example, we will attempt to develop a class and a synchronized wrapper for the class. We will develop a Book Collection library and Figure 4 shows the UML representation of the Book Collection library.

Figure 4

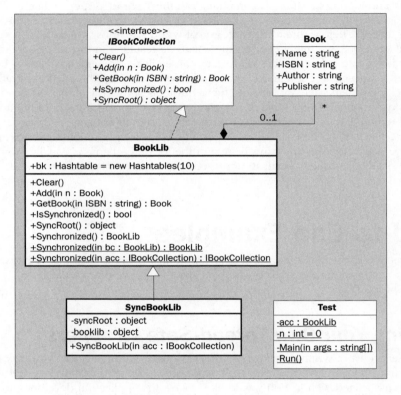

The program is very simple, but the concept of having intrinsic synchronization support is very important. By adding intrinsic synchronization support to our library, we will allow the developer to choose between a synchronized and non-synchronized environment for the same class. For example, programmers who do not need synchronization can instantiate an object as follows:

```
BookLib b = new BookLib()
```

while programmers who use our type in a thread-hot environment can use the thread-safe wrappers as follows:

```
BookLib b = new BookLib()
b = b.Synchronized()
```

The following is the complete `BookLib.cs` source along with its synchronized wrapper:

```csharp
using System;
using System.Threading;
using System.Collections;

interface IBookCollection
{
  void Clear();
  void Add(Book n);
  Book GetBook(string ISBN);
  bool IsSynchronized { get; }
  object SyncRoot { get; }
}

public class Book
{
  public string Name;
  public string ISBN;
  public string Author;
  public string Publisher;
}

class BookLib : IBookCollection
{
  internal Hashtable bk = new Hashtable(10);

  public virtual void Clear()
  {
    this.bk.Clear();
  }

  public virtual void Add(Book b)
  {
    Console.WriteLine("Adding Book for ThreadID:" +
                      Thread.CurrentThread.GetHashCode());
    Thread.Sleep(2000);
    bk.Add(b.ISBN, b);
  }

  public virtual Book GetBook(string ISBN)
  {
    Console.WriteLine("Getting Book for ThreadID:" +
                      Thread.CurrentThread.GetHashCode());
    return (Book)bk[ISBN];
  }

  public virtual bool IsSynchronized
  {
    get { return(false); }
  }
```

```csharp
  public virtual object SyncRoot
  {
    get { return(this); }
  }

  public BookLib Synchronized()
  {
    return Synchronized(this);
  }

  public static BookLib Synchronized(BookLib bc)
  {
    if (bc == null)
    {
      throw new ArgumentNullException("bc");
    }

    if (bc.GetType() == typeof(SyncBookLib))
    {
      throw new InvalidOperationException(
          "BookLib reference is already synchronized.");
    }

    return new SyncBookLib(bc);
  }

  public static IBookCollection Synchronized(IBookCollection acc)
  {
    if (acc == null)
    {
      throw new ArgumentNullException("acc");
    }

    if (acc.GetType() == typeof(SyncBookLib))
    {
      throw new InvalidOperationException(
          "BookLib reference is already synchronized.");
    }

    return new SyncBookLib(acc);
  }
}

sealed class SyncBookLib : BookLib
{
  private object syncRoot;
  private object booklib;

  internal SyncBookLib(IBookCollection acc)
  {
    booklib = acc;
    syncRoot = acc.SyncRoot;
  }
```

```
   public override void Clear()
   {
     lock(syncRoot)
     {
       base.Clear();
     }
   }

   public override void Add(Book b)
   {
     lock(syncRoot)
     {
       base.Add(b);
     }
   }

   public override Book GetBook(string ISBN)
   {
     lock(syncRoot)
     {
       return (Book)bk[ISBN];
     }
   }

   public override bool IsSynchronized
   {
     get{ return(true); }
   }

   public override object SyncRoot
   {
     get { return(syncRoot); }
   }
}

class Test
{
  private static BookLib acc;
  private static int n = 0;

  static void Main(string[] args)
  {
    acc = new BookLib();

    if (args.Length > 0)
    {
      acc = acc.Synchronized();
      //OR BookLib.Synchronized(acc);
    }

    Thread[] threads = {new Thread(new ThreadStart(Run)),
                        new Thread(new ThreadStart(Run)),
                        new Thread(new ThreadStart(Run))};
```

```
      foreach (Thread t in threads)
      {
        t.Start();
      }

      foreach (Thread t in threads)
      {
        t.Join();
      }

      for (int i = 0; i < n; i++)
      {
        Book bk = acc.GetBook(i.ToString());

        if (bk != null)
        {
          Console.WriteLine("Book : " + bk.Name);
          Console.WriteLine("ISBN : " + bk.ISBN);
          Console.WriteLine("Publisher : " + bk.Publisher);
          Console.WriteLine("Author : " + bk.Author);
        }
      }
      Console.WriteLine("Total Number of books added " + n);
    }

    static void Run()
    {
      for (int i = 0; i < 2; i++)
      {
        Book bk = new Book();
        bk.Author = "Tejaswi Redkar";
        bk.Name = "A" + i;
        bk.Publisher = "Wrox";
        bk.ISBN = (n++).ToString();
        acc.Add(bk);
      }
    }
  }
}
```

In the above example, we first declare an interface IBookCollection, which has the following methods and properties for handling collection of books:

❑   Clear() – Method to clear the book collection

❑   Add() – Method to add a book to the book collection

❑   GetBook() – Method to get a book from the book collection

❑   IsSynchronized() – Read-only property used to check whether the collection is synchronized or not

❑   SyncRoot() – Read-only property to get the synchronized root of the collection

Next we declare a class called `Book` representing a book in the collection. For example, the collection might be a library or a book store, but the representation of the `Book` class is the same in both.

The `BookLib` class implements the `IBookCollection` interface. As a result, the `BookLib` class must implement all the methods and properties of the `IBookCollection` interface. We declare a `Hashtable` called bk as the collection that will contain our books. The `Key` of the `Book` object will be its ISBN number. In the `Add()` method, we add a `Book` object to the `Hashtable`. In the `GetBook()` method, we retrieve the `Book` object if its ISBN number is supplied.

Now we must address any synchronization issues. In the `Synchronized()` method, we create an object of type `SyncBookLib` and return a reference to it. `SyncBookLib` is the synchronized version of the `BookLib` class. `SyncBookLib` inherits from the `BookLib` class, thus inheriting all the properties and methods that the `BookLib` class has already implemented. The difference between `SyncBookLib` and `BookLib` class is that in the `SyncBookLib` class, we lock all the critical sections using monitors (using the lock keyword). For example, the `Clear()`, `GetBook()`, and `Add()` methods have locks in their implementations thus making them thread-safe, whereas, in the `BookLib` class, there are no locks in any of the methods.

In the `Test` class, we create a synchronized `BookLib` if we pass any command-line argument. If there are no command-line arguments passed, we create a non thread-safe `BookLib` object. Then we create three threads that add some books to our book library. When you run the application, the difference between the execution of synchronized `BookLib` and non-synchronized `BookLib` will be clear. In the synchronized version, only one thread can access the library at any point of time. So, the other two threads have to wait until the first thread has finished adding books to the `BookLib`. This is not the case if we use the non-synchronized version; all the threads are given concurrent access to the `BookLib` object instance.

The output from `BookLib` with a command-line argument (thread-safe) will be as follows:

```
Adding Book for ThreadID:2
Adding Book for ThreadID:3
Adding Book for ThreadID:4
Adding Book for ThreadID:2
Adding Book for ThreadID:3
Adding Book for ThreadID:4
Book : A0
ISBN : 0
ISBN : Wrox
Author : Tejaswi Redkar
Book : A0
ISBN : 1
ISBN : Wrox
Author : Tejaswi Redkar
Book : A0
ISBN : 2
```

```
ISBN : Wrox
Author : Tejaswi Redkar
Book : A1
ISBN : 3
ISBN : Wrox
Author : Tejaswi Redkar
Book : A1
ISBN : 4
ISBN : Wrox
Author : Tejaswi Redkar
Book : A1
ISBN : 5
ISBN : Wrox
Author : Tejaswi Redkar
Total Number of books added 6
```

The output from BookLib with no command-line argument (non-thread-safe) will be as follows:

```
Adding Book for ThreadID:3
Adding Book for ThreadID:4
Adding Book for ThreadID:2
Adding Book for ThreadID:3
Adding Book for ThreadID:4
Adding Book for ThreadID:2
Getting Book for ThreadID:7
Book : A0
ISBN : 0
ISBN : Wrox
Author : Tejaswi Redkar
Getting Book for ThreadID:7
Book : A0
ISBN : 1
ISBN : Wrox
Author : Tejaswi Redkar
Getting Book for ThreadID:7
Book : A0
ISBN : 2
ISBN : Wrox
Author : Tejaswi Redkar
Getting Book for ThreadID:7
Book : A1
ISBN : 3
ISBN : Wrox
Author : Tejaswi Redkar
Getting Book for ThreadID:7
Book : A1
ISBN : 4
ISBN : Wrox
Author : Tejaswi Redkar
Getting Book for ThreadID:7
Book : A1
```

```
ISBN : 5
ISBN : Wrox
Author : Tejaswi Redkar
Total Number of books added 6
```

A Database Connection Pool

Object pools are very common in enterprise software development where instantiation of objects has to be controlled in order to improve the performance of the application. For example, database connections are expensive objects to be created every time we need to connect to a database. So, instead of wasting resources in instantiating the database connection for every database call, we can pool and reuse some connection objects that we have already created and thus gain a performance advantage by saving the time and resources required to create a new connection object for every database call.

Object pooling is similar to a book library. The book library maintains a pool of similar books. When the demand for that particular book increases, the library buys more, else the readers just keep on reusing the same books. In Object Pooling, first we check the pool to see whether the object has already been created and pooled, if it is pooled, we get the pooled object; else we create a new one and pool it for future use. Object pooling is extensively used in large-scale application servers like Enterprise Java Beans (EJB) Servers, MTS/COM+, and even the .NET Framework.

In this section, we will develop a database connection pool for pooling database connections. Database connections are expensive to create. In a typical web application there might be thousands of users trying to access the web site at the same time. If most of these hits need database access to serve dynamic data and we go on creating new database connection for each user, we are going to affect the application performance negatively. Creating a new object requires new memory allocation. Memory allocation reduces application performance and, as a result, the web site will either slow down considerably in delivering the dynamic content, or crash after a critical point is reached. Connection pooling maintains a pool of created objects, so the application that needs a database connection can just borrow a connection from the pool and then return it to the pool when the job is done, rather than creating a new database connection. Once data is served to one user, the connection will be returned back to the pool for future use.

Implementing the Pool

Let's start by taking a look at a UML diagram that depicts our database connection pool application. Figure 5 show the ObjectPool class and the DBConnectionSingleton class that inherits the ObjectPool class.

Figure 5

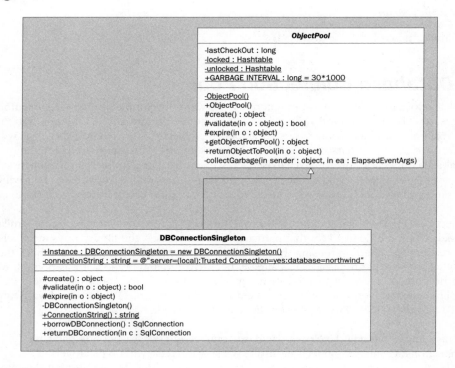

The ObjectPool Class

Let's start our discussion of the ObjectPool class by listing it in its entirety:

```
using System;
using System.Collections;
using System.Timers;

namespace WroxCS
{

  public abstract class ObjectPool
  {
    //Last Checkout time of any object from the pool.
    private long _lastCheckOut;

    //Hashtable of the checked-out objects
    private static Hashtable locked;

    //Hashtable of available objects
    private static Hashtable unlocked;

    //Clean-Up interval
    internal static long GARBAGE_INTERVAL = 90 * 1000; // 90 seconds
```

```
static ObjectPool()
{
  locked = Hashtable.Synchronized(new Hashtable());
  unlocked = Hashtable.Synchronized(new Hashtable());
}

internal ObjectPool()
{
  _lastCheckOut = DateTime.Now.Ticks;

  //Create a Time to track the expired objects for cleanup.
  System.Timers.Timer aTimer = new System.Timers.Timer();
  aTimer.Enabled = true;
  aTimer.Interval = GARBAGE_INTERVAL;
  aTimer.Elapsed += new
      System.Timers.ElapsedEventHandler(CollectGarbage);
}

protected abstract object Create();

protected abstract bool Validate(object o);

protected abstract void Expire(object o);

internal object GetObjectFromPool()
{
  long now = DateTime.Now.Ticks;
  _lastCheckOut = now;
  object o = null;

  lock(this)
  {
    try
    {
      foreach (DictionaryEntry myEntry in unlocked)
      {
        o = myEntry.Key;
        if (Validate(o))
        {
          unlocked.Remove(o);
          locked.Add(o, now);
          return(o);
        }
        else
        {
          unlocked.Remove(o);
          Expire(o);
          o = null;
        }
      }
    }
    catch (Exception){}
```

129

```
      o = Create();
      locked.Add(o, now);
    }
    return(o);
}

internal void ReturnObjectToPool(object o)
{
  if (o != null)
  {
    lock(this)
    {
      locked.Remove(o);
      unlocked.Add(o, DateTime.Now.Ticks);
    }
  }
}

private void CollectGarbage(object sender,
    System.Timers.ElapsedEventArgs ea)
{
  lock(this)
  {
    object o;
    long now = DateTime.Now.Ticks;
    IDictionaryEnumerator e = unlocked.GetEnumerator();

    try
    {
      while(e.MoveNext())
      {
        o = e.Key;

        if ((now - ((long) unlocked[ o ])) > GARBAGE_INTERVAL )
        {
          unlocked.Remove(o);
          Expire(o);
          o = null;
        }
      }
    }
    catch (Exception){}
  }
}
```

The ObjectPool base class contains two important methods; GetObjectFromPool(), which gets an object from the pool, and ReturnObjectToPool(), which returns object to the Pool. The object pool is implemented as two hashtables, one called locked and the other called unlocked. The locked hashtable contains all the objects that are currently in use and unlocked contains all the objects that are free and available for use. The ObjectPool also contains three MustOverride methods Create(), Validate(), and Expire(), that must be implemented by the derived classes.

In total, there are three critical sections in the ObjectPool class:

❑　While getting an object to the pool, GetObjectFromPool() is used – A lock is needed while adding an object to the pool because the content of the locked and unlocked hashtables change and we do not want any race condition here.

❑　While returning an object to the pool, ReturnObjectToPool() is used – Again, a lock is needed while returning an object to the pool because the content of the locked and unlocked hashtables will change and a new object will be available for use. Here also we cannot afford to have a race condition, because, we do not want multiple threads accessing the same hashtable at the same time.

❑　While cleaning up the expired objects from the pool, CollectGarbage() – In this method, we go over the unlocked hashtable to find and remove expired objects from the pool. The content of the unlocked hashtable may change and we need the removal of expired objects to be atomic.

In the GetObjectFromPool() method, we iterate over the unlocked hashtable to get the first available object. The Validate() method is used to validate the specific object. The Validate() method may vary in specific implementations based on the type of the pooled object. For example, if the object is a database connection, the derived class of the object pool needs to implement the Validate() method to check whether the connection to the database is open or closed. If the validation of the pooled object succeeds, we remove the object from the unlocked hash table and put it in the locked hashtable. The locked hashtable contains the objects that are currently in use. If the validation fails, we kill the object with the Expire() method. The Expire() method also needs to be implemented by the derived class and is specific to the specific type of pooled object. For example, in the case of a database connection, the expired object will close the database connection. If a pooled object is not found, that is if the unlocked hashtable is empty, we create a new object using the Create() method and put the object in the locked hashtable.

131

The `ReturnObjectToPool()` method implementation is much simpler. We just have
to remove the object from the `locked` hashtable and put it back in the `unlocked` hash
table for recycling. In this whole recycling process, we have to take into consideration
the memory usage of the application. Object pooling is directly proportional to
memory usage. So, the more objects we pool, the more memory we will be using. To
control memory usage, we should periodically garbage-collect the objects that are
pooled. This can be achieved by assigning a timeout period to every pooled object. If
the pooled object is not used within the timeout period, it will be garbage-collected. As
a result, the memory usage of the object pool will vary depending on the load on the
system. The `CollectGarbage()` method is used for handling the garbage collection
of the pooled object. This method is called by the `aTimer` delegate that is initialized in
the `ObjectPool` constructor. In our example, we set the garbage-collection interval to
90 seconds in the `GARBAGE_COLLECT` constant.

> **We haven't implemented any database connection-specific
> code so we can assume that the `ObjectPool` class can be used
> for the pooling any type of .NET Framework objects.**

The DBConnectionSingleton Class

The `DBConnectionSingleton` class is the implementation of a database connection-
specific object pool. The main purpose of this class is to provide database connection-
specific implementations of the `Create()`, `Validate()`, and `Expire()` methods
inherited from the `ObjectPool` class. The class also provides methods called
`BorrowDBConnection()` and `ReturnDBConnection()` for borrowing and returning
database connection objects from the object pool.

The complete listing of the `DBConnectionSingleton` class is as follows:

```csharp
using System;
using System.Data.SqlClient;

namespace WroxCS
{
  public sealed class DBConnectionSingleton : ObjectPool
  {
    private DBConnectionSingleton() {}

    public static readonly DBConnectionSingleton Instance =
        new DBConnectionSingleton();

    private static string _connectionString =
        @"server=(local);Trusted_Connection=yes;database=northwind";

    public static string ConnectionString
    {
      set
```

```
      {
        _connectionString = value;
      }
      get
      {
        return _connectionString;
      }
}

protected override object Create()
{
  SqlConnection temp = new SqlConnection(_connectionString);
  temp.Open();
  return(temp);
}

protected override bool Validate(object o)
{
  try
  {
    SqlConnection temp = (SqlConnection)o;
    return(
      !((temp.State.Equals(System.Data.ConnectionState.Closed))));
  }
  catch (SqlException)
  {
    return false;
  }
}

protected override void Expire(object o)
{
  try
  {
    ((SqlConnection) o ).Close();
  }
  catch (SqlException)
  {
  }
}

public SqlConnection BorrowDBConnection()
{
  try
  {
    return((SqlConnection)base.GetObjectFromPool());
  }
  catch (Exception e)
  {
    throw e;
  }
}
```

```
      public void ReturnDBConnection(SqlConnection c)
      {
        base.ReturnObjectToPool(c);
      }
    }
  }
```

As you are dealing with the `SqlConnection` object, the `Expire()` method closes the `SqlConnection`, the `Create()` method creates the `SqlConnection`, and the `Validate()` method checks whether the `SqlConnection` is open or not. The whole synchronization issue is hidden from the client application using the `DBConnectionSingleton` object instance.

Why Use a Singleton?

The Singleton is a popular creational design pattern, which is used when you need to have only one instance of an object. The intent of the Singleton pattern as defined in *Design Patterns (ISBN 0-201-70265-7)* is to ensure a class has only one instance, and provide a global point of access to it. To implement a Singleton, we need a `Private` constructor so that the client application is not able to create a new object whenever it wants to, and the `static ReadOnly` property instance is used to create the only instance of the Singleton class. The .NET Framework, during the JIT process, will initialize the `static` property when (and only when) any method uses this `static` property. If the property is not used, then the instance is not created. More precisely, the class gets constructed and loaded when *any* `static` member of the class is used by *any* caller. This feature is called lazy initialization and gives the effect of the creation of the object only on the first call to the instance property. The .NET Framework guarantees the thread safety of shared type initializations inherently. So we do not have to worry about the thread safety of the `DBConnectionSingleton` object because only one instance of it will ever be created during the lifetime of the application. The `static` variable instance holds the only instance of the `DBConnectionSingleton` class object.

Using the Database Connection Pool

The database connection pool is now ready for use and the `ObjectPoolTester` application in the code download for this chapter can be used to test it.

Below we show some code snippets of how to instantiate and use the database connection pool:

```
// Initialize the Pool
DBConnectionSingleton pool;
pool = DBConnectionSingleton.Instance

// Set the ConnectionString of the DatabaseConnectionPool
DBConnectionSingleton.ConnectionString =
    "server=(local);User ID=sa;Password=;database=northwind"
```

```
// Borrow the SqlConnection object from the pool
SqlConnection myConnection = pool.BorrowDBConnection()

// Return the Connection to the pool after using it
pool.ReturnDBConnection(myConnection)
```

In the above examples, we initialize the DBConnectionSingleton object from the instance property of the DBConnectionSingleton class. As discussed above, we are assured that with the use of the Singleton design pattern we have one and only one instance of the DBConnectionSingleton object. We set the ConnectionString property of the database connection to the Northwind database on the local SQL Server machine. Now, we can borrow database connections from the object pool using the BorrowDBConnection() method of the pool object, and return the database connection by calling the returnDBConnection() method of the pool object. The following screenshot shows the ObjectPoolTester application in action. If you really want to explore how the pooling application works, the best way is to open the project in Visual Studio .NET and step through the ObjectPoolTester application in Debug mode.

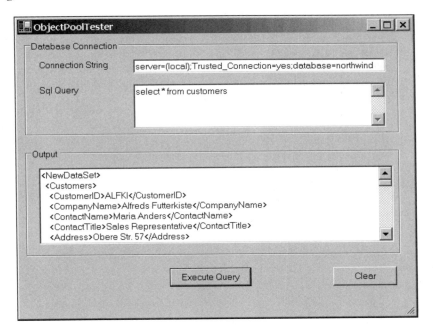

135

Summary

Synchronization is an extremely important concept in this multithreaded world of enterprise computing. It is extensively used in popular applications like databases, message queues, and even web servers. Any developer developing multithreaded applications needs to have their synchronization concepts crystal clear. Rather than getting overwhelmed with the locking features and trying to make every object thread-safe, the developer should focus on deadlock scenarios and try to resolve as many deadlock conditions as possible right from the design stage of the application. It is also important to understand the performance hit associated with synchronization and how it will affect the overall performance of your application. In this chapter, along with the synchronization support in the .NET Framework, we also developed a couple of useful applications:

❏ A custom thread-safe wrapper. In this example, you learned how you can add intrinsic synchronization support to your library and give the application developer the choice of using synchronization or not. This will help the developer focus on their own application rather than worrying about the thread safety of the library.

❏ A database connection pool. In this example, you developed a generic object pool that can be used for pooling any type of similar objects. Following that, we developed a database connection pool inheriting from the object pool. The object pool can be reused to pool any kind of object.

C# Threading

Handbook

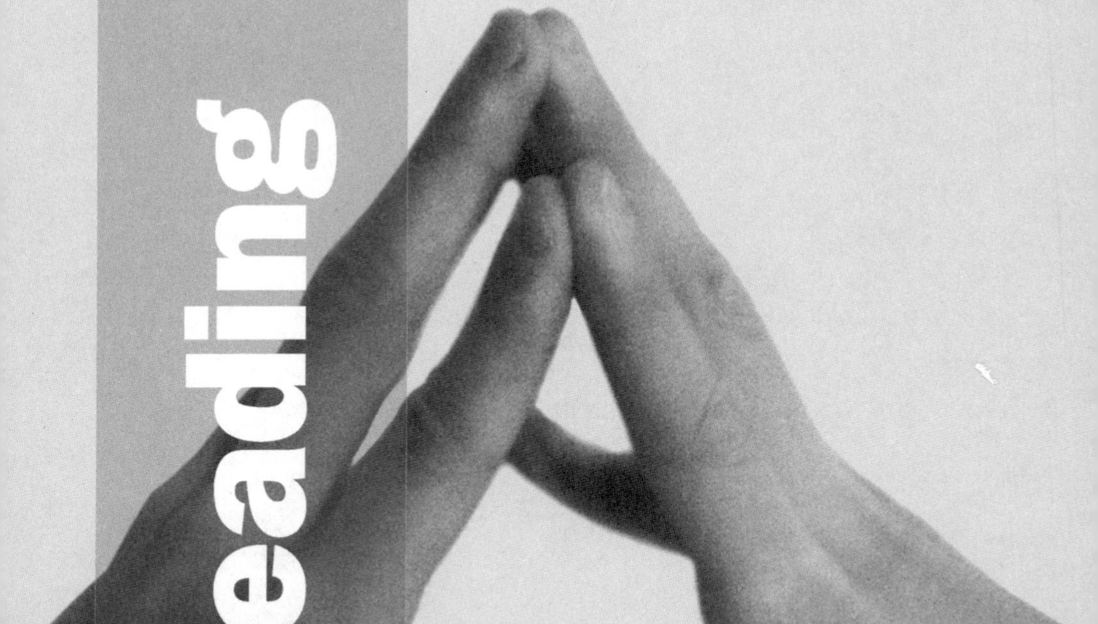

4

4

Threading Design Principles

Most highly scalable systems are highly concurrent in nature, meaning the existence of more than one request for the same object at the same time. However, it is a huge challenge to write code that is both highly concurrent and thread safe, which means that when one or more threads are accessing shared data, there is no possibility that the data could be corrupted or made inconsistent.

If we use multithreading techniques with a formal threading model, we can write highly scalable code that can work in a concurrent fashion. In the previous chapters, we learned when to use threading and all the details about threading, including the threading traps. In this chapter, we'll learn all about the threading models supported by .NET and how to take advantage of these threading models, as well as some models we can impose on top of .NET to help us design our code.

By default all the .NET applications are multithreaded, which was not the case in VB6. In Windows Forms applications, there is a special thread called the UI thread that controls all the user interface-related functions such as keyboard activities and mouse activities. When long-running, time-consuming processes are running on the UI thread, the application will become unresponsive. If you run such tasks on a newly spun thread different from the default UI thread, your application will behave better, and your user interface will respond better. However, if you thought that creating numerous Thread objects is the only way to achieve this, you would be wrong. You can use several techniques in addition to multithreading, including implementing asynchronous programming and using Timer-based functions, as you saw in Chapter 2.

Multiple Threads in Applications

If you programmed in versions of VB prior to .NET, you might know that VB supported multiple threads within a COM container, such as MTS or COM+. Well, although multiple threads were supported by VB5/6, the threading model they supported was **Single Threaded Apartments** (**STA**). If you come from Visual C++ then you'd have options to build both MTA (**Multi Threaded Apartments**) and STA applications. However, the .NET Framework does not retain the concept of Apartments and it manages all of the threads within AppDomains. By default, all .NET applications are multithreaded and any code can access any object at any time. Thus, we have to be very careful with static resources in the managed code.

The .NET Framework supports both managed and unmanaged threads and all the Win32 threading models such as STA and MTA. When you are trying to access COM components from managed code, unmanaged threads are created by the legacy COM components. Threads in the .NET Framework are created using the Thread object, whether managed or unmanaged.

If you have ever programmed multithreaded programs using the Win32 APIs, you may remember that Win32 supported *user-interface* threads and *worker* threads. As you learned in Chapter 1, the threading names have now changed into **Apartment Model Threading** and **Free Threading** respectively. The .NET Framework supports two basic threading models, which are *Apartment Model Threaded* or **Single Threaded Apartment** (**STA**) components, and *Free Threaded* or **Multi Threaded Apartment** (**MTA**) components. When we create a thread in .NET, by default it is an MTA thread.

> **You should only use the STA threading model when you're going to access STA-based COM components such as VB6 COM components. Otherwise, you shouldn't mark the current thread as STA, since it involves a significant performance hit to the application.**

To reiterate what you learned earlier, an apartment is the logical container within the AppDomain for sharing threads in the same context. Objects reside inside an AppDomain and the context is created when an object is created during the activation process.

STA Threading Model

An STA thread apartment works using a concept called **Object-per-Client** model, meaning the code that creates the STA thread apartment owns its threads. There will only be one thread in any apartment as shown in Figure 1.

In STA threading, all the calls to a thread will be placed in a queue and the calls will be processed one by one. Therefore, the STA thread will never execute multiple methods simultaneously. STA threads have their own private data and they don't share data between threads. This makes the threading model safe and avoids any data corruption and synchronization problems. However, this does restrict the options available to the developer, and performance suffers, as data has to be copied with every thread created.

Figure 1

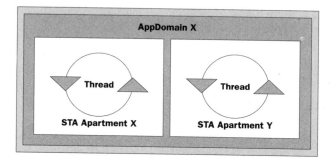

As you can see from the diagram, AppDomain X has two STA threads, X and Y, running inside, and each of the STA Apartments has only one thread. The term **Thread Affinity** is used when defining the relationship between the thread and the code that creates the thread. When a call is made to an STA apartment thread, then calls between the caller and the thread are handled by the contexts in the AppDomain, and the contexts maintain the thread affinity.

If your managed application is going to use unmanaged legacy COM components, then it is very important to know the threading model of the COM components before accessing them. If you don't mark the correct threading mode in your application, there could be some unexpected bugs and catastrophic errors in your application. The threading model information can be found in the registry under the HKEY_CLASSES_ROOT\CLSID\{Class ID of the COM component}\InProcServer32 key.

If you want to specify that you are using the Apartment Threading model, then apply the STAThreadAttribute attribute on the Main() method.

```
[STAThreadAttribute]
static void Main()
{
    ...
}
```

This attribute should only be used if we're trying to access legacy STA components from the managed code. Otherwise, mark the Main() method as MTAThreadAttribute:

```
[MTAThreadAttribute]
static void Main()
{
    ...
}
```

The same principal applies for ASP.NET applications. If your ASP.NET page is accessing an STA COM component, then you have to use the ASPCompat directive at the top of the ASP.NET page:

```
<%@ Page AspCompat="true" %>
```

By default, all the ASP.NET pages are multithreaded and when we use the AspCompat directive, the ASP.NET page is marked as STA. This will ensure the ASP.NET page is compatible with the threading model of a COM component.

> **When you mark the ASP.NET page to run under the STA threading model, the performance of the application may suffer.**

! If you are using VB.NET then you can use CreateObject statement to instantiate COM objects. Since C# doesn't allow late binding, the only way to call COM objects in late binding mode is to use reflection.

MTA Threading Model

The biggest difference between an STA and an MTA threaded apartment is that an MTA apartment can have more than one thread running simultaneously in the same apartment using all the shared data available in the apartment. This is illustrated in Figure 2.

Figure 2

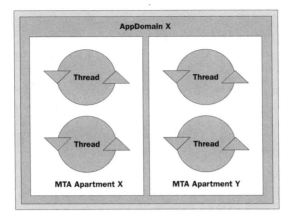

Since the MTA model supports simultaneous multiple thread execution, it becomes the caller's responsibility to synchronize the global data between multiple threads. Many of these issues were covered in the previous chapter.

Specifying the Threading Model

The threading model for a thread can be set using the `ApartmentState` property of the `Thread` class. The `ApartmentState` enumeration defines the types of threading models supported by .NET.

Enumeration Value	Meaning
MTA	Creates a multi-threaded apartment
STA	Creates a single-threaded apartment
Unknown	The apartment property of the `Thread` class is not set

As we've already learned, you should only mark the thread as STA thread if you are going to access an STA-threaded legacy COM component. Otherwise, your threading model is in the default MTA threading model.

Designing Threaded Applications

A multithreaded program has two or more threads (flows of control) and can achieve significant performance gains with concurrency, with or without parallel thread execution. Concurrent thread execution means that two or more threads are executing at the same time. Parallelism occurs when two or more threads execute simultaneously across two or more processors.

In this section, we'll talk about real threading considerations and issues. Before you start developing applications, you should ask yourself these questions:

1. Is it possible to subdivide the application to run on different threads?

2. If it is possible to subdivide, how do I subdivide and what are the criteria for subdividing?

3. What would be the relationship between the main thread and the worker threads? This defines how the tasks in the application will relate to each other.

You can determine the answer to the first question by inspecting the application. For example, does your application require heavy I/O operations, such as reading an XML file or querying a database, or perform a lot of CPU-intensive processing, such as encrypting and decrypting data, or hashing? If so, these operations could block your application's main thread.

If you've identified that parts of your application are potential candidates for separate threads, then you should ask yourself the following questions:

1. Does each of the tasks identified use separate global resources?

   For example, if you've identified two potential threads for your application and they are both going to use the same global resource, such as a global variable or a `DataSet` object, then if both threads try to access the global resource at the same time, you could get inconsistent or corrupt data, as shown in the previous chapter. The only way to prevent this kind of problem is by using locks on the global resources, which could leave the other thread waiting. If both of the tasks are going to use the same global resource then it is not a good idea to break the task into two. For some resources, you could use the `Monitor` class to prevent the threads from locking up. Again, this was shown in Chapter 3.

2. Over how long a period may the thread need to be blocked?

   It is not always possible to build applications that use independent global resources. For example, let's say two tasks in your application rely on a single global `DataSet` object. If the first task takes a long time to fill the `DataSet` object (let's say it fills about 50,000 rows from the database), then you would typically lock the `DataSet` object to prevent concurrency problems. Here a pseudo-code version of the first task:

```
1. Open the Database connection
2. Lock the global DataSet object
3. Perform the query
4. Fill the DataSet with 50,000 rows from the database
5. Unlock the DataSet object
```

In this case, the second task needs to wait for a long time before it can access the `DataSet` object, which happens only when the first task finishes its execution and releases the lock. This is a potential problem and it will likely remove the concurrency of your application. There is a better way to address this problem:

1. Open the Database connection
2. Perform the query
3. Fill the local DataSet with 50,000 rows from the database
4. Lock the global DataSet object
5. Set the local database to global dataset (DSGlobal = DSLocal)
6. Unlock the global DataSet object

In this way, we're not locking the global `DataSet` object until we need to update it and so we're reducing the time the lock on the global object is held.

3. Does the execution of one task depend on the other task?

For example, the tasks that you've identified could be querying the database and displaying the data in a `DataGrid` control. You can split the task into two by querying the database as the first task, and displaying the result in the `DataGrid` as the second task. The second task does not want to start until the first task has complete. Therefore, separating the querying and displaying the data in a `DataGrid` into two separate concurrently running tasks is not a viable option. One way around this is to have the first task raise an event when completed, and fire a new thread when this happens. Alternatively, you could use a timer that checks to see if is completed through a public field, and continues the execution of the thread when it has.

Threads and Relationships

The threads spun from a multithreaded application may or may not be related to each other. For example, in every application there will be a main thread that spins other threads and so the main thread becomes the controller of all other threads in the application. There are few common methods that can be used to define the relationship between the threads in a multithreaded application:

❑ Main and Worker thread model

❑ Peer thread model

❑ Pipeline thread model

We will detail each of these models, including some code so that you can see how they might be implemented in your applications.

Main and Worker Thread Model

This is the commonest model and the one used throughout this book so far. It is illustrated in Figure 3:

Figure 3

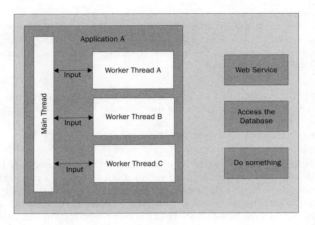

In the Main and Worker thread model, the main thread receives all input and passes it to other threads to perform particular tasks. The main thread may or may not wait for the worker threads to finish. In this model, the worker threads don't interact directly with the input sources as they read their input from the main thread. For example, we could have three buttons on a Windows Forms application that trigger three separate events:

❑ Get data from a web service

❑ Get data from a database

❑ Do something else such as parsing an XML file

This is the simplest threading model. The main thread is contained within the `Main()` method, and the model is very common in client GUI applications.

Let's look at some code to demonstrate this. We'll use a form like the following:

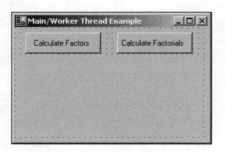

When you click on a button, it will fire off a worker thread that will perform some calculations and return the results in the space below the buttons. We won't detail the UI code here; the full code can be downloaded from the Wrox web site, but here are the relevant sections:

```
public class MainWorker
{
  public ArrayList CalculateFactors(int number)
  {
    if (number < 3)
      return null;
    else
    {
      ArrayList factors = new ArrayList();
      factors.Add("1");
      for (int current = 2; current <= number - 1; current++)
      {
        if ((int)(Math.Floor(number / current) * current) == number)
          factors.Add(current.ToString());
      }
      factors.Add(number.ToString());
      return factors;
    }
  }

  public long CalculateFactorial(int number)
  {
    if (number < 0)
      return -1;

    if (number == 0)
      return 1;
    else
    {
      long returnValue = 1;
      for (int current=1; current <= number; current++)
        returnValue *= current;
      return returnValue;
    }
  }
}
```

The above methods are quite straightforward and are wrapped in a class for modularity reasons. The first returns an ArrayList containing all of the factors of the number passed to it, whereas the second simply returns a Long. Remember that factorials very quickly get very large. The factorial of 13 is 6,227,020,800. The factorial method doesn't tie up the processor for very long, but it can be used to illustrate this model.

```
public frmCalculate()
{
  //
  // Required for Windows Form Designer support
  //
  InitializeComponent();

  //Add any initialization after the InitializeComponent() call
  threadMethods = new MainWorker();
}
```

The constructor just contains an instantiation of a new `MainWorker` object that will be used in the methods. Below we show the methods used for the button click event handlers:

```
private void cmdFactors_Click(object sender, System.EventArgs e)
{
  Thread calculateFactors = new
      Thread(new ThreadStart(FactorsThread));
  calculateFactors.Start();
}

void FactorsThread()
{
  ArrayList val = threadMethods.CalculateFactors(200);
  StringBuilder sb = new StringBuilder();

  for (int count = 0; count <= val.Count - 1; count++)
  {
    sb.Append((string)val[count]);
    if (count < val.Count - 1)
      sb.Append(", ");
  }

  //Create and invoke the delegate with the new value
  UpdateValue updVal = new UpdateValue(DisplayValue);
  string[] Arugs = {sb.ToString()};
  this.Invoke(updVal,Arugs);
}
```

The `cmdFactors_Click()` method instantiates a new thread with the `FactorsThread()` method, which formats and acts upon the result contained in `MainWorker.CalculateFactors()`.

> **This method will need to be wrapped because thread methods cannot have return values.**

```
private void cmdFactorial_Click(object sender, System.EventArgs e)
{
  Thread calculateFactorial =
     new Thread(new ThreadStart(FactorialThread));
  calculateFactorial.Start();
}

private void FactorialThread()
{
  long val = threadMethods.CalculateFactorial(20);
  //Create and invoke the delegate with the new value
  UpdateValue updVal = new UpdateValue(DisplayValue);
  string[] Arugs = {val.ToString()};
  this.Invoke(updVal,Arugs);
}
```

The `FactorialThread()` method is much simpler. Whenever the `cmdFactorial` button is clicked, the main thread fires off a new thread and updates the `lblResult` text label when the results have been achieved.

This was a straightforward example of main and worker threads in actions. Obviously, this example can easily be changed to deal with a connection to a database, or other more time-consuming activities.

However, you need to take care of several issues relating to threads when you use this mode. You can have threads spawning threads, threads accessing the same resource, and threads going into an infinite loop.

This is the simplest model, but also the one that requires most work from the developer.

In addition, the threads are completely independent of each other, each being controlled entirely by its parent – in this case the main thread.

Peer Thread Model

The next threading model we will describe is the Peer threading model. In this threading model, each thread will receive its own input from the appropriate sources and process that input accordingly. This model is illustrated in Figure 4.

Figure 4

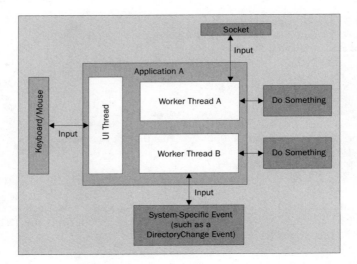

In the figure above, the UI thread will receive the input from the keyboard and mouse and it can work accordingly. Worker Thread A will listen to a particular socket and process input as it comes in from that socket, and in the same way Worker Thread B will wait for a system event and act accordingly. In this model, all the threads execute concurrently without blocking or waiting for other threads.

We can amend the previous example so that the `CalculateFactors()` method notices when the factorial thread finishes, and discovers the factors of this number. We will use the factorial of 8 in this example. In this example, however, we won't be using a socket, but just the setting of a variable. The principles will be the same for sockets; you would either continuously listen, or to save processor cycles, sleep intermittently.

So, let's change the `WorkerThread` class first:

```
public class PeerThread
{
  private int factorial;

  public ArrayList CalculateFactors(int number)
  {
    if (number < 3)
      return null;
    else
    {
      ArrayList factors = new ArrayList();
      factors.Add("1");
      for (int current = 2; current <= number - 1; current++)
```

```
    {
      if ((int)(Math.Floor(number / current) * current) == number)
        factors.Add(current.ToString());
    }
    factors.Add(number.ToString());
    return factors;
  }
}
```

```
public ArrayList CalculateFactors()
{
  for(int count = 1; count<=30; count++)
  {
    Thread.Sleep(TimeSpan.FromSeconds(1));
    if (factorial > 0)
      break;
    else if (count == 30 && factorial == 0)
      return null;
  }
  ArrayList returnValue = CalculateFactors(factorial);
  return returnValue;
}
```

```
public long CalculateFactorial(int number)
{
  factorial = 0;
  if (number < 0) return -1;
  if (number == 0) return 1;
  int returnValue = 1;

  for (int current = 1; current <= number; current++)
    returnValue *= current;
  factorial = returnValue;
  return returnValue;
}
```

First, we'll explain the small changes. A `private` field has been created that will store the result of the factorial when it has been calculated. In addition, the class has been renamed to `PeerThread`. The `CalculateFactors()` method now has an overload, so that if it isn't passed an argument it performs the business end of this model.

All that happens is that the thread monitors the state of the `factorial` field, as if it were a socket, say. It checks to see if it is anything other than 0, and if so, it calls the `CalculateFactors()` method with the value of `factorial` as its argument and returns the `ArrayList` that it produces. We have also made a change in that we reset the `factorial` field at the start of the `CalculateFactorial()` method so there will always be some work to do. At the end of this method, we set `factorial` to equal the factorial.

Now, the `frmCalculate` class needs altering also. Observe the following changes:

```
...
  private PeerThread threadMethods;
  ...
  public frmCalculate()
  {
    //
    // Required for Windows Form Designer support
    //
    InitializeComponent();

    //Add any initialization after the InitializeComponent() call
    threadMethods = new PeerThread();
  }
```

```
  ...
  private void NewFactorsThread()
  {
    ArrayList val = threadMethods.CalculateFactors();
    calculateFactorial.Join();

    StringBuilder sb = new StringBuilder();
    for (int count = 0; count <= val.Count - 1; count++)
    {
      sb.Append((String)val[count]);
      if (count < val.Count - 1)
        sb.Append(", ");
    }
    //Create and invoke the delegate with the new value
    UpdateValue updVal = new UpdateValue(DisplayValue);
    string[] Arugs = {sb.ToString()};
    this.Invoke(updVal,Arugs);
  }
```

```
  ...

  private void cmdFactorial_Click(object sender, System.EventArgs e)
  {
    Thread calculateFactors = new
        Thread(new ThreadStart(NewFactorsThread));
    Thread calculateFactorial = new
        Thread(new ThreadStart(FactorialThread));
    calculateFactors.Start();
    calculateFactorial.Start();
  }
```

Apart from defining the new `threadMethods` field as a new `PeerThread` class, there are two important changes. We define a new method called `NewFactorsThread()`, which will call the `CalculateFactors()` method of the `PeerThread` class with no arguments. The rest of this method is the same.

In the `cmdFactorial_Click()` method, instead of just firing up the `FactorialThread()` method in a thread, we fire up the `FactorsThread()` as well, and execute them out of sequence so that `calculateFactors` may have to wait for `calculateFactorial`. You should be able to see how this can be tied into a network socket, and we will see an example of monitoring such a socket in Chapter 7.

The common problems that could occur with this kind of model are those of deadlocks and blocking. If you have a thread continually listening at a socket and getting its parameters from that socket, then that socket may need to be locked from other threads. This means, therefore, that this is a very good model to use for manager classes. We could use a thread to monitor a socket and then fire off new threads to process the contents. However, do not have more than one thread monitoring the same socket. In addition, if the thread is continually checking the socket or other resource, then it may consume more processor cycles than is necessary. As seen in the above example, you can use `Thread.Sleep()` to reduce the processor cycles expended.

As you will see, this example is also very similar to the Pipeline Thread Model in concept, but we are simulating a Peer Thread Model. If you click on the Calculate Factorials button, unless you have a very fast machine, you should have time to click on Calculate Factors, which will enable you to calculate and display the factors of 200, before it overwrites the textbox with the factors of 8!, or 40320.

Pipeline Thread Model

The Pipeline thread model is based on a series of tasks, each of which depends on the previous task. Have a look at Figure 5 which illustrates the situation:

Figure 5

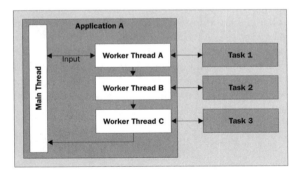

In the figure above, the main thread creates a series of threads, each of which will wait until the previous thread is finished executing. This kind of threading relationship is good if your task has certain stages and each of these stages is dependent on another. For example, your task could be processing input data and the process could have a few sub-tasks such as:

- ❏ Filter all the non-valid characters, such as <, >, !, etc.

- ❏ Check if the data is formatted correctly

- ❏ Format all the numbers with currency sign and decimal points

- ❏ Process the input

In this kind of situation, the next task can only be started if the previous task has finished. In the previous model, this is in effect what we were doing, as the factorial field was only set at the end of the thread. However, the proper way to implement the Pipeline thread model is to explicitly test that the thread has ended.

A few changes need to be made to the Peer thread example to make it part of the Pipeline model. First, we'll show the code for frmCalculate:

```
...
private PipelineThread threadMethods;
private Thread calculateFactorial;
...
public frmCalculate()
{
   ...
  threadMethods = new PipelineThread();
   ...
}
void NewFactorsThread()
{
  ArrayList val = threadMethods.CalculateFactors();
  calculateFactorial.Join();
   ...
```

As you can see, the changes are minimal here. The only interesting changes are the line that rescopes calculateFactorial, and the calculateFactorial.Join() line. This instructs the calculateFactors thread to wait until calculateFactorial has completed before executing. The Join() call has to be within the thread whose execution you want to pause, and it is called on the thread it is waiting for. This inevitably means that the thread variable has to be rescoped to be at least class wide so that it can be accessed from other threads.

```
public class PipelineThread
  ...
  public ArrayList CalculateFactors()
  {
    ArrayList returnValue = CalculateFactors(factorial);
    return returnValue;
  }
```

Again, the changes here are small. The above method no longer has to check if `factorial` has been set, and is able to thus execute since it can assume the factorial has been calculated. This example could be useful when, for instance, you are waiting on a `DataSet` to fill, before performing some further calculations. This would enable the thread to fire as soon as the thread that fills the `DataSet` is complete. Of course, in a real application, error checking would have to be implemented as the thread could have completed but ended abruptly because of an error, or because of an `Abort()` instruction from another thread.

The traps you have to watch out for are the same traps that can occur with any thread. The first thread could be placed in an infinite loop, in which case, the second thread would never execute. By ensuring this can never happen in your first thread, you ensure that the second thread will execute and complete. In addition, you have to watch out for the thread ending unpredictably, due to an error or otherwise, as mentioned in the previous paragraph.

This concludes the discussion of the three models that can be applied to threading. By modeling your application to one of these, you should become familiar with the structure of the code you would need to use.

Summary

In this chapter, the various threading models that can be applied to your application, why you should use them, and how to implement them have been described. You should now be confident in your knowledge of:

❑ Different types of basic threading model, such as STA and MTA apartments

❑ How to specify the threading model

❑ The different models of threads that can be applied and their relationships to each other

This chapter should help you design your threaded application – your application will fit into one or more of the models described above, and so the code examples given should help you to build the code you need. With the .NET Framework, threads are far more powerful, but also far more prone to errors than they used to be. By being aware of which model your application fits into, you can look out for these potential errors.

C#

Threading

Handbook

5

5

Scaling Threaded Applications

The goal of multithreading our applications so far has been to try to make as much use of the computer's processor as possible. So, it would seem that all we need to do is allocate each independent task to a different thread, and let the processor make sure that it's always processing commands on one of them. Well, for small systems this is pretty much the case. But as systems grow larger, and the number of threads grows, the operating system can spend much of its time allocating locks, and sorting out contention between threads, and little of its time actually processing our program's instructions. In order to make our applications scale, we'll have to take a bit more control of threads.

For some situations where the threads are short-lived, for example, it is efficient to use a pool of threads for performing tasks rather than creating and then subsequently deleting an entirely new thread for each task. A task, in this context, could be a single method execution, or a number of methods. The process of pre-allocating a collection, or pool, of threads prior to their actual usage and for reuse later in an application is known as **thread pooling**.

This chapter aims to provide a detailed insight into thread pooling, and covers the following topics:

- ❑ What thread pooling is
- ❑ The need for thread pooling
- ❑ The concept of thread pooling
- ❑ The role of the CLR in thread pooling
- ❑ Glitches involved in thread pooling and their solutions
- ❑ The size of a thread pool

   ❑   Exploring the .NET `ThreadPool` class

   ❑   Programming thread pools in C#

As you'll discover, the Common Language Runtime (CLR) of the .NET Framework plays a major role in the thread pooling process.

What is Thread Pooling?

Thread pooling is the process of creating a collection of threads during the initialization of a multithreaded application, and then reusing those threads for new tasks as and when required, instead of creating new threads. The number of threads for the process is usually fixed depending on the amount of memory available, and the needs of the application. However, it might be possible to increase the number of available threads. Each thread in the pool is given a task and, once that task has completed, the thread returns to the pool and waits for the next assignment.

The Need for Thread Pooling

Thread pooling is essential in multithreaded applications for the following reasons.

   ❑   Thread pooling improves the response time of an application as threads are already available in the thread pool waiting for their next assignment and do not need to be created from scratch

   ❑   Thread pooling saves the CLR from the overhead of creating an entirely new thread for every short-lived task and reclaiming its resources once it dies

   ❑   Thread pooling optimizes the thread time slices according to the current process running in the system

   ❑   Thread pooling enables us to start several tasks without having to set the properties for each thread

   ❑   Thread pooling enables us to pass state information as an object to the procedure arguments of the task that is being executed

   ❑   Thread pooling can be employed to fix the maximum number of threads for processing a particular request

The Concept of Thread Pooling

One of the major problems affecting the responsiveness of a multithreaded application is the time involved in spawning threads for each task.

For example, a web server is a multithreaded application that can service several client requests simultaneously. Let's suppose that ten clients are accessing the web server at the same time:

❑   If the server operates a *one thread per client* policy, it will spawn ten new threads to service these clients, which entails the overhead of first creating those threads and then of managing them throughout their lifetime. It's also possible that the machine will run out of resources at some point.

❑   Alternatively, if the server uses a pool of threads to satisfy those requests, then it will save the time involved in the spawning of those threads each time a request from a client comes in. It can manage the number of threads created, and can reject client requests if it is too busy to handle them. This is exactly the concept behind thread pooling.

The .NET CLR maintains a pool of threads for servicing requests. If our application requests a new thread from the pool, the CLR will try to fetch it from the pool. If the pool is empty, it will spawn a new thread and give it to us. When our code using the thread terminates, the thread is reclaimed by .NET and returned to the pool. The number of threads in the thread pool is limited by the amount of memory available.

To recap then, the factors affecting the threading design of a multithreaded application are:

❑   The responsiveness of the application

❑   The allocation of thread management resources

❑   Resource sharing

❑   Thread synchronization

Responsiveness of the application and resource sharing are addressed by this chapter on thread pooling. The remaining factors have been covered in the previous chapters of this book.

The CLR and Threads

The CLR was designed with the aim of creating a managed code environment offering various services such as compilation, garbage collection, memory management, and, as we'll see, thread pooling to applications targeted at the .NET platform.

Indeed, there is a remarkable difference between how Win32 and the .NET Framework define a process that hosts the threads that our applications use. In a traditional multithreaded Win32 application, each process is made up of collections of threads. Each thread in turn consists of Thread Local Storage (TLS) and Call Stacks for providing time slices in the case of machines that have a single CPU. Single processor machines allot time slices for each thread to execute based on the thread priority. When the time slice for a particular thread is exhausted, it is suspended and some other thread is allowed to perform its task. In the case of the .NET Framework, each Win32 process can be sub-divided logically into what are known as Application Domains that host the threads along with the TLS and call stack. It's worthwhile to note that communication between application domains is handled by a concept called Remoting in the .NET Framework.

Having gained a basic understanding on concepts of thread pooling and the .NET process, let's dig into how the CLR provides us with thread pooling functionality for .NET applications.

The Role of the CLR in Thread Pooling

The CLR forms the heart and soul of the .NET Framework offering several services to managed applications, thread pooling being one of them. For each task queued in the thread pool (**work items**), the CLR assigns a thread from the pool (a **worker thread**) and then releases the thread back to the pool once the task is done.

Thread pools are always implemented by the CLR using a multithreaded apartment (MTA) model by employing high performance queues and dispatchers through **preemptive multitasking.** This is a process in which CPU time is split into several time slices. In each time slice, a particular thread executes while other threads wait. Once the time slice is exhausted, other threads are allowed to use the CPU based on *the highest priority of the remaining threads*. The client requests are queued in the task queue and each item in this queue is dispatched to the first available thread in the thread pool.

Once the thread completes its assigned task, it returns to the pool and waits for the next assignment from the CLR. The thread pool can be fixed or of dynamic size. In the former case, the number of threads doesn't change during the lifetime of the pool. Normally, this type of pool is used when we are sure of the amount of resources available to our application, so that a fixed number of threads can be created at the time of pool initialization. This would be the case when we are developing solutions for an intranet or even in applications where we can tightly define the system requirements of the target platform. Dynamic pool sizes are employed when we don't know the amount of resources available, as in the case of a web server that will not know the number of client requests it will be asked to handle simultaneously.

Caveats to Thread Pooling

There is no doubt that thread pooling offers us a lot of advantages when building multithreaded applications, but there are some situations where we should avoid its use. The following list indicates the drawbacks and situations where we should avoid using thread pooling:

❑ The CLR assigns the threads from the thread pool to the tasks and releases them to the pool once the task is completed. There is no direct way to cancel a task once it has been added to the queue.

❑ Thread pooling is an effective solution for situations where tasks are short lived, as in the case of a web server satisfying the client requests for a particular file. A thread pool should not be used for extensive or long tasks.

❏ Thread pooling is a technique to employ threads in a cost-efficient manner, where cost efficiency is defined in terms of quantity and startup overhead. Care should be exercised to determine the utilization of threads in the pool. The size of the thread pool should be fixed accordingly.

❏ All the threads in the thread pool are in multithreaded apartments. If we want to place our threads in single-thread apartments then a thread pool is not the way to go.

❏ If we need to identify the thread and perform various operations, such as starting it, suspending it, and aborting it, then thread pooling is not the way of doing it.

❏ Also, it is not possible to set priorities for tasks employing thread pooling.

❏ There can be only one thread pool associated with any given Application Domain.

❏ If the task assigned to a thread in the thread pool becomes locked, then the thread is never released back to the pool for reuse. These kinds of situations can be avoided by employing effective programmatic skills.

The Size of the Thread Pool

The .NET Framework provides the ThreadPool class located in the System.Threading namespace for using thread pools in our applications. The number of tasks that can be queued into a thread pool is limited by the amount of memory in your machine. Likewise, the number of threads that can be active in a process is limited by the number of CPUs in your machine. That is because, as we already know, each processor can only actively execute one thread at a time. By default, each thread in the thread pool uses the default task and runs at default priority in a multithreaded apartment. The word default seems to be used rather vaguely here. That is no accident. Each system can have default priorities set differently. If, at any time, one of the threads is idle then the thread pool will induce worker threads to keep all processors busy. If all the threads in the pool are busy and work is pending in the queue then it will spawn new threads to complete the pending work. However, the number of threads created can't exceed the maximum number specified. By default, 25 thread pool threads can be created per processor. However, this number can be changed by editing the CorSetMaxThreads member defined in mscoree.h file. In the case of additional thread requirements, the requests are queued until some thread finishes its assigned task and returns to the pool. The .NET Framework uses thread pools for asynchronous calls, establishing socket connections, and registered wait operations.

Exploring the ThreadPool Class

In this section, we will be exploring the various aspects of the `ThreadPool` class and will see how they can be employed to create thread pools in our .NET applications. The `ThreadPool` class provides a pool of threads that can be used to do the following things:

❑ Process work items

❑ Process asynchronous I/O calls

❑ Process timers

❑ Wait on behalf of other threads

The following table gives the list of methods of the `ThreadPool` class and their functionality.

Method Name	Functionality
`BindHandle`	This method binds the OS handle to the thread pool
`GetAvailableThreads`	This method indicates the number of work items that can be added to the work items queue
`GetMaxThreads`	This method indicates the number of requests that the thread pool can queue simultaneously
`QueueUserWorkItem`	This method queues a work item to the thread pool
`RegisterWaitForSingleObject`	This method registers a delegate, which waits for a `WaitHandle`
`UnsafeQueueUserWorkItem`	This is the unsafe version of the `QueueUserWorkItem()` method
`UnsafeRegisterWaitForSingleObject`	This is the unsafe version of the `RegisterWaitForSingleObject()` method

Of the above methods, `QueueUserWorkItem()` and `RegisterWaitForSingleObject()` play the most important roles in thread pooling. Let's dig into the details of each method. Here we'll see both their syntax and a sample call in C#:

The `BindHandle()` method binds an operating system handle to the thread pool. It's a way to call `BindIoCompletionCallback`; Several classes in the BCL – such as `Socket` and `FileStream` – use it internally to bind their handles to an I/O completion port of the CLR-created thread-pool. The client application usually doesn't need to call this method directly; this functionality is indirectly accessed when methods such as `BeginRead` or `BeginReceive` are called.

```
public static bool BindHandle(IntPtr osHandle);
```

`osHandle` refers to the `IntPtr` type holding the OS handle. The return value is a Boolean where `true` indicates binding to the handle. This method throws a `SecurityException` if the caller does not have the required permission.

The `GetAvailableThreads()` method indicates the number of thread pool requests that can be added before reaching the maximum specified limit:

```
public static void GetAvailableThreads(out int workerThreads,
                                        out int completionPortThreads);
```

`workerThreads` refers to the number of worker threads of the thread pool while `completionPortThreads` refers to the number of asynchronous I/O threads.

The `GetMaxThreads()` method returns the maximum number of concurrent requests that a thread pool can handle. Any requests above this limit are queued until some of the threads in the thread pool are freed up:

```
public static void GetMaxThreads(out int workerThreads,
                                 out int completionPortThreads);
```

`workerThreads` refers to the number of worker threads of the thread pool while the `completionPortThreads` refers to the number of asynchronous I/O threads.

`QueueUserWorkItem()` is an overloaded method that queues a work item to the thread pool. It may be called in the following two forms. In the first case, the method queues the specified work item to the thread pool and calls the specified delegate associated with it. This case has the following syntax:

```
public static bool QueueUserWorkItem(WaitCallback callBack);
```

Here `callBack` refers to the delegate to be invoked when the thread in the thread pool takes the work item. The return value `true` indicates the method succeeded and `false` indicates failure.

In the second case, the method queues the specified work item to the thread pool, invokes the specified delegate, and specifies the object to be passed to the delegate when the work item is executed in the pool. In this case the method call has the following syntax:

```
public static bool QueueUserWorkItem(WaitCallback callback,
                                     object state);
```

callBack refers to the delegate to be invoked when the thread in the thread pool services the work item, while state refers to the object containing the state that is being passed to the delegate when the servicing of the work item occurs. The return value true indicates the method succeeded and fFalse indicates failure.

RegisterWaitForSingleObject() is also an overloaded method. It registers a delegate that waits for a WaitHandle. This class encapsulates all the objects of the operating system that wait for exclusive access to shared resources.

The method takes the following four forms. In the first case, the method registers a delegate and waits for the WaitHandle indicated by the timeout in milliseconds, which is given by a 32-bit signed integer. This overloaded form of the method has the following syntax in C#:

```
public static RegisteredWaitHandle RegisterWaitForSingleObject(
    WaitHandle waitObject,
    WaitOrTimerCallback callBack,
    object state,
    int millisecondsTimeOutInterval,
    bool executeOnlyOnce);
```

In the above syntax, the waitObject refers to the WaitHandle and the callBack refers to the WaitOrTimerCallback delegate to be invoked. The state parameter refers to the Object to be passed to the delegate. The millisecondsTimeOutInterval parameter refers to the timeout in milliseconds; if its value is 0 then the function tests the object state and returns immediately, on the other hand if its value is -1 the function waits forever. The executeOnlyOnce parameter indicates whether the thread has to wait on the waitObject parameter after the delegate has been invoked or not. The RegisteredWaitHandle parameter encapsulates the native handle.

This method throws an ArgumentOutOfRangeException if the millisecondsTimeOutInterval parameter is less than -1.

In the second case, the method does the same thing as specified in the first case but waits for the WaitHandle indicated by a timeout in milliseconds that is given by a 32-bit unsigned integer. This overloaded form of the method has the following syntax:

```
public static RegisteredWaitHandle RegisterWaitForSingleObject(
    WaitHandle waitObject,
    WaitOrTimerCallback callBack,
    object state,
    long millisecondsTimeOutInterval,
    bool executeOnlyOnce);
```

164

In the third case, the method waits for the `WaitHandle` indicated by the timeout given by the `TimeSpan` value. This overloaded form of the method has the following syntax:

```
public static RegisteredWaitHandle RegisterWaitForSingleObject(
    WaitHandle waitObject,
    WaitOrTimerCallback callBack,
    object state,
    TimeSpan timeout,
    bool executeOnlyOnce);
```

In the fourth case, the timeout is given in milliseconds by an unsigned integer and because unsigned integers are not part of the common type system, this method is not CLS compliant:

```
public static RegisteredWaitHandle RegisterWaitForSingleObject(
    WaitHandle waitObject,
    WaitOrTimerCallback callBack,
    object state,
    uint millisecondsTimeOutInterval,
    bool executeOnlyOnce);
```

The `UnsafeQueueUserWorkItem()` method is the unsafe version of the `QueueUserWorkItem()` method. It is unsafe because it does not propagate the calling stack to the worker thread, which means that the code can lose the calling stack and, in doing so, gain security privileges it should not be able to. It has the following syntax:

```
public static bool UnsafeQueueUserWorkItem(WaitCallback callBack,
                                           object state);
```

The `UnsafeRegisterWaitForSingleObject()` method is the unsafe version of the `RegisterWaitForSingleObject()` method and takes the following four forms:

```
public static RegisteredWaitHandle UnsafeRegisterWaitForSingleObject(
    WaitHandle waitObject,
    WaitOrTimerCallback callBack,
    object state,
    int millisecondsTimeOutInterval,
    bool executeOnlyOnce);
```

```
public static RegisteredWaitHandle UnsafeRegisterWaitForSingleObject(
    WaitHandle waitObject,
    WaitOrTimerCallback callBack,
    object state,
    long millisecondsTimeOutInterval,
    bool executeOnlyOnce);
```

```
public static RegisteredWaitHandle UnsafeRegisterWaitForSingleObject(
    WaitHandle waitObject,
    WaitOrTimerCallback callBack,
    object state,
    TimeSpan timeout,
    bool executeOnlyOnce);
```

```
public static RegisteredWaitHandle UnsafeRegisterWaitForSingleObject(
    WaitHandle waitObject,
    WaitOrTimerCallback callBack,
    object state,
    uint millisecondsTimeOutInterval,
    bool executeOnlyOnce);
```

These unsafe methods should not be used when queuing work items from code you
don't fully trust, and in general should not normally be used.

Programming the Thread Pool in C#

The previous sections of the chapter dealt with theoretical aspects of using thread
pools in the .NET Framework. Now it's time for us to cover the programmatic aspects
of creating and using thread pools in .NET applications from a C# perspective. As
described in the previous section, the `System.Threading` namespace contains the
`ThreadPool` class that we can use to create a thread pool in .NET applications.

Before we start coding, there are two important rules that we must be clear about
concerning the `ThreadPool` class. They are:

❑   There can be only one `ThreadPool` object per application domain

❑   A `ThreadPool` object is created for the first time when we call the
    `ThreadPool.QueueUserWorkItem()` method, or when a callback
    method is called through a timer or registered wait operation (which use
    the application domain thread pool internally)

First, let's see through examples how a `ThreadPool` class can be beneficial over
starting individual `Threads`. In the next example (`ThreadDemo.cs`) we will use
independent `Threads` to start two long tasks and in the following example
(`ThreadPoolDemo.cs`), we will start the same two tasks, but using a `ThreadPool`:

```
using System;
using System.Threading;

class ThreadDemo
{
  public void LongTask1()
```

```
{
  for (int i = 0; i <= 999; i++)
  {
    Console.WriteLine("Long Task 1 is being executed");
  }
}

public void LongTask2()
{
  for(int i = 0; i <= 999; i++)
  {
    Console.WriteLine("Long Task 2 is being executed");
  }
}

static void Main()
{
  ThreadDemo td = new ThreadDemo();
  for(int i = 0; i < 50; i++)
  {
    Thread t1 = new Thread(new ThreadStart(td.LongTask1));
    t1.Start();
    Thread t2 = new Thread(new ThreadStart(td.LongTask2));
    t2.Start();
  }

  Console.Read();
}
}
```

In the above example, we start two separate tasks LongTask1 and LongTask2 using independent threads t1 and t2. Note that we call threads repeatedly, in a loop, to stress the processing power of the operating system, so that we can get a better view of the benefits of using a ThreadPool. The ThreadPoolDemo class below shows the usage of the ThreadPool class.

```
using System;
using System.Threading;

class ThreadPoolDemo
{
  public void LongTask1(object obj)
  {
    for(int i = 0; i <= 999; i++)
    {
      Console.WriteLine("Long Task 1 is being executed");
    }
  }
}
```

```
public void LongTask2(object obj)
{
  for(int i = 0; i <= 999; i++)
  {
    Console.WriteLine("Long Task 2 is being executed");
  }
}

static void Main()
{
  ThreadPoolDemo tpd = new ThreadPoolDemo();
  for(int i = 0; i < 50; i++)
  {
    ThreadPool.QueueUserWorkItem(new WaitCallback(tpd.LongTask1));
    ThreadPool.QueueUserWorkItem(new WaitCallback(tpd.LongTask2));
  }

  Console.Read();
}
}
```

Let's dissect the above example. It comprises two separate tasks called LongTask1 and LongTask2 that do the simple job of outputting a message to the console in a loop. A ThreadPool class can be employed to start these two tasks without setting the properties of threads for each individual task by passing the delegate of the procedure to the WaitCallback() method, as given by the following block of code:

```
ThreadPool.QueueUserWorkItem(new WaitCallback(tpd.LongTask1));
ThreadPool.QueueUserWorkItem(new WaitCallback(tpd.LongTask2));
```

Note that the QueueUserWorkItem is a static method in the ThreadPool class and hence can be called directly by the class (ThreadPool). The example also has a Console.Read() statement, which holds the input on the console until the user presses the *Enter* key (or any other key).

By running the ThreadDemo and ThreadPoolDemo applications (separately, one after the other), we can compare the thread usage using the Windows Task Manager. The numbers on each operating system will be different depending on the power of the operating system, but relatively, results will be the same.

Threads usage of `ThreadDemo` application:

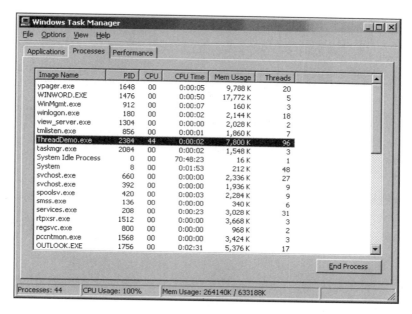

Thread usage of the `ThreadPoolDemo` application:

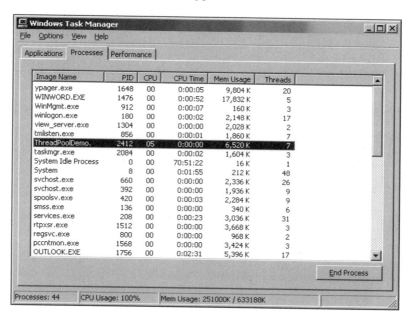

By comparing these screenshots, it is evident that using a `ThreadPool` not only helps reduce the thread usage of the application, but also reduces the CPU time, as well as the memory used by the application.

The next example (`ThreadPoolState.cs`) shows how to pass and return values from a thread in a thread pool. The thread pool framework only allows us to pass a single object parameter, but often we may want to pass several parameters to the method that we wish to be executed by a thread from the pool. However, we can easily wrap up all of the necessary parameters into a class and can pass an instance of that class as an argument to the `QueueUserWorkItem()` method:

```
using System;
using System.Threading;

class ObjState
{
  protected internal String inarg1;
  protected internal String inarg2;
  protected internal String outval;
}

class ThreadPoolState
{
  public void Task1(object stateObj)
  {
    ObjState StObj;
    StObj = (ObjState)stateObj;

    Console.WriteLine("Input Argument 1 in task 1: " + StObj.inarg1);
    Console.WriteLine("Input Argument 2 in task 1: " + StObj.inarg2);
    StObj.outval = "From Task1 " + StObj.inarg1 + " " + StObj.inarg2;
  }

  public void Task2(object stateObj)
  {
    ObjState StObj;
    StObj = (ObjState)stateObj;
    Console.WriteLine("Input Argument 1 in task 2: " + StObj.inarg1);
    Console.WriteLine("Input Argument 2 in task 2: " + StObj.inarg2);
    StObj.outval = "From Task2 " + StObj.inarg1 + " " + StObj.inarg2;
  }

  static void Main()
  {
    ObjState StObj1 = new ObjState();
    ObjState StObj2 = new ObjState();
    StObj1.inarg1 = "String Param1 of task 1";
    StObj1.inarg2 = "String Param2 of task 1";
    StObj2.inarg1 = "String Param1 of task 2";
    StObj2.inarg2 = "String Param2 of task 2";

    ThreadPoolState tps = new ThreadPoolState();
```

```
    // Queue a task
    ThreadPool.QueueUserWorkItem(new WaitCallback(tps.Task1), StObj1);
    // Queue another task
    ThreadPool.QueueUserWorkItem(new WaitCallback(tps.Task2), StObj2);
    Console.Read();
  }
}
```

The output from `ThreadPoolState` will be:

```
Input Argument 1 in task 1: String Param1 of task 1
Input Argument 2 in task 1: String Param2 of task 1
Input Argument 1 in task 2: String Param1 of task 2
Input Argument 2 in task 2: String Param2 of task 2
```

Let's explore the above example step by step. This example is pretty similar to the previous example except for the passing of an object; we are passing the input and output parameters to tasks queued in the thread pool using the `ObjState` object.

The `ObjState` object contains two input parameters and one output parameter, all of type `String`, as given by the following code block:

```
internal class ObjState
{
  protected internal String inarg1;
  protected internal String inarg2;
  protected internal String outval;
}
```

Next we define two methods, `task1` and `task2`, and pass an instance of `ObjState` as a parameter to each of them. The procedures `task1` and `task2` concatenate the values of the input parameters `inarg1` and `inarg2` of the passed `ObjState` object and store the result in the `outval` class variable. This is given by the following code block:

```
public void Task1(object stateObj)
{
  ObjState StObj;
  StObj = (ObjState)stateObj;

  Console.WriteLine("Input Argument 1 in task 1: " + StObj.inarg1);
  Console.WriteLine("Input Argument 2 in task 1: " + StObj.inarg2);
  StObj.outval = "From Task1 " + StObj.inarg1 + " " + StObj.inarg2;
}

public void Task2(object stateObj)
{
  ObjState StObj;
  StObj = (ObjState)stateObj;
```

171

```
      Console.WriteLine("Input Argument 1 in task 2: " + StObj.inarg1);
      Console.WriteLine("Input Argument 2 in task 2: " + StObj.inarg2);
      StObj.outval = "From Task2 " + StObj.inarg1 + " " + StObj.inarg2;
   }
```

In the `Main()` method we queue these two tasks in the thread pool employing the
`QueueUserWorkItem()` method of the `ThreadPool` class, as given by the following
code block:

```
static void Main()
{
   ObjState StObj1 = new ObjState();
   ObjState StObj2 = new ObjState();
   StObj1.inarg1 = "String Param1 of task 1";
   StObj1.inarg2 = "String Param2 of task 1";
   StObj2.inarg1 = "String Param1 of task 2";
   StObj2.inarg2 = "String Param2 of task 2";

   ThreadPoolState tps = new ThreadPoolState();

   // Queue a task
   ThreadPool.QueueUserWorkItem(new WaitCallback(tps.Task1), StObj1);
   // Queue another task
   ThreadPool.QueueUserWorkItem(new WaitCallback(tps.Task2), StObj2);
   Console.Read();
}
```

We can also queue work items that have wait operations involved with them to the
thread pool by employing `RegisterWaitForSingleObject()` to which
`WaitHandle` is passed as an argument. This `WaitHandle` signals the method wrapped
in a `WaitOrTimerCallback` delegate. In this case, the thread pool creates a
background thread to invoke the callback method. The following example
(`RegWait.cs`) demonstrates this concept:

```
using System;
using System.Threading;

public class RegWait
{
   private static int i = 0;

   public static void Main()
   {
      AutoResetEvent arev = new AutoResetEvent(false);
      ThreadPool.RegisterWaitForSingleObject
          (arev, new WaitOrTimerCallback(workitem), null, 2000, false);
      arev.Set();
      Console.Read();
   }
```

```
public static void workitem(object O ,bool signaled)
{
  i += 1;
  Console.WriteLine("Thread Pool Work Item Invoked: " +
                    i.ToString());
}
}
```

The output from the above example will be something like:

```
Thread Pool Work Item Invoked: 1
Thread Pool Work Item Invoked: 2
Thread Pool Work Item Invoked: 3
Thread Pool Work Item Invoked: 4
```

The output will continue with a new line printed every 2 seconds and the value of i incremented by one until the user presses the *Enter* key to invoke the `Console.Read()` statement.

To start, an `AutoResetEvent` object called `arev` is created with an initial state of non-signaled to signal the execution of queued work items:

```
AutoResetEvent arev = new AutoResetEvent(false);
```

We invoke the `RegisterWaitForSingleObject()` method with `null` for the state parameter, 2000 milliseconds as the timeout value and `false` for the `executeOnceOnly` parameter. `RegisterWaitForSingleObject()` registers a delegate and signals the work item at the specified time interval. In our example, it is set to 2 seconds as given by the following piece of code:

```
ThreadPool.RegisterWaitForSingleObject
    (arev, new WaitOrTimerCallback(workitem), null, 2000, false);
```

To raise the event we need to use the `Set()` method of the `AutoResetEvent` object:

```
arev.Set()
```

This example concludes the practical session on using thread pools in C# applications; in the next section we will examine scalability and build a thread pool manager application.

A Multi-Threaded Microsoft Message Queue (MSMQ) Listener

In this section, we will leverage the `ThreadPool` to send and listen to the messages from MSMQ. MSMQ is a distributed queue in which one application can send messages to another application asynchronously.

In a typical scenario, we have an MSMQ server that maintains the list of queues we want to send messages to. MSMQ Senders make a connection to the MSMQ Server (to a particular queue) and send messages to that queue. An MSMQ receiver receives messages sent by the MSMQ Senders. The MSMQ Receiver has to listen on a specific queue to receive messages sent on that queue. Thus, the MSMQ Server acts as a broker between the MSMQ Sender(s) and the MSMQ Receiver. The MSMQ Sender is unaware of the MSMQ Receiver and vice-versa.

In our application, we will develop an MSMQ Sender Windows Forms Application and an MSMQ Receiver as a Console application. In our MSMQ Sender Application (MSMQUI.cs), we send the messages to the queue using a ThreadPool:

```
int count = Convert.ToInt32(countTxt.Text);
while(count > 0)
{
    ThreadPool.QueueUserWorkItem(new WaitCallback(SendMessage),
                                 count.ToString());
    count--;
}
```

In the above code snippet (from MSMQUI.cs), we create a counter to send messages to the MSMQ. We put the messages into the ThreadPool as the state object and give a reference of the SendMessage() method to the WaitCallback delegate. SendMessage() is the method that will be called by the ThreadPool to send the message. In other words, the SendMessage() method will do the actual job of sending the message to the MSMQ.

```
public void SendMessage(object state)
{
    messageQueue1.Send (state.ToString());
}
```

The SendMessage() method converts the state object to string and send it to the MSMQ.

The MSMQUI application looks like the following screenshot when executed.

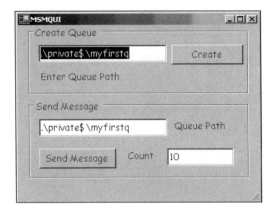

In the MSMQ Receiver (`MSMQListener.cs`), we receive the message notification from the MSMQ Server asynchronously whenever a message arrives into the queue. For this reason, we create the MSMQ Event Handler and pass the `MessageReceived()` method name to the `ReceiveCompletedEventHandler` delegate.

```
this._mq1.ReceiveCompleted += new
System.Messaging.ReceiveCompletedEventHandler(this.MessageReceived);
```

To start receiving messages from MSMQ, we need to call the `BeginReceive()` method on the message queue object.

```
_mq1.BeginReceive(new TimeSpan(0,0,2));
```

The `BeginReceive()` method takes a `TimeSpan` object to indicate how long the Receiver should wait till the message arrives into the queue. If the `TimeSpan` is not supplied, the application will block on the `BeginReceive()` method till a message arrives into MSMQ.

The `MessageReceived()` method is called by the MSMQ event handler when a message arrives into the queue:

```
public void MessageReceived(object source,
    System.Messaging.ReceiveCompletedEventArgs asyncResult)
{
  MessageQueue mq = null;
  try
  {
    // Connect to the queue.
    mq = (MessageQueue)source;
    System.Messaging.Message m =
        mq.EndReceive(asyncResult.AsyncResult);
    // Process the message here.
    //Console.WriteLine(m.Body.ToString());
    ThreadPool.QueueUserWorkItem
        (new WaitCallback(InvokeMDAO), m.Body);
```

```
      }
      catch(MessageQueueException)
      {

      }
      catch(Exception ex)
      {
         Console.WriteLine(ex.Message);
      }
      finally
      {
         this._mq1.BeginReceive(new TimeSpan(0,0,2));
      }
   }

   static void InvokeMDAO(object state)
   {
      MDAO md = new MDAO();
      md.AccessDatabaseOrDoSomeImportantWork(state);
   }
```

To get the arrived message, we have to call the EndReceive() method on the
message queue object. After we get the System.Messaging.Message object, it is up
to us to do whatever processing we want on to this object. Typically in a real-world
application, we would call System.EnterpriseServices (COM+) object and that
would in-turn update some database or forward the message to some other object for
processing. Here we can use the ThreadPool to keep the object invocation under
control. We put the body of the message into the ThreadPool and pass the name of
the InvokeMDAO() method to the WaitCallback delegate. The InvokeMDAO()
method invokes a method on the object and prints message on the console. As
discussed earlier, we can invoke a System.EnterpriseServices (COM+)
component in the InvokeMDAO() method. This would indirectly control the number of
created COM+ objects, which would be directly proportional to the numbers of threads
created by the ThreadPool. Finally, we have to call the BeginReceive() method
again to restart the async wait. If this method is not called, the message receiver stops
receiving messages from the MSMQ.

Scalability in .NET

If you have a multiprocessor system, then you'll see threads really show their worth.
The Windows OS manages the allocation of threads to processors and, as you have
seen throughout this book, firing any process automatically starts a thread. The .NET
Framework does not provide fine-grained control of the processor allocation, preferring
to allow the operating system to control the scheduling, as it will have more
information on the loading of the processors than the CLR would. It does, however,
provide some control over which processor an entire process runs on. However, this
applies to *all* of its threads, so its use is not applicable to this book.

If you have only one thread, the main thread, then every task within that thread will operate on the same processor. However, if a new thread is fired, then the operating system schedules which processor it should be executed on. This decision as to which processor will run the thread does itself consume some processor resources and so, for small tasks, it isn't generally worth it as the time to execute may be only as long as the time it takes for the OS to allocate the task to a processor. However, this allocation has been taking less and less time in successive versions of Windows, and for anything other than the most trivial of tasks, when using threads, you should find a performance improvement by creating a new thread to execute your task. It is in symmetric multi-processor (SMP) systems that the benefits of threading are really shown, as the processors can be used to their full effect to distribute the load of the application.

In the next section, we describe how to create a thread pool manager with which you can create and manage threads, and which will ensure that a maximum and minimum number of threads exist in a pool and that idle threads get reused.

A Thread Pool Manager

Throughout this book, you have seen different ways of creating threads and in this chapter we have described the `ThreadPool` class to make use of the operating system's own thread pool for short-lived threads. We can implement a half-way house between the two, however. We can create a class that will keep a pool of a specified number of threads to be supplied to any requesting application. This will enable the threads to be managed more easily by your code, and also allow for faster thread execution as you may be able to use a previously instantiated thread object. This class will draw together much of the knowledge acquired so far, and you will be able to use it in your own multithreaded applications. We will explain this class as we go along, and at the end provide an application to test that this assembly is working as expected.

So, let's get started and explain the code of our thread pool manager contained in a file named `MyThreadPool.cs`:

```
using System;
using System.Text;
using System.Threading

namespace GenThreadPool
{
```

The above declarations show that the only additional external assembly needed is `System.dll`. The `GenThreadPool` namespace is defined to contain all of the relevant classes for this project. Below we show the interface called `IThreadPool` that will be used for the `GenThreadPoolImpl` class:

```
public interface IThreadPool
{
    void AddJob(System.Threading.Thread jobToRun);
```

```
      Stats GetStats();
   }
}
```

This defines two methods for the thread pool, AddJob() and GetStats(), which will be detailed in the following definitions of the GenThreadPoolImpl class, which generates the thread pool that we will be using:

```
public class GenThreadPoolImpl : IThreadPool
{
  private int _maxThreads;
  private int _minThreads;
  private int _maxIdleTime;
  private static bool _debug;
  private ArrayList _pendingJobs;
  private ArrayList _availableThreads;

  public bool Debug
  {
    get
    {
      return _debug;
    }
    set
    {
      _debug = value;
    }
  }

  public ArrayList PendingJobs
  {
    get
    {
      return this._pendingJobs;
    }
    set
    {
      this._pendingJobs = value;
    }
  }

  public ArrayList AvailableThreads
  {
    get
    {
      return this._availableThreads;
    }
  }
```

```
public int MaxIdleTime
{
  get
  {
    return this._maxIdleTime;
  }
  set
  {
    this._maxIdleTime = value;
  }
}

public int MaxThreads
{
  get
  {
    return this._maxThreads;
  }
  set
  {
    this._maxThreads = value;
  }
}

public int MinThreads
{
  get
  {
    return this._minThreads;
  }
  set
  {
    this._minThreads = value;
  }
}
```

This class implements the IThreadPool interface, which we defined earlier, and then goes on to define a few Private fields. The properties are just wrappers around the relevant Private members to prevent users from altering the values directly, in case further rules need to be added later. The fields m_maxThreads, m_minThreads, and m_maxIdleTime specify the maximum and minimum number of threads in the pool, and how long in milliseconds to allow a thread to remain idle before removing it from the pool. There are three constructors for this class:

```
public GenThreadPoolImpl()
{
  _maxThreads = 1;
  _minThreads = 0;
  _maxIdleTime = 300;
```

```
    this._pendingJobs =
        ArrayList.Synchronized (new ArrayList() );

    this._availableThreads =
        ArrayList.Synchronized (new ArrayList());

    _debug = false;
}
```

The default constructor only permits one thread to be present in the pool, and will destroy it after only 0.3 seconds. It also performs some lazy initialization, creating an array list to contain the jobs awaiting a thread, and the threads not yet allocated to a method call. The m_debug flag, when set to true, would allow further debugging information while testing:

```
public GenThreadPoolImpl(int maxThreads, int minThreads,
                         int maxIdleTime)
{
    _maxThreads = maxThreads;
    _minThreads = minThreads;
    _maxIdleTime = maxIdleTime;

    this._pendingJobs =
        ArrayList.Synchronized (new ArrayList());
    this._availableThreads =
        ArrayList.Synchronized (new ArrayList());

    _debug = false;
    InitAvailableThreads();
}
```

When a GenThreadPoolImpl class is instantiated with three integers, we specify how the minimum and maximum number of threads, and the idle time of the threads. It also fires off the InitAvailableThreads() method, detailed below:

```
private void InitAvailableThreads()
{
    if(this._minThreads > 0)
        for(int i = 0; i < this._minThreads; i++)
        {
            Thread t = new
                Thread(new ThreadStart(new GenPool (this, this).run ));
            ThreadElement e = new ThreadElement (t);
            e.Idle = true;
            _availableThreads.Add (e);
        }

    Console.WriteLine("Initialized the ThreadPool. "
                    + " Number of Available threads: "
                    + this._availableThreads.Count);
}
```

This creates the threads needed for the pool on instantiation. The default constructor only specified one thread, so it wasn't necessary before. This cycles through, creating the maximum number of threads allowed by the pool, specified in m_maxThreads. Below is the constructor for four arguments:

```
public GenThreadPoolImpl(int maxThreads, int minThreads,
                         int maxIdleTime, bool debug_)
{
    _maxThreads = maxThreads;
    _minThreads = minThreads;
    _maxIdleTime = maxIdleTime;

    this._pendingJobs =
        ArrayList.Synchronized (new ArrayList());
    this._availableThreads =
        ArrayList.Synchronized (new ArrayList());

    _debug = debug_;
    InitAvailableThreads();
}
```

This constructor does the same as the above, only allowing us to set the debugging flag. We now go on to describe the business end of this class, the AddJob() method:

```
public void AddJob(Thread job)
{
    if(job == null) return;

    lock(this)
    {
```

The above method actually adds a job to the pool. If the job passed as a parameter is non-existent, then it exits the method. Otherwise, it provides a lock on the GenThreadPoolImpl instance to ensure that no other thread or process can add or remove a job:

```
        _pendingJobs.Add (job);

        int index = findFirstIdleThread();

        if(_debug)
            Console.WriteLine("First Idle Thread is " + index);

        if(index == -1)
        {
            if((_maxThreads == -1)
                || ( _availableThreads.Count < _maxThreads))
            {
                if(_debug)
                    Console.WriteLine("Creating a new thread");
```

```
           Thread t = new Thread(new
               ThreadStart (new GenPool(this, this).run ));
```

The job is added to an `ArrayList`, which will store all the jobs awaiting execution and completion. The `FindFirstIdleThread()` method returns the index of a thread contained within m_availableThreads that is currently idle and so available for use. If the method returns -1, then there are no idle threads and the pool needs to attempt to create a new one. The `Run()` method of the `GenPool` class is fired inside this thread:

```
           ThreadElement e = new ThreadElement (t);

           e.Idle = false;
           e.getMyThread().Start();

           try
           {
             _availableThreads.Add (e);
           }
           catch(OutOfMemoryException)
           {
             Console.WriteLine("Out of Memory");
             _availableThreads.Add (e);
             Console.WriteLine("Added Job again");
           }

           return;
           }

       if(_debug)
           Console.WriteLine("No Threads Available .."
                               + this.GetStats().ToString());
```

The `ThreadElement` class is another helper class that will be defined later. It adds some additional properties to a standard thread so that the pool can manage it effectively. The thread's `Start()` method is fired before it is added to the m_availableThreads collection.

```
   else
   {
     try
     {
       if(_debug)
           Console.WriteLine("Using an existing thread...");

       ((ThreadElement)_availableThreads[index]).Idle = false;
```

Above, we start to detail the condition whereby a thread is deemed idle and so free for allocation to a new job. Firstly, we convert the thread explicitly into a `ThreadElement` and change its idle flag:

```
lock(((ThreadElement)_availableThreads[index]).getMyThread ())
{
  Monitor.Pulse((
      (ThreadElement)_availableThreads[index]).getMyThread ());
}
```

Here we lock the thread so that it cannot be affected by any other process. We then alert all waiting threads that it is now available for use, so we issue a `Monitor.Pulse()` instruction, and then release the lock:

```
}
catch(Exception ex)
{
    Console.WriteLine ("Error while reusing thread " + ex.Message );

    if(_debug)
    {
      Console.WriteLine("Value of index is " + index );
      Console.WriteLine ("Size of available threads is " +
                        this._availableThreads.Count);
      Console.WriteLine ("Available Threads is "
                        + this._availableThreads .IsSynchronized );
    }
  }
}//end of else

}//lock
}//end of method
```

Finally, we catch any exceptions and output the results to the command line, providing more useful debugging information if the this.Debug flag has been set. That completes the AddJob() method so now let's look at the implementation of the GetStats() method:

```
public Stats GetStats()
{
    Stats stats = new Stats();

    stats.maxThreads = _maxThreads;
    stats.minThreads = _minThreads;
    stats.maxIdleTime = _maxIdleTime;
    stats.pendingJobs = _pendingJobs.Count;
    stats.numThreads = _availableThreads.Count;

    stats.jobsInProgress =
        _availableThreads.Count - findIdleThreadCount();

    return stats;
}
```

The GetStats() method returns a Stats() structure, which we will define later. As we will see, it contains the minimum and maximum number of threads, as well as other values set in the constructor. Now let's look at the FindIdleThreadCount() method:

```
public int FindIdleThreadCount()
{
   int idleThreads = 0;

   for (int i = 0; i < _availableThreads.Count; i++)
   {
      if(((ThreadElement)_availableThreads[i]).Idle)
         idleThreads++;
   }

   return idleThreads;
}
```

This method is one called earlier in the class and it simply goes through the array list of threads and returns the how many of them are idle. We also used the FindFirstIdleThread() method so let's see it:

```
public int FindFirstIdleThread()
{
   for (int i = 0; i < _availableThreads.Count; i++)
   {
      if(((ThreadElement)_availableThreads[i]).Idle )
         return i;
   }

   return -1;
}
```

As we can see, the method returns the index of the first idle thread in the array list. We will also need the following method:

```
public int FindThread()
{
   for(int i = 0; i < _availableThreads.Count; i++)
   {
      if(((ThreadElement)_availableThreads[i])
         .GetMyThread()
         .Equals(Thread.CurrentThread ))
      return i;
   }

   return -1;
}
```

This method is used to determine in which index position in the array list the current thread is located. We'll also need the following method:

```
public  void RemoveThread()
{
  for(int i = 0 ; i < _availableThreads.Count; i++)
  {
    if(((ThreadElement)_availableThreads[i])
        .GetMyThread()
        .Equals (Thread.CurrentThread ))
    {
      _availableThreads.RemoveAt (i);
      return;
    }
  }
}
```

This removes the current thread from the array list of threads. This is, of course, used to remove a thread from the pool when it is finished with and has been idle for longer than the time specified in this.MaxIdleTime. Now we start to define the rest of the classes for this assembly:

```
public class GenPool
{
  private Object _lock;
  private GenThreadPoolImpl _gn;

  public GenPool(Object lock_, GenThreadPoolImpl gn)
  {
    this._lock = lock_;
    this._gn = gn;
  }
```

The GenPool class executes all of the pending threads, and once complete, after the period specified in MaxIdleTime, will remove them from the pool. It checks to see if there are any threads available on the GenThreadPoolImpl passed as a reference to the constructor, and it locks the values of the object passed as the first parameter. In general, this will be the same GenThreadPoolImpl object passed as the second argument:

```
public void Run()
{
  Thread job = null;
  try
  {
    while(true)
    {
      while(true)
      {
        lock(this._lock )
```

```
            {
              if(_gn.PendingJobs.Count == 0)
              {
                int index = _gn.findThread();
                if(index == -1)return;

                ((ThreadElement)_gn.AvailableThreads[index]).Idle =
                    true;
                break;
              }

              job = (Thread)_gn.PendingJobs[0];
              _gn.PendingJobs.RemoveAt (0);
            }//end of lock
```

This Run() method starts a loop to attempt to find a thread in the pool that matches the current thread, and begin its execution. You can see above that it locks the object passed in as a parameter to the constructor, and if there are no pending jobs, then it just finds the thread in the pool that matches the current one, returning -1 if there isn't one. If there is a pending job, then it retrieves the first one, and then removes it from the queue:

```
          //run the job
        job.Start();
      }
```

It then begins execution of the method on the pending thread, and returns to the start of the loop:

```
    try
    {
      lock(this)
      {
        if(_gn.MaxIdleTime == -1)
          Monitor.Wait (this);
        else Monitor.Wait (this, gn.MaxIdleTime);
      }
    }
```

In the next part of the loop (once it has no more pending jobs), it locks the current object and waits for the thread to be free for execution for the period specified in MaxIdleTime.

```
    lock(_lock)
    {
      if(_gn.PendingJobs.Count == 0)
      {
        if(_gn.MinThreads != -1 && _gn.AvailableThreads.Count >
          _gn.MinThreads)
```

```
      {
        _gn.removeThread();
        return;
      }
    }
  }
}
```

Finally, it locks the object again, and if there are no pending jobs and there are more than the minimum required number of threads, then it removes the thread from the pool. We now move on to the ThreadElement class:

```
public class ThreadElement
{
  private bool _idle;
  private Thread _thread;

  public ThreadElement(Thread th)
  {
    this._thread = th;
    this._idle = true;
  }
```

A ThreadElement is what is stored in the thread pool, and takes a thread as the parameter for its constructor. It sets the thread as idle on construction of this object:

```
public bool Idle
{
  get
  {
    return this._idle;
  }
  set
  {
    this._idle = value;
  }
}
public Thread GetMyThread(){return this._thread;}
```

The above code is straightforward. The Idle property essentially defines when the thread's execution is complete, and the GetMyThread() method just returns the Thread object. Now look at the following structure:

```
public struct Stats
{
  public int maxThreads;
  public int minThreads;
  public int maxIdleTime;
  public int numThreads;
  public int pendingJobs;
  public int jobsInProgress;
```

Here we define the Stats structure that we mentioned earlier, which stores all of the statistics of the thread pool. The fields are self-describing. ToString() is the only method:

```
public override String ToString()
{
  StringBuilder sb = new StringBuilder ("MaxThreads = ");
  sb.Append(maxThreads);
  sb.Append("\nMinThreads = ");
  sb.Append(minThreads);
  sb.Append("\nMaxIdleTime = ");
  sb.Append(maxIdleTime);
  sb.Append("\nPending Jobs = ");
  sb.Append(pendingJobs);
  sb.Append("\nJobs In Progress = ");
  sb.Append(jobsInProgress);

  return sb.ToString ();
}
```

This ToString() method returns the structure in a string format, using StringBuilder to build up the string. The 107 argument initializes the StringBuilder's size to 107 characters, as it is fair to assume that there are not likely to be more than 99,999 threads. If so, then StringBuilder will resize itself anyway. This capacity specification allows a small performance boost.

If you have an application that is firing methods repeatedly on different threads, this class can manage the process and help ensure that too many threads aren't spawned. Apart from containing a maximum and minimum number of threads, it will reuse an existing thread if possible. You can now compile this project into a DLL, and use this class from within other projects. Below is code that will allow you to test this thread pool class, TestGenThreadPool.cs:

```
using System;
using System.Threading;
using GenThreadPool;

namespace TestGenThreadPool
{

  public class TestPerformance
  {
    public int count;
    private Object _lock = new Object();

    public TestPerformance(IThreadPool pool, int times)
    {
      count = 0;
      DateTime start =System.DateTime .Now;
```

```
Console.WriteLine("Start Time for Job is "
                  + System.DateTime .Now);

for (int i = 0; i < times; i++)
{
  Thread t1 = new Thread(
      new ThreadStart (new Job(this).Run ));
  pool.AddJob(t1);
}

Console.WriteLine("End Time for Job is " +
                  System.DateTime .Now);

Console.WriteLine("Performance using Pool[in ms]: ");
Console.WriteLine(""
                  + (System.DateTime.Now - start).ToString());

count = 0;
start = System.DateTime.Now;

Console.WriteLine("Start Time for JobThread is " +
                  System.DateTime.Now.ToString());

for (int i = 0; i < times; i++)
{
  Thread jt = new Thread(new ThreadStart(new Job(this).Run));
  jt.Start();
}

while (true)
{
  lock (_lock)
  {
    if (count == times)
        break;
  }
  try
  {
    Thread.Sleep(1000);
  }
  catch
  {
  }
}

Console.WriteLine("End Time for JobThread is "
                  + System.DateTime.Now.ToString());
Console.WriteLine("Performance using no Pool[in ms]: ");
Console.WriteLine(""
                  + (System.DateTime.Now - start).ToString());
}
```

```csharp
sealed class JobThread
{
  private Object _lock = new Object();
  private TestPerformance tpf;

  public JobThread(TestPerformance tpf_)
  {
    this.tpf = tpf_;
  }

  public void Run()
  {
    lock(_lock)
    {
      tpf.count++;
    }
  }
}

sealed class Job
{
  private Object _lock = new Object();
  private TestPerformance tpf;

  public Job(TestPerformance tpf_)
  {
    this.tpf = tpf_;
  }

  public void Run()
  {
    tpf.count++;
  }
}
  }
}

class TestPool
{
  static void Main(string[] args)
  {
    GenThreadPool.IThreadPool tp =
        new GenThreadPoolImpl(200, 300, 300, true);
    TestPerformance p = new TestPerformance(tp, 100);
  }
}
```

The above application just mechanically attempts to add new threads to an instance of the thread pool, with the debug flag set to true. It is quite straightforward, but the best way to see this thread pool in action is to try it out in your own applications. You can use this class, once it is compiled.

Summary

In this chapter, we have seen how thread pooling can be used when a thread is required for a relatively short duration. Thread pooling allows recycling of threads. A thread is assigned a task and, when that task has completed, it returns to the pool and waits for the next assignment. We also covered the various aspects of using thread pools in .NET applications. We started defining what a thread pool is and then why we might choose to use one in our applications. We also covered the role of CLR in creating the thread pool followed by the glitches involved in using a thread pool.

We later covered some more scalability issues, as the ThreadPool class isn't suitable for applications that may need to fire a number of long-lived threads. We discussed the creation of a ThreadPool manager class and mentioned how SMP systems can dramatically increase the performance of an application if it is threaded.

C#

Threading

Handbook

6

6

Debugging and Tracing Threads

Debugging and tracing are two techniques frequently, and often necessarily, employed by developers. The former allows a developer to analyze an application's variables and code, and step through the program's code flow. The latter allows us to trace the behavior of our application, displaying information in a **listener** (a log file, the Windows event log, or similar). They are fundamental to creating robust applications because they provide an easy way to monitor and understand how our application is working. The big difference between the two techniques is that tracing can be done during an application's run time, while the debugger is used at design time, before releasing the final version of our application.

Desktop application developers have traditionally had access to excellent debugging support, with the ability to use breakpoints and examine the contents of variables. .NET is no exception in this regard, but the issues inherent in using breakpoints in a multithreaded application deserve some attention, and will be the focus of this chapter.

Outside the desktop, developers have long suffered from the lack of a good debugger for web applications written in environments such as ASP. In order to understand a variable's value, or the code's flow, and every common task usually done with a debugger, ASP developers often had to populate their code with `Response.Write()` statements, echoing messages like Entered the function, Exited from the loop, and so on. Then when they had finished testing the ASP application, they needed to remove all the undesired statements. That's not the best way to debug a program.

Fortunately, .NET brings debugging functionality to the next generation of ASP developers by providing four useful classes: `Trace`, `Debug`, `BooleanSwitch`, and `TraceSwitch`. In addition, any .NET language can use these classes so every developer who chooses to use Visual Studio .NET to create applications can perform debugging operations using its visual tools.

The various tracing and debugging techniques are especially useful for applications that use threads. If implemented well, these techniques allow developers to trace each thread's behavior, discovering any application anomalies, such as unexpected resource consumption, contention bugs, and so on.

In this chapter, we will analyze both tracing and debugging aspects in the following order:

❑ Using Visual Studio .NET debugging analysis and its powerful tools

❑ Using the .NET tracing classes in order to implement these features in our code

❑ Putting it all together by creating an application that uses tracing

For this chapter, Visual Studio .NET is necessary to make use of much of the tracing and debugging features shown. However, by using the /d:TRACE=TRUE switch, some tracing functionality can be achieved using the command line.

Creating the Application Code

Usually, when you create an application (or part of one), you write the code and then try to run the application. Sometimes it works as you expected it to; often it doesn't. When it doesn't, you try to discover what could be happening by examining more carefully the code that you wrote. In Visual Studio .NET, you can use the debugger by choosing some breakpoints to stop the application's execution near or just before the guilty method, then step through lines of code, examining variable values to understand precisely what went wrong. Finally, when all is working you can build the release version (a version without the symbols used by the debugging tools) of our application, and distribute it.

In this type of program, during the development process, you can also insert tracing functionality. In fact, even if the program works very well, there will be always a case where something has not been foreseen (especially when some external, possibly third-party, components fail). In that case, if you have filled the code with tracing instructions, you can turn on tracing and examine the resulting log file to understand what might have happened. Moreover, tracing functionality is useful to discover where an application consumes resources or where it spends too much time performing a task. In applications that use threads, you should use tracing functionality because otherwise it can be difficult to observe each thread's behavior, identify race conditions, and spot potential deadlocks or time-consuming contention.

Tracing, debugging, and performance techniques are often known as **instrumentation**. This term refers to the capacity to monitor an application's performance and behavior, and diagnose errors and bugs. So, an application that supports instrumentation has to include:

❑ Debugging: Fixing errors and bugs during an application's development

❏   Code tracing: Receiving information in a listener program during an application's execution

❏   Performance counters: Using techniques to monitor an application's performance

Let's examine what the .NET Framework provides for us to add instrumentation to our applications.

Debugging Your Code

Usually, when you test your application and see that its behavior is not what you expect it to be, you start examining more carefully the code written. If you are using Visual Studio .NET to create your application, it provides many amazing tools to visually debug the application. In addition, whatever language you choose to develop your application in, it will use the same debugger with the same tools. Moreover, the basic debugger's functionalities have been inherited from the Visual Basic 6 and Visual C++ IDEs, resulting in something that should be familiar for most developers. However, we will not spend too much time on the debugger in general, and will focus this discussion mostly on those features directly relevant to threading.

The new debugger provides:

❏   The same tool to debug different applications created using different languages, and the ability to debug applications written in mixed languages

❏   The ability to debug SQL Server stored procedures

❏   The ability to debug .NET Framework and Win32 native code, so that if you are debugging your Visual C# .NET application and your thread uses a COM+ component, you can debug both the applications using the same debugger

❏   A more powerful and enhanced remote debugger

If you already have experience with the Visual Basic 6 debugger, you will know that some functionality has been removed. The most relevant is the ability to change the code and continue with its execution. Using the Visual Studio .NET debugger, this feature is no longer available, because each modification to the code requires a new compilation.

In this section of the book, we will analyze the debugging tools provided by the Visual Studio .NET IDE that are especially useful during the testing and error discovery phase of multithreaded application development.

Visual Studio .NET Debugger

Using the Visual Studio .NET debugger, as you know, you can break the execution of
your application at a specified point simply by inserting a breakpoint near the line of
the code you wish to inspect. When the application is suspended, the debugger
provides many tools to examine and edit the content of variables, examine the memory
and call stack, and more.

Configuring Debugger Parameters

In order to make use of the Visual Studio .NET debugger, you have to build the
application using the Debug configuration. In that way, you will fill the application with
symbolic debugging information rather than optimize the code. When everything
appears to work fine, you would release your application after recompiling the code,
choosing the Release configuration, which removes debugging information and
optimizes the code.

When a new debugger session begins, a lot of resources are loaded into the memory.
In fact, the debugger fills the memory with various code to allow us to debug
unmanaged code, SQL Server stored procedures, and more. It is therefore a good idea
to remove these features when you don't need them. You can change the debugger's
settings inside the Property Pages dialog box that can be found by right-clicking on the
project in the Solution Explorer and selecting Properties. For a Windows application, the
following dialog box will appear:

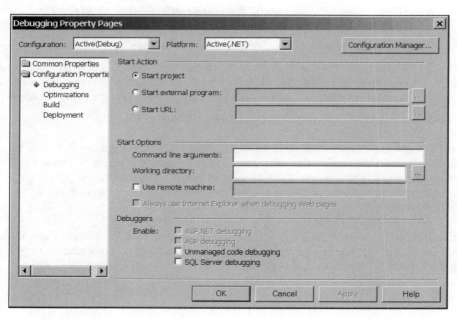

After compiling a Debug configured project, the output directory will contain the exe or dll file and a pdb (program database) file. Because IL keeps the values of parameters and private members inside arrays, the original names of these variables are lost – as well as some other information relevant to debugging. When a project is compiled for debugging, or the /debug:full switch is used on the command-line compiler, a pdb file is generated at the same time. The exe or dll file contains an absolute path pointing to the pdb file and if the debugger doesn't find the program database file, it starts to search in the same application path and in the directory specified in the Property Pages dialog box. Finally, if the debugger can't find the pdb file in any directory, it will regenerate a new one.

Debugger Windows

Once you have loaded your project into Visual Studio .NET you are ready to debug your application by simply running it, waiting for the code to reach a breakpoint, then using either the *F10* or *F11* key to step over and step into method calls in our code, respectively. If you are not working with the release version of your application, you will see the IDE showing many docked windows. During your debugging session these windows will be filled with the variables' values, objects' dumps, call stack, disassembly code, and more. Let's start examining more closely these debugging tools, and how they can be used to assist in the debugging of your threaded application.

The Locals Window

This window allows you to examine and modify each variable's content defined locally in the method you are debugging (including parameters to the method). For example, debugging the following Main() method of TraceSwitchExample, you will retrieve just the content of two variables: fs and t, as shown in the following screenshot:

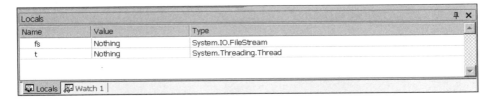

You can activate this window selecting the Debug | Window | Locals menu, or you can press *Ctrl+Alt+V*, release, and press *L*.

The Watch Window

You can drag variables from the source code and drop them over the Watch window in order to inspect their values and structure. In the following screenshot, a BooleanSwitch object from an example later in the chapter has been dropped into the window.

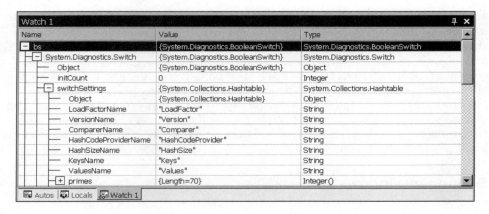

You can expand tree nodes by clicking the plus sign and then examine and change object property values. You can activate up to four Watch windows by pressing *Ctrl+Alt+W*, then releasing, and pressing a key between *1* and *4*.

> *You can also add a variable to the* Watch *window by selecting it in the source code and choosing* Add Watch *from the context menu.*

The Command Window – Immediate Window

This window provides a text field where you can query a variable's contents and change variable values. When you need to retrieve the variable's content you have to use a question mark before the expression. In the following screenshot, the `Enabled` property of the `BooleanSwitch` object has been examined, changed to `false`, and displayed again.

In addition, this window allows you to make use of various IDE commands, such as creating a new file or project, finding a string, or whatever else you usually do within the Visual Studio .NET menu. To switch from Immediate mode to Command mode you simply have to write the `>cmd` statement. Once in Command mode, you will be assisted by the IDE in finding the desired commands by the IntelliSense functionality. You switch back to Immediate mode by using the `>immed` command.

You can activate this window by selecting Debug | Window | Immediate, or you can press *Ctrl+Alt+I*.

Stepping Through the Code

Now that we have briefly described the more useful debugger windows, we can focus our attention on code navigation. The Visual Studio .NET debugger allows developers to step between code lines of both single and multiple source code files, observing the program behavior at run time. Moreover, you can debug unmanaged code and Microsoft SQL Server stored procedures. The debugger provides three different ways to step through the code:

- ❏ **Step Into**: Pressing the *F11* key you will go through the code one step at a time, entering method bodies that you find on your way (where source code and debug symbols are available).

- ❏ **Step Over**: Pressing the *F10* key you will go one step forward in the code executing every method you encounter but without stepping into it (executing the method as one line).

- ❏ **Step Out**: Pressing *Shift+F11*, you will execute all the remaining code within the body of the method that you are currently stepped into, and step onto the next line in the method that called it.

Each time you step to the next line of code by pressing these keys, you are executing the highlighted code.

Another useful feature provided by the Visual Studio .NET debugger is the Run To Cursor functionality. Selecting it from the context menu over the source code, you can execute all the lines between the highlighted line and the line where the cursor is placed.

Finally, the Visual Studio .NET debugger provides a way to change the execution point of our application. You can decide to move your application's execution point by launching the debugger and choosing the Set Next Statement item in the context menu. Be careful when using this feature, because every line of code between the old and the new position will fail to be executed.

Setting Breakpoints

In large source code applications, it is not practical to step through all the preceding code before arriving at the method you are interested in debugging. The debugger offers the possibility to set breakpoints in the code. As the name says, a breakpoint is a point where the execution of your program is to be suspended. You can specify breakpoints both before and after launching the debugger session, by simply placing the cursor on the line and pressing the *F9* key – or by clicking in the left margin. A red highlight will be placed over the line to let you know that you have just added a breakpoint to the code, and a glyph will be added to the left margin of the source window. In order to remove a breakpoint you can either click over the glyph or press the *F9* key again.

You can manage all the set breakpoints from a single dialog by using the Breakpoints window.

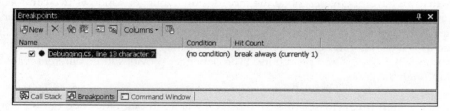

Using this window, you can add a new breakpoint, delete one or all breakpoints, disable all breakpoints, add and remove window's columns, and view breakpoint properties.

> **By using breakpoints, you can suspend execution of a thread and examine its current stackframe contents.**

Selecting the breakpoint properties option from the window above a new dialog box will be shown and you can specify to activate a breakpoint only when a specific variable changes its content. You have to specify the variable's name choosing the has changed radio button in the breakpoint property pages. This again can be useful in threaded scenarios, as you can detect when something unexpected occurs.

Finally, the Hit Count... button from the same dialog box allows developers to enable a breakpoint only when it has reached the specified hit count. Again this is useful in debugging threads as it allows you to see how often a thread is spawned.

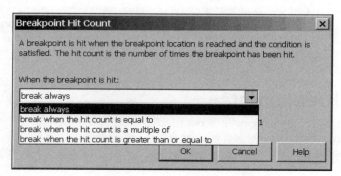

From the combo box, you can select the condition that you want to assign to the breakpoint. For example, you can activate the breakpoint in a loop only when you are near to exiting from it. You can select the break when the hit count is equal to an item by assigning a value to the text field that will appear next to the combobox.

In order to execute all the code lines until the breakpoint is reached you have to press the *F5* key, select the Debug | Start menu, or press the Start button on the standard toolbar.

Debugging Threads

The Visual Studio .NET debugger provides a special window to manage threads during debugging sessions. You can display this window by selecting Debug | Windows | Threads, or by pressing *Ctrl+Alt+H*.

The Threads window contains the following columns:

Column name	Description
ID	The thread's unique identifier assigned by the operating system.
Name	The thread's name. You can specify it in the code using the Name property of the Thread object.
Location	The method or memory address in which the thread is currently executing.
Priority	The thread's priority.
Suspend	A counter for determining how often the thread has been suspended. The counter zero in the screenshot above indicates that the thread has never been suspended.

You can switch between threads by simply double-clicking on the item within the Threads window. Moreover, by right-clicking on a thread, you can choose the Freeze menu item that will pause the thread's execution. To roll back the frozen thread state, you select the Thaw menu item.

Code Tracing

The next code instrumentation technique that we will analyze is tracing. In a multi-threaded application, this technique is especially important. You can trace a thread's behavior and interaction when more than one task has been started. As we will see later, this is not possible using the debugger. The .NET Framework provides some useful classes that allow developers to implement tracing functionality simply. Let's examine the tracing classes from the `System.Diagnostics` namespace that the .NET Framework offers:

- ❑ `Trace`: This class has many static methods that write messages to a listener. By default, the debug output windows in VS.NET will be used as the listener application, but thanks to the `Listeners` collection, you can add different listeners such as a text file listener, or the Windows event log listener.

- ❑ `Debug`: This class has the same methods as the `Trace` class, writing information to a listener application. The largest difference between these two classes is in their usage; `Trace` is useful at run time, `Debug` is used at development time.

- ❑ `BooleanSwitch`: This class allows us to define a switch that turns on or off the tracing messages.

- ❑ `TraceSwitch`: This class provides four different tracing levels allowing developers to choose the severity of the messages to send to the listener.

The Trace Class

In this section, we will analyze the most frequently used methods of the `Trace` class. It is provided by the .NET Framework and encapsulates all the necessary methods to implement tracing functionality easily. The `Trace` class is contained in the `System.Diagnostics` namespace and provides many static methods for sending messages to the listener application. As you know, static methods mean that you do not have to instantiate a new object from the `Trace` class and can use the method directly. For example:

```
static void Main()
{
    Trace.WriteLine(t.ThreadState);
}
```

The code snippet above uses the `WriteLine()` method to output the thread state, followed by a carriage return, to the listener application. The following table lists some of the other static methods provided by the `Trace` class:

Method	Description
Assert (*condition, message*)	Displays the specified string *message* when the *condition* provided to the method evaluates to `false`. When you do not specify the message text, the Call Stack is displayed instead.
Fail (*message*)	Similar to the `Assert()` method, this writes the specified text to the Call Stack when a failure occurs. The `Assert()` method differs because `Fail()` cannot specify a condition before displaying the error. In fact, the `Fail()` method is usually placed in the `catch` statement of a `try-catch-finally` instruction. You could also place it anywhere in your code that you are sure could never be reached – such as in the default case of a switch statement where you believe you've allowed for all possibilities.
Write (*message* | *object*)	Writes the specified text *message*, or object name, to the listener application.
WriteIf (*condition, message*)	Writes the specified *message* text into the listener application if the specified *condition* is `true`.
WriteLine (*message* | *object*)	Writes the specified *message* text, or object name, followed by a carriage return.
WriteLineIf (*condition, message*)	Writes the specified *message* text followed by a carriage return if the specified *condition* is `true`.

The behavior of these methods depends on the listener application chosen. For example, the `Assert()` method displays a message box when the default listener is specified.

Default Listener Application

The `Trace` class provides a `Listeners` collection that allows us to add a new listener application. When no new listener object is added to the collection, the `Trace` class uses the default listener application: the Output debug window. This window is provided by the Visual Studio .NET IDE during debugging. Let's see a simple example, `TraceExample1`:

```
static void Main()
{
  Trace.WriteLine("Entered Main()");

  for (int i = 0; i < 6; i++)
    Trace.WriteLine(i);

  Trace.WriteLine("Exiting from Main()");
}
```

The code is really simple; it writes tracing information when entering and exiting from the `Main()` method, plus the variable's values in the loop. In the next screenshot, you can see how the Visual Studio .NET Output listener shows the information:

```
Output                                                                    x
Debug                                                                     ▼
 'DefaultDomain': Loaded 'c:\winnt\microsoft.net\framework\v1.0.3705\mscorlib.dll ▲
 'TraceExample1': Loaded 'C:\7132\Chapter04\TraceExample1\bin\TraceExample1.exe',
 'TraceExample1.exe': Loaded 'c:\winnt\assembly\gac\system\1.0.3300.0__b77a5c5619
 'TraceExample1.exe': Loaded 'c:\winnt\assembly\gac\system.xml\1.0.3300.0__b77a5c
 Entered in Main()
 0
 1
 2
 3
 4
 5
 Exiting from Main()
 The program '[1308] TraceExample1.exe' has exited with code 0 (0x0).
                                                                          ▼
◄                                                                   ►
```

The `Trace` class also provides two useful methods to assert error notification: `Assert()` and `Fail()`. The former allows developer to check a condition provided as parameter and write a message into the listener when this condition is `false`. The latter writes a message into the listener each time a failure occurs. When no other listener is added to the collection, the `Assert()` method displays a message box to inform the user about an assertion failure. The following snippet of code, `TraceAssert.cs`, can be tested when the SQL Server service has been stopped deliberately in order to raise a connection exception:

```csharp
using System;
using System.Data;
using System.Data.SqlClient;
using System.Threading;
using System.Diagnostics;

namespace TraceAssert
{
  class Class1
  {
    [STAThread]
    static void Main(string[] args)
    {
      // Create a thread
      Thread t;
      t = new Thread(new ThreadStart(DBThread));

      // Start the thread
      t.Start();
    }
```

```
private static void DBThread()
{
  // Create a connection object
  SqlConnection dbConn = new
      SqlConnection("server=.;database=pubs;uid=sa;pwd=");

  // Create a command object to execute a SQL statement
  SqlCommand dbComm = new
      SqlCommand("SELECT * FROM " + "authors", dbConn);

  SqlDataReader dr = null;

  Trace.WriteLine(DateTime.Now + " - Executing SQL statement");

  try
  {
    // Open the connection to the database
    dbConn.Open();

    // Assert that the connection opened
    Trace.Assert(dbConn.State == ConnectionState.Open,
        "Error", "Connection failed...");

    // Execute the SQL statement
    dr = dbComm.ExecuteReader(CommandBehavior.CloseConnection);

    // Assert that the statement executed OK
    Trace.Assert(dr != null, "Error",
        "The SqlDataReader is null!");

    while (dr.Read())
    {
      // Reading records
    }
  }
  catch
  {
    // Log the error to the Trace application
    Trace.Fail("An error occurred in database access");
  }
  finally
  {
    if ((dr.IsClosed == false) && (dr!=null))
      dr.Close();
  }
}
}
}
```

In the `Main()` method, a new thread is created and started. The new thread runs the code within the `DBThread()` method. This code simply tries to contact the pubs SQL Server database, and retrieve all the data contained within the `authors` table. If the SQL Server service were not available, the following assertion failure would be displayed upon execution of the code:

The row that raises that assertion is:

```
Trace.Assert(dbConn.State == ConnectionState.Open,
        "Error", "Connection failed...");
```

As you can see, the first parameter checks whether the state of the connection is `Open`. It will be set to `false` when the connection has not been opened, so the assertion will be displayed. As you will see later in the chapter, you can deactivate tracing messaging using the application configuration file. In that way, you can decide whether or not to display assert messages at run time.

Using Different Listener Applications

In this section, we will see how to change the default listener application. The `Trace` class (and the `Debug` class as you will see later) exposes the `Listeners` collection, which contains a collection of listener applications. Without adding any new listener class, the `DefaultTraceListener` will point to the Output debug window provided by Visual Studio .NET. However, the .NET Framework provides another two classes that can be used as listener applications:

Class	Description
`EventLogTraceListener`	Using this class, you will redirect tracing messages to the Windows Event Log
`TextWriterTraceListener`	Using this class you will redirect tracing messages to a text file, or to a stream

In a multi-threaded application, you change the default listener with one of the listed listeners if you need to trace an application's behavior during its execution outside of Visual Studio .NET. Naturally, the Output debug window is available only during debug. Using these two classes, you could choose whether trace messages are placed in the Windows Event log, or inside a text file. Usually, when you know that your application will run in an operating system equipped with the Event Log, the EventLogTraceListener class is the best solution to choose. The reasons include:

❑ The Event Log is managed by the operating system.

❑ The Event Log allows administrators to specify security settings for the log.

❑ The Event Log has to be read with the Event Viewer. This displays in a better visual environment than occurs with text file in Notepad.

Changing the default listener is simple, so let's see an example, TraceEventLog.cs:

```
static void Main(string[] args)
{
    // Create a trace listener for the event log.
    EventLogTraceListener eltl = new EventLogTraceListener("TraceLog");

    // Add the event log trace listener to the collection.
    Trace.Listeners.Add(eltl);

    // Write output to the event log.
    Trace.WriteLine("Entered in Main()");
}
```

Firstly, we have to create a new listener object. In the example above, a new EventLogTraceListener has been created in order to use the Windows event log as listener application. The class constructor accepts a string where we can specify the name of the source that has written an entry. The constructor will instantiate a new EventLog object assigning the specified source name to the Source property of the EventLog class, automatically.

The next step is adding the new listener object to the Listeners collection using the Add() method and providing the reference to the listener object. Finally, we can start to write tracing messages that will be redirected to the listener application.

Opening up the Windows event log using the Event Viewer application, you should see the new entry appearing in the Application Log section:

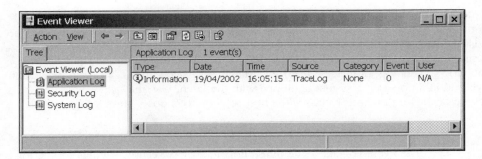

You can double-click the item inside the Application Log report to examine the message:

The code that we have examined above adds a new listener to the `Listeners` collection so that you will receive tracing messages both in the Output debug window, and in the event log. If you want to remove the default listener in order to use just the event log application, you have to call the `RemoveAt()` method, as illustrated in the code below:

```
static void Main(string[] args)
{
    // Create a trace listener for the event log.
    EventLogTraceListener eltl = new EventLogTraceListener("TraceLog");
```

```
// Remove the default listener
Trace.Listeners.RemoveAt(0);

// Add the event log trace listener to the collection.
Trace.Listeners.Add(eltl);

// Write output to the event log.
Trace.WriteLine("Entered in Main()");
}
```

The TextWriterTraceListener Class

We are going to conclude our listener explanation by examining the
TextWriterTraceListener class. It is useful when you have to write our tracing
messages to a text file or directly in a console application. In fact, during the creation
of a TextWriterTraceListener object, you can specify either a TextWriter object,
or a Stream object. Using a Stream object allows you to specify more details on how
the file stream is handled. The following snippet of code, TraceConsole.cs, shows
how to trace messages in a Console application:

```
static void Main(string[] args)
{
    // Remove the default listener
    Trace.Listeners.RemoveAt(0);

    // Add a console listener
    Trace.Listeners.Add(new TextWriterTraceListener(Console.Out));

    // Write a trace message
    Trace.WriteLine("Entered in Main()");
}
```

Specifying the Console.Out streaming in the class's constructor, our Console
application will display tracing messages:

Finally, let's see how to add text log files as listener. We have to add a new
TextWriterTraceListener object, specifying a FileStream object in its
constructor. When the application ends, you have to use the static Close() method
provided by the Trace class in order to close the log writing all the tracing messages.
In the following code, Debugging.cs, a thread is started that traces both main and
secondary thread messages:

209

```
private static void WritingThread()
{
    // Trace an info message
    Trace.WriteLine(DateTime.Now + " - Entered WritingThread()");

    // Sleeping for one sec....
    Thread.CurrentThread.Sleep(1000);

    // Trace an info message
    Trace.WriteLine(DateTime.Now + " - Slept for 1 second...");
}
```

The WritingThread() method is simply used by the thread to sleep for a second and write some tracing messages.

Here, we create a new FileStream object, either creating or opening the Debugging.log file, if it already exists. Then, we add the new listener into the Listeners collection by creating a new instance of the TextWriterTraceListener class within the Add() method:

```
static void Main(string[] args)
{
    // Create a file listener
    FileStream fs = new
        IO.FileStream("C:\Debugging.log", IO.FileMode.OpenOrCreate);
    Trace.Listeners.Add(new TextWriterTraceListener(fs));
```

After starting the thread, the code waits for the carriage return key from the user and then closes the listener application and flushes all the tracing messages to the log file:

```
    // Write the line only when the switch is on
    Trace.WriteLine(DateTime.Now + " - Entered Main()");

    // Create a thread
    Thread t;
    t = new Thread(new ThreadStart(WritingThread));

    // Start the thread
    t.Start();

    // Wait for the user carriage return
    Console.Read();

    // Close the file listener flushing the trace messages
    Trace.Close();
}
```

The output of the code will be something similar to this:

30/04/2002 16:38:15 - Entered Main()
30/04/2002 16:38:15 - Entered into WritingThread()
30/04/2002 16:38:16 - Slept for one second...

The Trace class provides a useful property called IndentLevel for indenting tracing messages. For instance, you could use different indent levels for tracing messages written by the main and secondary threads. Adding the following lines to the code above, we can accomplish this task easily:

```
private static void WritingThread()
{
    // Setting indent level
    Trace.IndentLevel = 2;

    // Trace an info message
    Trace.WriteLine(DateTime.Now + " - Entered WritingThread()");

    // Sleeping for one sec....
    Thread.CurrentThread.Sleep(1000);

    // Trace an info message
    Trace.WriteLine(DateTime.Now + " - Slept for 1 second...");
}
```

The output of the modified code is:

30/04/2002 16:40:07 - Entered Main()
    30/04/2002 16:40:07 - Entered into WritingThread()
    30/04/2002 16:40:08 - Slept for one second...

> You can increment or decrement the level of the indentation using the Indent() and Unindent() methods, respectively.

Tracing Switches

When you are near to the application deployment phase, you will probably want to remove all the tracing and debugging messages from the code. However, you do not have to look for every trace instruction and remove it. You can use compilation flags during the application building. From the Visual Studio .NET IDE, you can right-click on the project name within the Solution Explorer window, selecting the Properties item from the context menu. The following dialog box will appear:

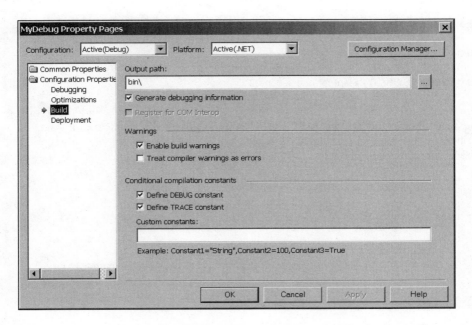

You simply need to uncheck the Define DEBUG constant and Define TRACE constant checkboxes, recompile the solution, and all the Trace and Debug statements will be stripped from the application.

> **In order to remove tracing functionalities, you can even use the `csc.exe` command-line compiler. Simply use the `/d:TRACE=FALSE /d:DEBUG=FALSE` switches when compiling.**

Adding switches to the traced code allows us to activate/deactivate tracing messages at run time. By simply declaring a value in the configuration file of our application, you can activate the trace functionality without rebuilding the entire solution. Naturally, you have to build the application to maintain tracing information, and this results in a greater final application size and slower performance, even when the switches are turned off.

The `BooleanSwitch` and `TraceSwitch` classes are provided by the .NET Framework to implement these switches. Let's first examine the `BooleanSwitch` class.

The BooleanSwitch Class

Using this class in the traced code, you can decide to activate/deactivate messages by simply changing a value in the application configuration file. The `WriteLineIf()` and `WriteIf()` methods will be useful to write messages depending on the `Enabled` property provided by the `BooleanSwitch` class. In order to add switches to your application you have to follow these few steps:

1. Add an application configuration file either manually, or by selecting Add New Item... from the Project menu within Visual Studio .NET, and choosing the Text File template from the dialog box choosing the App.config filename.

2. Open the configuration file in order to insert the necessary XML tags to inform the application about the switch name and value. Specifying a value equal to 0 will deactivate tracing functionality, and a value of 1 activate it:

```xml
<?xml version="1.0" encoding="utf-8" ?>
<configuration>
  <system.diagnostics>
    <switches>
      <add name="MySwitch" value="1" />
    </switches>
  </system.diagnostics>
</configuration>
```

3. Create a new BooleanSwitch object in the code that has the same name as that specified in the configuration file. You could also use the Enabled property in conjunction with the Trace static methods. Let's continue our Debugging example, by declaring a global BooleanSwitch object in order to use it everywhere in the code:

```csharp
BooleanSwitch bs;

static void Main(string[] args)
{
    // Create a Boolean switch called MySwitch
    bs = new BooleanSwitch("MySwitch",
        "Enable/Disable tracing functionalities");

    // Create a file listener
    FileStream fs = new FileStream("C:\Debugging.log",
        FileMode.OpenOrCreate);
    Trace.Listeners.Add(new TextWriterTraceListener(fs));

    // Write the line only when the switch is on
    Trace.WriteLineIf(bs.Enabled, DateTime.Now +
        " - Entered in Main()");

    ...
}
```

In the Main() method we create the object, specifying the same name used in the configuration file plus a brief description. The WriteLineIf() method will write the message only if the Enabled property has been set to 1 in the configuration file.

The TraceSwitch Class

This class is an enhanced version of the `BooleanSwitch` class because it allows us to choose whether to deactivate tracing functionality or display messages using an importance-based hierarchy. The following table lists the levels:

Trace level	Description
0	None: Tracing is deactivated.
1	TraceError: Only the error messages will be written to the listener application.
2	TraceWarning: Error and warning messages will be written to the listener application.
3	TraceInformation: Error, warning, and information messages will be written to the listener application.
4	TraceVerbose: All kinds of messages will be written to the listener application.

So, when an error occurs, you can change the application configuration file, specifying to write just the error messages that you have added to the code to focus our attention just on these messages. The configuration file is the same as for the `BooleanSwitch` example. What changes is the code, as we have to instantiate an object from the `TraceSwitch` class. Moreover, we will use the enumeration values within the class to specify the level of the tracing messages. Let's see an example, `TraceSwitchExample.cs`:

```
using System;
using System.Threading;
using System.IO;
using System.Data;
using System.Data.SqlClient;
using System.Diagnostics;

namespace TraceSwitchExample
{
  class Class1
  {
    private static TraceSwitch ts;

    [STAThread]
    static void Main(string[] args)
    {
      // Create a boolean switch called MySwitch
      ts = new TraceSwitch("MySwitch", "Four different trace levels");
```

```
    // Create a file listener
    FileStream fs = new FileStream(@"C:\Debugging.log",
        FileMode.OpenOrCreate);
    Trace.Listeners.Add(new TextWriterTraceListener(fs));

    // Write the line only when the switch is set
    // to TraceInformation level or above.
    Trace.WriteLineIf(ts.TraceInfo, DateTime.Now +
        " - Entered in Main()");

    // Create a thread
    Thread t;
    t = new Thread(new ThreadStart(DBThread));

    // Start the thread
    t.Start();

    // Wait for the user carriage return
    Console.Read();

    // Close the file listener flushing the trace messages
    Trace.Close();
}
```

We start by declaring a global TraceSwitch object and then create a new object, giving it the name specified in the configuration file. We add a text file log listener to the application. We then start a new thread that contacts the pubs database within SQL Server in order to retrieve all the records from the authors table.

If the thread has been omitted, the Open() method raises an exception that generates a trace error message:

```
private static void DBThread()
{
  // Trace an info message
  Trace.WriteLineIf(ts.TraceInfo, DateTime.Now +
          " - Entered in DBThread()");

  // Create a connection object
  SqlConnection dbConn = new
      SqlConnection("server=.;database=pubs;uid=sa;pwd=");

  // Create a command object to execute a SQL statement
  SqlCommand dbComm = new SqlCommand("SELECT * FROM authors", dbConn);
  SqlDataReader dr = null;

  try
  {
    Trace.WriteLineIf(ts.TraceInfo, DateTime.Now +
            " - Executing SQL statement");
```

215

```
      // Execute the SQL statement
      dr = dbComm.ExecuteReader(CommandBehavior.CloseConnection);

      while (dr.Read())
      {
        // Reading records
      }
    }
    catch (Exception ex)
    {
      Trace.WriteLineIf(ts.TraceError, DateTime.Now +
          " - Error: " + ex.Message);
    }
    finally
    {
      if ((dr.IsClosed == false) && (dr != null))
        dr.Close();
    }
  }
```

Here is the output from the code when the value 1 is specified in the configuration file, which specifies `TraceError`:

19/04/2002 17:52:23 - Error: ExecuteReader requires an open and available Connection. The connection's current state is Closed.
Slept for 1 second...

Here is the output when the value 3 is specified in the configuration file, which specifies `TraceInformation`:

19/04/2002 17:54:23 - Entered Main()
19/04/2002 17:54:23 - Entered DBThread()
19/04/2002 17:54:24 - Executing SQL statement
19/04/2002 17:54:24 - Error: ExecuteReader requires an open and available Connection. The connection's current state is Closed.

The Debug Class

The `Debug` class provides the same functionality as the `Trace` class. You will find that it exposes the same methods and properties, with the same tracing results.

> **When you change the listener application using the `Listeners` collection provided by the `Trace` class, you will change the listener application for `Debug` messages as well.**

The big difference between these two classes is in the context in which you should use them. The Debug class is useful when you need to add information during debugging sessions. Before deploying our application, you will build the release version that will remove debug information from our code, automatically. Therefore, you would add Trace class functionalities when you need to check our application during the run time phase.

The DataImport Example

At this point we are ready to concentrate our attention on a practical example that will be useful to demonstrate what we have seen thus far. The DataImport example, included here, is a typical application that waits for files to arrive in a specific directory before importing them into a SQL Server database. The code for this application, as with the rest of the code in this book, can be found at the Wrox web site. Below we outline the classes that will be used in this example:

❑ FileSystemWatcher: This allows developers to specify the directory to monitor and to raise an event when something changes (for example, a new file is created or removed). This class is contained in the System.IO namespace of the .NET Framework class library.

❑ TextWriterTraceListener: This implements our own tracing functionality.

❑ Thread: This, which you've seen many times before, allows us to start a new thread to import data into the database.

❑ Many classes from the SqlClient namespace necessary to manage the SQL Server database connection and update.

The first release of the DataImport application contains some logical errors that you will discover using tracing functionality. In that way you can have a good example about log (trace) files and their importance.

> **To learn more about the ADO.NET classes, please refer to one of the Wrox Press releases such as *Professional ADO.NET Programming* (ISBN 1-86100-527-X), or *ADO.NET Programmer's Reference* (ISBN 1-86100-558-X).**

The Code

Let's start analyzing the code of the DataImport example:

```
using System;
using System.IO;
using System.Data;
using System.Data.SqlClient;
using System.Threading;
using System.Diagnostics;

namespace DataImport1
{
    class DataImport
    {
```

First of all, we referenced all the necessary namespaces to use the
FileSystemWatcher, Thread, and SQL Server classes:

```
public static BooleanSwitch bs;

[STAThread]
static void Main(string[] args)
{
    // Remove the default listener
    Trace.Listeners.RemoveAt(0);

    // Create and add the new listener
    bs = new BooleanSwitch("DISwitch", "DataImport switch");
    Trace.Listeners.Add(new TextWriterTraceListener(
        new FileStream(@"C:\DataImport.log", FileMode.OpenOrCreate)));
```

Then the code removes the default listener and creates a new
TextWriterTraceListener object that points to C:\DataImport.log:

```
    // Create a FileSystemWatcher object used to monitor
    // the specified directory
    FileSystemWatcher fsw = new FileSystemWatcher();

    // Set the path to watch and specify the file
    // extension to monitor for
    fsw.Path = @"C:\temp";
    fsw.Filter = "*.xml";

    // No need to go into subdirs
    fsw.IncludeSubdirectories = false;

    // Add the handler to manage the raised event
    // when a new file is created
    fsw.Created += new FileSystemEventHandler(OnFileCreated);
```

```
// Enable the object to raise the event
fsw.EnableRaisingEvents = true;
```

Here the code creates a `FileSystemWatcher` object used to monitor the `C:\temp` directory specified in the `Path` property. The `Filter` property is useful to filter through each file within the directory looking for just the ones with the specified file extension. The `IncludeSubdirectories` property determines whether to extend the file monitoring to subdirectories. Next, we want to receive file creation events so we have to specify the `Created` event provided by the `FileSystemWatcher` class. Using the `FileSystemEventHandler` we can specify the event handler that will be called when a new XML file is created in the target directory. Finally, the code enables the `FileSystemWatcher` object to raise events.

```
try
{
    // Call the waitforchanged method in
    // an infinite loop. When the event is raised
    // the OnFileCreated will be contacted.
    WaitForChangedResult res;
    while(true)
    {
        res = fsw.WaitForChanged(WatcherChangeTypes.Created);
        Trace.WriteLineIf(bs.Enabled, DateTime.Now +
            " - Found: " + res.Name + " file");
    }
}
```

The above code implements an infinite loop, which waits for the file creation event to be raised. The `WaitForChangedResult` object will contain information about the file created. For example, the code uses the `Name` property to trace the name of the discovered file.

```
catch (Exception e)
{
    Trace.WriteLineIf(bs.Enabled, DateTime.Now +
        " - An exception occurred while waiting for file: ");
    Trace.Indent();
    Trace.WriteLineIf(bs.Enabled, DateTime.Now + " - " + e.ToString());
    Trace.Unindent();
}
finally
{
    fsw.EnableRaisingEvents = false;
    Trace.WriteLineIf(bs.Enabled, DateTime.Now +
        " - Directory monitoring stopped");
    Trace.Close();
}
```

The above Main() method ends by tracing some useful messages and any exceptions. The OnFileCreated() static method is detailed below:

```
private static void OnFileCreated(Object source,
                                      FileSystemEventArgs e)
{
  try
  {
    // Create a new object from the
    // ImportData class to process the
    // incoming file
    ImportData id = new ImportData();
    id.m_strFileName = e.FullPath;

    // Create and start the thread
    Thread t = new Thread(new ThreadStart(id.Import));
    t.Name = "DataImportThread";
    t.Start();
```

Inside the OnFileCreated event handler a new thread will be started. This thread will use the Import() method of the custom ImportData class to import the XML file into the database. Since at this point we know the full path of the discovered file (the FileSystemEventArgs parameter contains this information) and since we need it even in the ImportData class, we can use the m_strFileName variable provided by the class:

```
catch
{
  Trace.WriteLineIf(bs.Enabled, DateTime.Now +
      " - An exception occurred while queuing file : ");
  Trace.Indent();
  Trace.WriteLineIf(bs.Enabled, DateTime.Now + " - " + e.ToString());
  Trace.Unindent();
}
finally
{
  Trace.Flush();
}

class ImportData
{
  // Path and filename of the retrieved file
  public string m_strFileName = null;

  public void Import()
  {
    // Declare Sql objects to contact the database
    SqlConnection dbConn = new
        SqlConnection("server=.;database=pubs;uid=sa;pwd=");
    SqlDataAdapter da = new SqlDataAdapter(
        "SELECT * FROM authors", dbConn);
```

```
DataSet ds = new DataSet();

SqlCommandBuilder sa = new SqlCommandBuilder(da);
```

Inside the `Import()` method, the code starts by creating and setting all the necessary classes to contact the `authors` table within the SQL Server pubs database. The `SqlConnection` object allows us to specify database connection parameters. The `SqlDataAdapter` object connects to the database using the connection object executing the SQL statement specified as the first parameter. Finally, the `SqlCommandBuilder` examines the SQL statement specified in the `SqlDataAdapter` constructor, creating INSERT, MODIFY, and DELETE statements automatically. They are needed when we use the `Update()` method exposed by the `SqlDataAdapter` class to physically change the database with new information:

```
try
{
  Trace.WriteLineIf(DataImport.bs.Enabled, DateTime.Now +
      " - Filling the DataSet.");
  // Fill a dataset with data within the authors table
  da.Fill(ds);
```

Here the `Fill()` method from the `SqlDataAdapter` class is used to fill the `DataSet` object specified in its parameter, with the results of the SQL query specified earlier. The `DataSet` is an in-memory representation of the database data and so it will be formatted as the `authors` table and filled with every record contained in the table:

```
// Read the XML file filling another dataset
DataSet dsMerge = new DataSet();

Trace.WriteLineIf(DataImport.bs.Enabled, DateTime.Now +
    " - Reading XML file.");
dsMerge.ReadXml(m_strFileName, XmlReadMode.InferSchema);
Trace.WriteLineIf(DataImport.bs.Enabled, DateTime.Now +
    " - DataSet filled with data.");
```

Here the code uses the discovered file to fill another `DataSet` object. This time the `ReadXml()` method has been used. The power of the `DataSet` object is just right in front of you. You can manage data provided by both database and XML document in exactly the same way. The `DataSet` object maintains an XML data representation of the records within itself:

```
// Update the database tracing the
// total time needed to conclude the operation
DateTime time;
time = DateTime.Now;
Trace.WriteLineIf(DataImport.bs.Enabled, time +
    " - Updating database.");
da.Update(dsMerge);
```

```
DateTime time2;
time2 = DateTime.Now;
Trace.WriteLineIf(DataImport.bs.Enabled, time2 +
        " - Database updated successfully.");
Trace.Indent();
Trace.WriteLineIf(DataImport.bs.Enabled, DateTime.Now +
    " - Total TIME: " + time2.Subtract(time) + " second/s");
Trace.Unindent();
```

Finally, the code uses the Update() method provided by the SqlDataAdapter class to write new records to the authors table. Note the tracing information used in this snippet of code; this provides detailed information by adding performance messages. The DateTime class has been used to retrieve the total time in seconds needed to update the database:

```
catch (SqlException sex)
{
  Trace.WriteLineIf(DataImport.bs.Enabled, DateTime.Now +
      " - A SQL exception occurred during file processing: ");
  Trace.Indent();
  Trace.WriteLineIf(DataImport.bs.Enabled, DateTime.Now
      + " - " + sex.ToString());
  Trace.Unindent();
}
catch (Exception ex)
{
  Trace.WriteLineIf(DataImport.bs.Enabled, DateTime.Now +
      " - A general exception occurred during file processing: ");
  Trace.Indent();
  Trace.WriteLineIf(DataImport.bs.Enabled, DateTime.Now +
      " - " + ex.ToString());
  Trace.Unindent();
}
finally
{
  Trace.Flush();
}
```

Then, after writing the code for catching and dealing with any exceptions that may occur, the code is complete.

Testing the Application

To test the application you have to follow these steps:

❑ Create a C:\temp directory to contain the XML file

❑ Run the DataImport application

❑ Copy the authors.xml file into the C:\temp directory

As a final result you should find the `DataImport.log` file in the `C:\` directory having content similar to this:

```
01/05/2002 12:23:01 - Found: authors.xml file
01/05/2002 12:23:01 - Filling the DataSet.
01/05/2002 12:23:02 - Reading XML file.
01/05/2002 12:23:02 - DataSet filled with data.
01/05/2002 12:23:02 - Updating database.
01/05/2002 12:23:02 - Database updated successfully.
01/05/2002 12:23:03 - Total TIME: 0 second/s
```

The `authors.xml` file is not that large so the total time is less than one second.

Logical Errors

All seems to be working well, but obviously, everything hasn't been accounted for. So far, we have tested our application with a very small file size, so when the application receives the file creation event and opens the file, the process that copies it into the directory finishes its task of closing the file. What happens when you receive a huge file? Well, when the thread tries to access the XML file and fill the `DataSet` object, it receives an access-denied error caused by attempting to open a file already in use by the copier task. Try to test the application again by copying the `huge_authors.xml` file instead. Since you have used tracing messages, you may find the following error in the log file:

```
4/14/2002 1:29:00 PM - Found: huge_authors.xml file
4/14/2002 1:29:00 PM - Filling the DataSet.
4/14/2002 1:29:00 PM - Reading XML file.
4/14/2002 1:29:00 PM - A general exception occurred during file processing:
    4/14/2002 1:29:00 PM - System.IO.IOException: The process cannot access the file
"C:\temp\huge_authors.xml" because it is being used by another process.
    at System.IO.__Error.WinIOError(Int32 errorCode, String str)
    at System.IO.FileStream..ctor(String path, FileMode mode, FileAccess access, FileShare share,
Int32 bufferSize, Boolean useAsync, String msgPath, Boolean bFromProxy)
    at System.IO.FileStream..ctor(String path, FileMode mode, FileAccess access, FileShare share)
    at System.Xml.XmlDownloadManager.GetStream(Uri uri, ICredentials credentials)
    at System.Xml.XmlUrlResolver.GetEntity(Uri absoluteUri, String role, Type ofObjectToReturn)
    at System.Xml.XmlTextReader.CreateScanner()
    at System.Xml.XmlTextReader.Init()
    at System.Xml.XmlTextReader.Read()
    at System.Xml.XmlReader.MoveToContent()
    at System.Data.DataSet.ReadXml(XmlReader reader, XmlReadMode mode)
    at System.Data.DataSet.ReadXml(String fileName, XmlReadMode mode)
```

This is a kind of error that the debugger often fails to catch because the time used to launch it and the time to step through the code is often sufficient to copy the file. It may also not occur on your machine. It depends on the speed of your disk access and the amount of memory you have (so how much the application is slowed down).

The error message suggests a possible solution that you should add to the application to resolve the error. Before calling the `ReadXml()` method, you should try to open the file with exclusive access. If an error occurs, then you can suspend the thread for few seconds, trying again when the file can be processed. Let's see how the code changes in `DataImport2`, by adding the `GetFileAccess()` method:

```
private bool GetFileAccess()
{
  Trace.WriteLineIf(DataImport.bs.Enabled, DateTime.Now +
      " - Trying to get exclusive access to the "
    + m_strFileName + " file.");

  try
  {
    FileStream fs = File.Open(m_strFileName,
                              FileMode.Append,
                              FileAccess.Write,
                              FileShare.None);
    fs.Close();
    Trace.WriteLineIf(DataImport.bs.Enabled, DateTime.Now +
        " - Access to the " + m_strFileName + " file allowed.");
    return true;
  }
  catch
  {
    Trace.WriteLineIf(DataImport.bs.Enabled, DateTime.Now +
        " - Access denied to the " + m_strFileName + " file.");
    return false;
  }
}
```

The `GetFileAccess()` method has been added in order to return a Boolean value indicating whether you can have exclusive access to the file or not. The method simply tries to open the file with the share access property set to `None`:

```
public void Import()
{
  // Declare Sql objects to contact the database
  SqlConnection dbConn = new
      SqlConnection("server=.;database=pubs;uid=sa;pwd=");
  SqlDataAdapter da = new SqlDataAdapter(
      "SELECT * FROM authors", dbConn);
  DataSet ds = new DataSet();

  SqlCommandBuilder sa = new SqlCommandBuilder(da);
```

```
try
{
    while (GetFileAccess() == false)
    {
        Thread.Sleep(5000);
        Trace.WriteLineIf(DataImport.bs.Enabled, DateTime.Now +
            " - Slept 5 seconds... Try to access to the "
            + m_strFileName + " file, again.");
    }

    Trace.WriteLineIf(DataImport.bs.Enabled, DateTime.Now +
        " - Filling the DataSet.");
    // Fill a dataset with data within the
    // authors table
    da.Fill(ds);
```

The `Import()` method provided by the `ImportData` class will try to get exclusive access to the file. If the file is still opened by the copier task, the thread will be suspended for five seconds. So, the `GetFileAccess()` method will be called until the source file can be opened.

We have seen practically how the tracing functionalities can be useful to understand the application behavior during run-time execution.

Summary

In this chapter we have seen how the Visual Studio .NET debugger can be used to observe an application's behavior during its execution. Also, we have seen which powerful tools the debugger provides, to allow us to examine and change a variable's value, and more.

In the second part of the chapter, we covered the tracing functionality provided by the .NET with three classes: `Trace`, `Debug`, and `Switch`. We started listing the most useful tracing functionalities focusing on the ability to activate tracing by modifying values within the application configuration file.

Finally, we have seen a practical example where the tracing technique helps developers to find and correct bugs and logical errors.

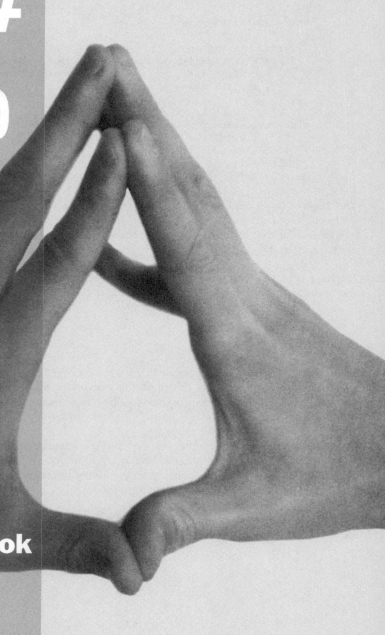

C#

Threading

Handbook

7

Networking and Threading

In the previous chapters of this book, we've taken an in-depth look at threading in C# and .NET and discussed the various concepts and techniques associated with programming multithreaded applications. Now that you are a threading expert, we're going to build a simple multithreaded client-server application in C# and put to use some of the concepts that we have discussed thus far.

There are certain application needs for which the effective use of threads and asynchronous programming is indispensable, such as network communication, effective user interfaces, and disk input/output, to just name a few. In all these cases, a single-threaded application can freeze or appear to have crashed while it's waiting for an operation to complete. This is also true in the case of a network application where latency is often the most important criterion, especially with users that have low speed connections. In the sample application showcased in this chapter, we are going to utilize the System.Net namespace and briefly explore the networking capabilities of .NET, especially since the multi-user and asynchronous nature of network applications make them ideal candidates for threading.

In particular, we will discuss the following:

- ❏ Developing network applications in .NET using the System.Net namespace
- ❏ Developing a simple multithreaded client-server application based on TCP/IP
- ❏ Using intrinsic .NET functionality to implement asynchronous operations
- ❏ Using asynchronous message transfers between a client and a remote server

Networking in .NET

Prior to the advent of the .NET Framework, the ability to develop sophisticated Windows-based networking applications was limited to advanced C++ programmers using the convoluted WinSock library for the most part. There was, of course, the `WinInet` control that Visual Basic developers could utilize in order to accomplish relatively simple tasks. Other controls were available for other languages. However, one did not have to attempt too much before facing functional impediments with the simple and limited services offered in that control.

Fortunately, the `System.Net` namespace within the .NET Framework brings a slew of effective functionality packaged in a simple and consistent object model. The ease of use of these classes does not compromise functionality, as almost all the core functions of WinSock 2.0 have been wrapped and abstracted in the `System.Net` namespace. Developers can easily develop at any level from sockets all the way up to HTTP. Also, unlike the raw use of the WinSock library, the `System.Net` namespace relieves developers from having the dubious pleasure of manually coding many imperative resource management tasks, such as dealing with overlapped IO and completion ports.

So, without further delay, let's briefly explore the `System.Net` namespace.

System.Net Namespace

The `System.Net` namespace actually comprises two namespaces, `System.Net` and `System.Net.Socket`.

We will primarily be using the `System.Net.Sockets` namespace in our application. The layered approach of the `System.Net` classes provides applications with the ability to access networks with various levels of control based on the demands of the application. In addition to the extensive support for sockets, `System.Net` classes also offer an impressive array of functionality to use with the HTTP protocol. For the most part, the `System.Net` offerings are categorized in three layers, Application protocols, Transport protocols, and Web protocols. The `System.Net.Sockets` namespace consists primarily of classes and utilities for dealing with the transport protocol. Let's look at some of the more important classes within the `System.Net` namespace, as listed in the table opposite.

Class	Description
Authorization	Provides authentication messaging for a web server.
Cookie	Provides a set of properties and methods used to manage cookies. This class cannot be inherited.
Dns	Simple domain name resolution functionality.
EndPoint	Identifies a network address. This is an abstract class.
GlobalProxySelection	Global default proxy instance for all HTTP requests.
HttpVersion	Defines the HTTP version numbers supported by the HttpWebRequest and HttpWebResponse classes.
HttpWebRequest	HTTP-specific implementation of the WebRequest class.
HttpWebResponse	HTTP-specific implementation of the WebResponse class.
IPAddress	Internet Protocol (IP) address.
IPEndPoint	A network endpoint consisting of an IP address and a port number.
IPHostEntry	Container class for Internet host address information.
NetworkCredential	Provides credentials for password-based authentication schemes such as basic, digest, NTLM, and Kerberos authentication.
SocketAddress	Stores serialized information from EndPoint-derived classes.
SocketPermission	Controls rights to make or accept socket connections.
WebClient	Provides common methods for sending data to and receiving data from a resource identified by a URI.
WebException	The exception that is thrown when an error occurs while accessing resources via the HTTP protocol.
WebPermission	Controls rights to access HTTP Internet resources.
WebPermissionAttribute	Specifies permission to access Internet resources.
WebProxy	Contains HTTP proxy settings for the WebRequest class.
WebRequest	Makes a request to a Uniform Resource Identifier (URI). This class is abstract.
WebResponse	Provides a response from a Uniform Resource Identifier (URI). This class is abstract.

As you can see, the System.Net namespace contains a cornucopia of classes and utilities that are quite useful for a wide range of web and network programming needs.

System.Net.Sockets Namespace

The System.Net.Sockets namespace primarily focuses on the transport layer: the socket layer for which it contains a comprehensive set of classes. These classes do an excellent job of abstracting much of the complexity associated with socket programming, while offering a powerful and productive socket stack that also adheres to the Berkeley socket. Lastly, built-in support for TCP and UDP is well integrated in the classes of the System.Net.Sockets. The table below lists the classes of the System.Net.Sockets namespace.

Class	Description
LingerOption	Contains information about the amount of time it will remain available after closing with the presence of pending data (the socket's linger time).
MulticastOption	Contains IP address values for IP multicast packets.
NetworkStream	Provides the underlying stream of data for network access.
Socket	Implements the Berkeley sockets interface.
SocketException	The exception that is thrown when a socket error occurs.
TcpClient	Provides client connections for TCP network services.
TcpListener	Listens for connections from TCP network clients. This is essentially the TCP server class.
UdpClient	Provides User Datagram Protocol (UDP) network services.

A varying level of control is offered to the developer, such as lower-level classes like the Socket class, and higher-level classes, such as the TcpClient class, which offers slightly less control with added productivity. An in-depth discussion of these classes would go beyond the scope of this book – *Professional .NET Network Programming* (Wrox Press, ISBN 1-86100-735-3) is the ideal book for this, but we will take a closer look at some of the above classes as we design and develop our sample application a little later in this chapter.

Creating the Sample Application

Now that you've had a brief introduction to network programming in .NET, let's actually start discussing the application that we are going to build in this chapter. The purpose of this example is to create a simple application to familiarize you with the use of threading in building networking applications in .NET. The application will actually consist of two small Windows Form applications, with one acting as the server and the other as the client. We will be using Visual Studio .NET to design and implement these applications.

Design Goals

We want to create two applications that interact with one another. The first application is a multithreaded/multi-user stock quote server program that looks up stock quotes from a database table and sends the data back to the requesting client asynchronously. The second application is the client and simply queries the server with a stock symbol for which it wishes to get the quote information. All this will happen asynchronously, such that the client's user interface is not paused while the server is responding to the request.

Within the .NET Framework there are a number of methods that will handle the asynchronous operations for us; with these methods the need to explicitly spawn and manage the required threads ourselves is removed.

The list below outlines and summarizes the basic requirements we are going to abide by when building the applications:

❑ There will be two autonomous applications (one serving as the client and the other as the server) that can communicate with each other over the Internet

❑ The user interface of the client should not pause or freeze because of slow network connections, or any other delays, when querying the server for stock quotes

❑ The server should be capable of handling numerous simultaneous client connections and queries, and have the ability to communicate with the client in an asynchronous manner

❑ Network settings must be abstracted away from the application and be modifiable

To help us understand the typical user interaction within the application, let's look at a simple UML sequence diagram overleaf.

Figure 1

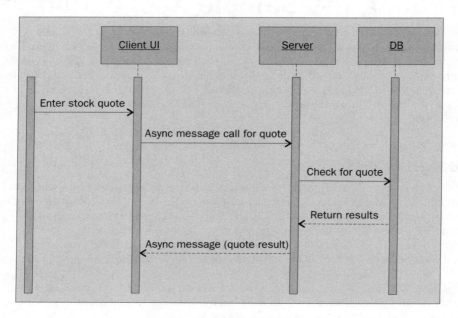

So far, we've discussed the basic design guidelines for the applications from a very high-level standpoint. If you are like most developers, you probably can't wait to see some code. So without further delay, let's actually start building the two applications and examining code segments and concepts as we go along (as always, the code is available at http://www.wrox.com).

Building the Application

As mentioned before, the sample application in this chapter really consists of two autonomous applications: a client and a server. The two applications will communicate with each other via a specific TCP/IP port, which can be changed by altering the configuration file of the application (as we'll see later, both the client and the server need the same configuration file). Enough said, let's start by building our client application, which performs the simple task of querying the server for the result of a stock quote.

Creating the Client

Before we start building the application, let's take a moment or two to see the UML view of the client form class, which is going to contain all the code for the client application:

Figure 2

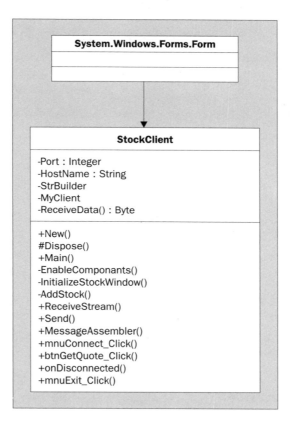

The `StockClient` application simply has a Windows form and contains all the code for the client application, such as the `private` member variables and the methods. To create the `StockClient` application, we start by creating a new Windows Application project in Visual Studio .NET and naming it `StockClient`. On the default form, we create three controls on the page; a textbox called `txtStock`, a button called `btnGetQuote` with its `Text` property set to `Get Quote`, and a new `ListView` control from the Visual Studio .NET Toolbox called `lstQuotes`. Change the `Name` and `Text` properties of the form to `StockClient`. Also, add a `MainMenu` control to your form, and create a menu item `&File` with two sub-items `&Connect` (called `mnuConnect`) and `E&xit` (called `mnuExit`). Lastly, ensure that all the controls on the form, except the menu, have their `Enabled` property set to `False`; these will remain disabled until the user connects to the server.

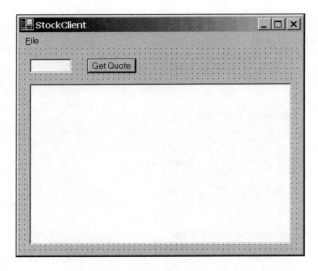

We'll start with the set of using directives that reference the namespaces we need:

```
using System.Threading;
using System.Net;
using System.Net.Sockets;
using System.Text;
using System.IO;
using System.Configuration;
```

We are going to need some private member variables that will be used throughout the StockClient application:

```
private int Port;
private string HostName;
private const int packetSize = 1024;
private byte[] ReceiveData = new byte[packetSize];
private TcpClient MyClient;
private StringBuilder StrBuilder = new StringBuilder();
```

We will examine the variables and their use later on, but for now let's amend our ListView control so that it can keep track of all the stock quotes that we enter. We need it to contain six columns: one column for each of the returned fields for the stock quote. The desired fields are Symbol, Price, Change, Bid, Ask, and Volume. Let's create a method called InitializeStockWindow() to add these columns to the ListView control as shown below:

```
private void InitializeStockWindow()
{
   lstQuotes.View = System.Windows.Forms.View.Details;
   lstQuotes.Columns.Add("Symbol", 60, HorizontalAlignment.Left);
```

```
lstQuotes.Columns.Add("Price", 50, HorizontalAlignment.Left);
lstQuotes.Columns.Add("Change", 60, HorizontalAlignment.Left);
lstQuotes.Columns.Add("Bid", 50, HorizontalAlignment.Left);
lstQuotes.Columns.Add("Ask", 50, HorizontalAlignment.Left);
lstQuotes.Columns.Add("Volume",170, HorizontalAlignment.Left);
}
```

The code segment above simply enables the grid lines of the ListView control, as well as assigning six columns of various widths to it. We will call this function upon connecting to the server when the application is ready to start retrieving stock quotes from the server. We also need a method to enable and disable the controls as required, for instance upon the successful connection, as listed below:

```
private void EnableComponents(bool enable )
{
  txtStock.Enabled = enable;
  btnGetQuote.Enabled = enable;
  lstQuotes.Enabled = enable;
}
```

Now we create a simple delegate called DisconnectedHandler, an event called Disconnected, and an implementation of the event handler called OnDisconnected() which would be called once the event is actually raised. The OnDisconnected() method simply enables the Connect option in the File menu as well as displaying an error message via a message box. It also disables the remaining input controls on the form:

```
public delegate void DisconnectedHandler ( object sender );
public event DisconnectedHandler Disconnected;
private void OnDisconnected(object sender)
{
  mnuConnect.Enabled = true;
  MessageBox.Show("The connection was lost!", "Disconnected",
                  MessageBoxButtons.OK, MessageBoxIcon.Error);
  EnableComponents(false);
}
```

To bind the OnDisconnected() method to the Disconnected event, we use the code below:

```
Disconnected += new DisconnectedHandler(OnDisconnected);
```

235

As you may know, one of the greatest features of .NET is its ability to dynamically bind and unbind event handlers to events at run time. You can use the += operator to assign a method to an event and, in much the same manner, use the -= operator to detach an event handler method from an event. Indeed, the ability to dynamically assign functionality to an event is very useful when you need to start or stop the event handler for an event or need to override the behavior of an event handler. In the case of the Disconnected event, we assign it to the OnDisconnected delegate. Technically, we have the opportunity to accomplish this anytime before the invocation of the event. However, it's usually best to declare all the event handlers early on in the application's execution, so we will declare it in our mnuConnect_Click event as soon as a connection to the server is established.

Speaking of the mnuConnect_Click event, double-click the Connect sub-item of the File menu to enter code for the actual connection to the server. This is where we start to get our feet wet in network programming. First we need to instantiate a TcpClient object, which is a member of the System.Net.Sockets namespace. In order to that, we are going to need a host address and a port with which the client contacts the server. We will abstract that information away from the core of the application by storing it in an application configuration file. .NET configuration files are well-formed XML files and are accompanied by a useful namespace in the .NET Framework, System.Configuration. With that in mind, let's look at the contents of the external configuration file that we can easily create in Notepad or Visual Studio.NET:

```
<configuration>
  <configSections>
    <section name="HostInfo"
             type="System.Configuration.SingleTagSectionHandler" />
  </configSections>
  <HostInfo hostname="localhost" port="6800" />
</configuration>
```

The XML above contains an entry with two attributes storing the host information. We used localhost, and the port could be just about any port (just as long as it's not a reserved port) and you can choose just about any port number between 1024 and 65000. Save the file as StockClient.exe.config (the configuration file has the name of the assembly followed by .config), and place it in the bin subdirectory where the compiled version of the application is going to reside.

Now add the following code to the mnuConnect_Click event handler:

```
private void mnuConnect_Click(object sender, System.EventArgs e)
{
    IDictionary HostSettings;
    try
    {
        HostSettings =
            (IDictionary)ConfigurationSettings.GetConfig("HostInfo");
        HostName = (string)HostSettings["hostname"];
        Port = (int)HostSettings["port"];
```

```
        MyClient = new TcpClient(HostName, Port);
        MyClient.GetStream().BeginRead(receiveData, 0,
        packetSize,new AsyncCallback(ReceiveStream), null);
        EnableComponents(true);
        InitializeStockWindow();
        mnuConnect.Enabled = false;
        Disconnected += new DisconnectedHandler( OnDisconnected );
    }
    catch
    {
        MessageBox.Show("Error: Unable to establish a connection!",
            "Disconnected", MessageBoxButtons.OK, MessageBoxIcon.Error);
        MyClient.Close();
    }
}
```

The first portion of the code above reads the host information from the configuration file. The HostName, Port, and MyClient fields have already been declared as private at the start of the class. At this point we just declare a local dictionary object to read in all the attributes of the HostInfo node in the configuration file.

An instance of the TcpClient class is instantiated by passing the DNS host name and a port number into the constructor. As you probably know, the host name maps to a specific host (or, more accurately, interface) on the network; the port number identifies the specific service on that host to connect to. The combination of host name and a service port is typically called an endpoint, which is represented in the .NET Framework by the EndPoint class. The TcpClient class constructor may take in an instance of the IPEndPoint class, but is also overloaded to accept a host name and a service port number.

> **You can use the DNS class to resolve a host name into an IP address and then use a service port to construct an IPEndPoint class.**

If we've done everything right and there is a server running with the same host name and port, a new connection will be established. Upon obtaining a connection, we must spawn a background thread to get data from the server asynchronously to enable the input controls for the user to receive stock symbols. Here's where things start to get a little interesting.

As mentioned previously, we need the receiving method of our application to be asynchronous. This is the only way the client can function without delays and serial user interaction. It is simply unacceptable to have the client application remain suspended while waiting for data to arrive from the server. Thanks to the .NET Framework, the solution is relatively simple and easy to implement. We first have to identify the `TcpClient`'s `NetworkStream` object. We can do that by calling the `GetStream()` method of the `TcpClient` object instance, which returns the underlying `NetworkStream` used to send and receive data. `GetStream()` creates an instance of the `NetworkStream` class using the underlying socket as its constructor parameter. The `NetworkStream` class inherits from the `Stream` class, which provides a number of methods and properties used to facilitate network communications. Once we have an underlying stream, we can use it to send and receive data over the network. Much like its cousin classes `FileStream` and `TextStream`, the `NetworkStream` class exposes read and write methods designed to send and receive data in a synchronous manner. `BeginRead()` and `BeginWrite()` are nothing more than the asynchronous versions of those methods. As a matter of fact, most of the methods in the .NET Framework whose names start with `Begin`, such as `BeginRead()` and `BeginGetResponse()`, are intrinsically asynchronous without the programmer having to provide additional code when they are used with delegates. Therefore, there's no need to manually spawn new threads, and as the process reading the data is running on a background thread, the main thread of the application is free to remain attentive and responsive to UI interaction. Let's look at the signature of the `BeginRead()` method:

```
public override IAsyncResult BeginRead(
    byte[] buffer,
    int offset,
    int size,
    AsyncCallback callback,
    object state
);
```

The table below explains each of the parameters of this method.

Parameter	Description
buffer	A byte array data buffer in which the data will arrive
offset	The location in buffer to begin storing the data to
size	The size of buffer
callback	The delegate to call when the asynchronous call is complete
state	An object containing additional information supplied by the client

Before we proceed further, let's take a moment to have a word or two about asynchronous calls, since they are a very important concept. As mentioned earlier, the problem with synchronous operations is that the working thread can be blocked until a certain operation is complete and that's not always desirable. Asynchronous calls run in a background thread and allow the initial thread (the calling thread) to continue as normal. .NET allows asynchronous calls via the help of delegates to just about any class and/or method. However, certain classes, such as the NetworkStream class, contain methods like BeginRead() that have asynchronous capabilities built into them. Delegates are used to act as placeholders for the functions against which asynchronous calls are made. Remember that delegates are essentially type-safe function pointers.

As you can see, the BeginRead() method requires byte arrays as opposed to strings or text streams and, as such, is going to require a little more processing. We have already defined a variable named ReceiveData and another integer constant for the size of the byte array named PacketSize. Now we need to pass in the name of the method that is going to actually receive the data – the method that is going to be invoked by the callback delegate when the data arrives. Bear in mind that this method is going to be running in a background thread, so we have to be careful if we wish to interact with the UI. Therefore, we simply spawn a background thread to receive the data as it arrives from the server over the network by just one line:

```
MyClient.GetStream().BeginRead(receiveData, 0, packetSize,
    new AsyncCallback(ReceiveStream), null);
```

We create a method called ReceiveStream() that deals with the data in the byte packets as it arrives:

```
private void ReceiveStream( IAsyncResult ar )
{
    int ByteCount;
    try
    {
        ByteCount = MyClient.GetStream().EndRead(ar);
        if(ByteCount < 1)
        {
            // MessageBox.Show("Disconnected")
            Disconnected(this);
            return;
        }
        MessageAssembler(receiveData, 0, ByteCount);
        MyClient.GetStream().BeginRead(receiveData, 0,
            packetSize, new AsyncCallback(ReceiveStream), null);
    }
    catch(Exception ex)
    {
        // Display error message
        object [] Params =
            {("An error has occurred" + ex.ToString()).ToString()};
        Invoke( new InvokeDisplay(this.DisplayData), Params);
    }
}
```

First off, we have to check to see if there are any bytes in the byte array packet. There always has to be something in there. You can think of this as the pulse of the connection; as long as the client is connected to the server, there will be some data in that incoming packet, however small. We use the `EndRead()` method of the `Stream` object to check the current size of the byte array. We pass an instance of `IAsyncResult` into the `EndRead()` method. The `BeginRead()` method of the `GetStream()` method initiates an asynchronous call to the `ReceiveStream()` method, which is followed by a series of under-the-hood actions built in by the compiler in order to expedite the asynchronous operation. The `ReceiveStream()` method is then queued on a thread-pool thread. If the delegate method, `ReceiveStream()` throws an exception, then the newly created `Async` thread is terminated, and another exception is generated in the caller thread. The diagram below further illustrates the situation:

Figure 3

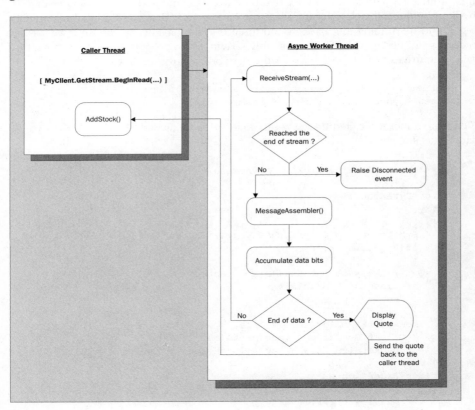

If the number returned from the EndRead() method is anything less than one, we know that the connection has been lost and we can raise the Disconnected event to take care of the appropriate work that needs to be done to handle that situation. However, if the number of bytes in the byte array is bigger than zero, we can start receiving the incoming data. At this point, we are going to need the assistance of a helper method to help us construct a string from the data that we retrieve from the server.

In fact, in .NET you can call almost any method asynchronously in much the same manner that we used the BeginRead() method. All you have to do is declare a delegate and call that delegate using the BeginInvoke() and the EndInvoke() methods – methods that are automatically added when you define a delegate. The intricacies of the asynchronous infrastructure are abstracted away from you and you don't have to worry about background threads and synchronization (not entirely, however). It is important to note that the BeginInvoke() and EndInvoke() methods are not found with IntelliSense within the VS.NET IDE. These methods are added at compile time.

OK, now let's move on to the next portion of the code in which you see a call to the MessageAssembler() method. Due to the asynchronous nature of the BeginRead() method, we really have no way of knowing for sure when and in what quantity the data will arrive from the server. It could arrive all at once, or it could arrive in a hundred smaller pieces, each being only one or two characters long. So, we have to perpetually read the data until we receive some sort of a signal indicating the end of the data for now. In this case, we will append a single character (#) to the end of our message, which will act as a trigger agent for the MessageAssembler() method indicating the end of the incoming string, at which point the MessageAssembler class can stop waiting for more data and work with the data. We'll make use of the StringBuilder class from the System.Text namespace – this class is designed for higher-performance string manipulation operations. Let's take a closer look at the MessageAssembler() method:

```
private void MessageAssembler(byte [] Bytes, int offset , int count)
{
    for(int ByteCount = 0; ByteCount < count - 1; ByteCount++)
    {
        if(Bytes[ByteCount] == 35)    // Check for '#' to signal the end
        {
            object [] Params = {StrBuilder.ToString()};
            Invoke(new InvokeDisplay(this.DisplayData), Params);
            StrBuilder = new StringBuilder();
        }
        else
        {
            StrBuilder.Append((char)Bytes[ByteCount]);
        }
    }
}
```

As you can see, the `MessageAssembler()` method loops through the byte array of data and accumulates the data as pieces of a string using the instance of the `StringBuilder` class until it encounters the # character. Once it encounters the # character, signaling the end of the incoming string, it will stop and flush out the string by calling the `ToString()` method of the `StringBuilder` instance. We don't have to worry about manual conversion of bytes to strings at this point since the `StringBuilder` class takes care of that for us. It will then call the `DisplayData()` method to process the data:

```
object [] Params = {StrBuilder.ToString()};
Invoke(new InvokeDisplay(this.DisplayData), Params);
```

This is the second time we've encountered something similar to the code above, and you may be wondering what it is doing. Remember that this method is running in the background worker thread and is in the same thread that the UI form is. Although we can call the methods anywhere in the application, it is definitely not a good idea since that operation would not be thread-safe. Windows Forms are based on Win32 Single Threaded Apartments (STA) and thus are not thread-safe, which means that a form can't safely switch back and forth between operating threads (including the background threads spawned by an asynchronous operation) once it has been instantiated. You must call the methods of a form on the same thread in which the form is residing. To alleviate this issue, the CLR supports the `Invoke()` method, which marshals calls between the threads.

If you doubt the above claim, you can always see for yourself by stepping through the code and looking at the Threads window and seeing the thread ID of the code that indicates the current thread in which the code is executing. By creating a delegate and calling it through the form's `Invoke()` method, it's executed in the form's thread and interaction with the form's controls is safely executed. Without marshaling, you often find that the code runs just fine and the desired functionality is accomplished initially, but you can run into problems later on as this can cause instability in the application, with at times unpredictable behavior. This can get worse the more the application spawns threads. Therefore, don't talk to the GUI without marshaling the threads. In addition, the signature of the delegate must always match that of the `Invoke()` method, and therefore we have to create an object array and insert the string in it; this is the only way we can use the `Invoke()` method. We call on the `DisplayData()` method to display the data as we wish:

```
private void DisplayData(string stockInfo)
{
    if(stockInfo == "-1")
    {
        MessageBox.Show("Symbol not found!", "Invalid Symbol",
            MessageBoxButtons.OK, MessageBoxIcon.Error);
    }
    else
    {
        AddStock(stockInfo);
    }
}
```

In the `DisplayData()` method, we simply check the string to see whether its value is
`-1`. As we shall see later, the server has been configured to simply return a `-1` string if
the requested stock quote cannot be returned as we've submitted an invalid symbol. Of
course, in our case, an invalid symbol is any symbol that does not happen to be in our
tiny database table of stocks, `tbl_stocks` (which we'll see later). Otherwise, we can
go ahead and pass the `stockInfo` variable to the `AddStock()` method, which will
gracefully add it to the `lstQuotes` control on the form:

```
private void AddStock(string stockInfo )
{
    string [] StockParameter = stockInfo.Split(new char[] {","});
    ListViewItem Item = new ListViewItem(StockParameter);

    if(double.Parse(StockParameter[2]) > 0)
    {
        Item.ForeColor = Color.Green;
    }
    else if(double.Parse(StockParameter[2]) < 0)
    {
        Item.ForeColor = Color.Red;
    }
    lstQuotes.Items.Add(Item);
}
```

We will be configuring the server to return the data values in a string with the
individual values being separated by a comma:

```
Symbol, Price, Change, Bid, Ask, Volume
```

So, the very first thing we have to do is to separate the individual values from one
another by using the `Split()` method of the string class. We then create a new
instance of the `ListViewItem` class and pass in the newly created string array as its
constructor parameter. Lastly, we want to be able to color-code the stock quotes in the
`lstQuotes` control such that if the price of a stock is down, the entire quote is
displayed in red, and if the stock price is up, it is displayed in green. To accomplish
this, we just have to convert the second value of the string array, which contains the
current stock price, into a `Double` and check its value. After setting the color, we can
just add a new entry into the `lstQuotes` control.

We are nearly done with the client code; we just need to create a few smaller methods
to finish off. First, we need to add code to the `click` event of `btnGetQuote`:

```
private void btnGetQuote_Click(object sender, System.EventArgs e)
{
    Send(txtStock.Text.Trim() + "#");
    txtStock.Text = "";
}
```

This method simply gets the string value of the txtStock textbox, appends a # character to the end of it to indicate the end of this string, and passes it to the Send() method. Remember that we needed the # character in the MessageAssembler() method to tell us when the end of the string was reached.

Once the data is passed on to the Send() method, the Send() method creates a new instance of the StreamWriter class by passing the underlying TcpClient stream to it as its constructor and calling its Write() method, which sends the data across the socket in the form a stream. We also call the Flush() method to ensure that the data is sent immediately and is not sitting in buffer until some point in the future:

```
private void Send(string sendData )
{
    StreamWriter writer = new StreamWriter(MyClient.GetStream());
    writer.Write(sendData);
    writer.Flush();
}
```

We're almost done here, but we have to do some minor clean-up code. For the most part, the Windows Form class does most of the cleanup by calling on its own Dispose() method and that of its base, but since .NET has non-deterministic garbage collection, it would a good idea for us to manually close the TcpClient connection. We can write a small function to do that, which will be called from the SocketClient_Closing() method, which is invoked when the user closes the form:

```
private void StockClient_Closing(object sender , EventArgs e )
{
    closeConnection();
}

private void closeConnection()
{
    if( MyClient != null)
    {
        MyClient.Close();
        MyClient = null;
    }
}
```

We also need to instantiate a copy of the StockClient form in the form's Main() method to kick start the application:

```
public static void Main()
{
    Application.Run(new StockClient());
}
```

Lastly, we need to call the `Application.Exit()` method on the `Click` event of the exit menu item to shut down the application:

```
private void mnuExit_Click(object sender, System.EventArgs e)
{
    Application.Exit();
}
```

We're done with the client portion of the application.

Creating the Server

OK, let's move on to creating the server application. Due to the multi-client nature of the target environment, we have to take a slightly different approach while creating the `StockServer` application. We want to be able to keep track of clients and know when they connect and disconnect. Client management would be far more effective with the use of a single class instance per client. Therefore, we are going to have to create a separate client class that will represent the clients that are connected to the server as you can see in the UML class diagram below:

Figure 4

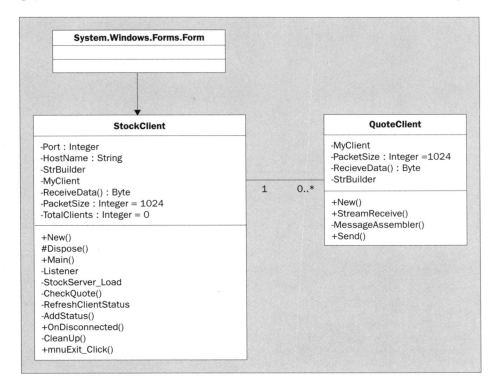

A new instance of the QuoteClient class is created for each new client that connects to the server and so the StockServer class and the QuoteClient class have a one-to-many relationship. The QuoteClient class is always instantiated in a newly spawned thread made to handle the new client that has just connected. The QuoteClient class takes in a TcpClient object, responsible for the new client, as its constructor. We will talk about the QuoteClient class a bit more later on. First, let's see what the user interface is going to look like. The server application is a bit simpler than the client in terms of the UI. We are going to have a single ListBox control to display some information along with the standard File menu with only the Exit sub-item. In addition to those controls, drag and drop a new StatusBar and change its Anchor property to Bottom, Right, such that you can place it in the lower right portion of the form. Be sure to change the Name and the Text property of the form to StockServer. Your form should now look something like the form below:

We will also need a class file that we will call QuoteClient.cs. This application is going to access a SQL Server database to get the stock quote information, and so we are going to need to make references to the necessary data namespaces in addition to the others shown below:

```
using System.Threading;
using System.Net;
using System.Net.Sockets;
using System.Text;
using System.Configuration;
using System.Data;
using System.Data.SqlClient ;
```

We are also going to need some `private` variables that will be used throughout the application. You will see their use as we explore the code for this application:

```
private Thread ListenerThread ;
private TcpListener MyListener ;
private int Port ;
private TcpClient MyClient ;
private int TotalClients = 0;
private const int PacketSize = 1024;
private byte[] ReceiveData = new byte[PacketSize];
```

The server application is going to start running just as soon as it is opened and so we will start by entering some code in the `StockServer_Load()` method of the application. We will discuss the server's `Listener()` method, which is the core of the server itself, shortly; but first we start by spawning a new thread to run our `Listener()` method in the background:

```
private void StockServer_Load(object sender, EventArgs e)
{
    IDictionary HostSettings ;

    try
    {
        HostSettings = ConfigurationSettings.GetConfig("HostInfo");
        Port = int.Parse(HostSettings("port"));
        ListenerThread = new Thread( new ThreadStart(Listener) );
        ListenerThread.Start();
        RefreshClientStatus();
    }
    catch( Exception ex )
    {
        AddStatus("An error has occurred. The server is not running." +
                ex.ToString());
        CleanUp();
    }
    finally
    {
        HostSettings = null;
    }
}
```

Just as we did in the client application, we assign the port number from the configuration file into the `Port` variable, which we have already defined. We don't need the host name when creating server listeners since the server itself is the host. Since this application is really two autonomous parts running entirely independently of each other, please be sure to use to the same configuration file for both the client and the server as nothing is going to work if the port numbers of the two applications don't match precisely. If an error occurs, we notify the user by using the `AddStatus()` method and do some manual cleaning up by calling the `CleanUp()` method, both of which we will see later. But for now, let's look at the `Listener()` method:

```
private void Listener()
{
    try
    {
        MyListener = new TcpListener(Port);
        MyListener.Start();

        object [] Message =
        {"Server started. Awaiting new connections..."};
        Invoke(new InvokeStatus(this.AddStatus), Message);

        while (true)
        {
            QuoteClient NewClient =
                new QuoteClient(MyListener.AcceptTcpClient());
            NewClient.Disconnected +=
                new DisconnectedHandler(onDisconnected);
            NewClient.QuoteArrived +=
                new QuoteArrivedHandler(CheckQuote);

            Object [] ConnectMessage = {"A new client just connected at "
                    + Now().ToShortTimeString()};
            Invoke(new InvokeStatus(this.AddStatus), ConnectMessage);
            TotalClients += 1;
            RefreshClientStatus();
        }
    }
    catch( Exception ex )
    {
        object [] Message  = {"The server stopped due to an unexpected"
                + "error\r\n" +  ex.ToString()};
        Invoke(new InvokeStatus(this.AddStatus), Message);
    }
}
```

This is a very important part of the server application since it basically represents the underlying engine of our server. As you can see, upon initialization of the port number, we called the `AcceptTcpClient()` method of the `TcpListener` class instance to accept incoming requests for connections. In essence, the `TcpListener` class is the server. It builds upon the `Socket` class to provide TCP services at a higher level of abstraction. However, the reason for spawning a new background thread to handle the `Listener()` method is the `AcceptClient()` method, which is a *synchronous* method that waits for connections while keeping the thread it's running on blocked, therefore we need to run it as a background thread. Once again, since this method is running in a background thread, we need to marshal between the current working thread and the thread in which the UI controls are running by using the `Invoke()` method of the form. We also start the *asynchronous* process of listening for incoming data, which in this case is going to be stock quote requests from the client. In much the same manner as we did in the client application, we will use the `StreamReceive()` method that is located in the `QuoteClient` class:

```
public void StreamReceive(IAsyncResult ar)
{
    int ByteCount;

    try
    {
        lock(MyClient.GetStream())
        {
            ByteCount = MyClient.GetStream().EndRead(ar);
        }
        if(ByteCount < 1)
        {
            Disconnected(this);
            return;
        }

        MessageAssembler(ReceiveData, 0, ByteCount);
        lock(MyClient.GetStream())
        {
            MyClient.GetStream().BeginRead(ReceiveData, 0, PacketSize,
                new AsyncCallback(StreamReceive), null);
        }.
    }
    catch( Exception ex )
    {
        Disconnected(this);
    }
}
```

The major difference between this and its sister method in the client application arises from the fact that we are now in a multithreaded, multi-user environment and that we can't just get the default stream and do whatever we want with it. There would be a very good chance of resource collisions, such that while we're reading data from it here, another thread in our server might attempt to send data to that same stream; and so we need to use synchronization. For simple synchronization, we are going to use the keyword lock to lock the requested stream while we read from it. lock is the most basic thread synchronization tool available. Don't forget to use good judgment when it comes to locking resources, as it can be detrimental to your application's performance if used in excess. For more sophisticated and custom tailored thread synchronizations, you can use some of the other classes available in the System.Threading namespace, such as Interlocked, which allows you to increment and decrement interlocks. Other than that, the ReceiveStream() method is more or less the same as the one in the client application.

The MessageAssembler() method also very closely resembles its counterpart defined in the client application. The only difference is that it calls the CheckQuote() method to connect to the database and retrieve the stock quote by raising the QuoteArrived event, which is dealt with in the Listener() method discussed previously:

```
private void MessageAssembler(byte [] Bytes, int offset, int count)
{
   for(int ByteCount = 0; ByteCount < count -1; ByteCount++)
   {
      if(Bytes[ByteCount] == 35) // Check for '#' to signal the end
      {
         QuoteArrived(this, StrBuilder.ToString());
         StrBuilder = new StringBuilder();
      }
      else
      {
         StrBuilder.Append((char)Bytes[ByteCount]);
      }
   }
}
```

Before we move on to the CheckQuote() method, let's briefly discuss the data source from which the server retrieves its quote information.

We need to start by creating a SQL Server database called StockDB, which will contain a single table called tbl_stocks with a structure as outlined in the following table.

> **Database setup and population scripts will be available at the Wrox Press web site http://www.wrox.com along with all the code from the book.**

Field	Description
Symbol	The actual stock symbol
Price	The last price of the stock
Change	The price change of the stock
Bid	The last bid price of the stock
Ask	The last bid price of the stock
Volume	The total traded volume of the stock in a trading session

That's all we need for the database so back to the code and the CheckQuote() method. The CheckQuote() method resides in the main form of the application and is called by the local event handler when the QuoteArrive() method is triggered. The role of this method is to make a connection to the database, query it to retrieve the quote information, and pass the data back to the client. You can use the SqlConnection control in Visual Studio .NET and follow the wizards to generate a connection string to the database, or you can simply instantiate the SqlConnection class, which resides in the System.Data.SqlClient namespace, and manually assign it a connection string, as shown here:

250

```csharp
private void CheckQuote(QuoteClient sender,
    string stockSymbol)
{

    // Connection string using SQL Server authentication
    SqlConnection SqlConn =
        new SqlConnection("Initial Catalog=StockDB;" +
        "Data Source=(local);User ID=sa;Password=");
    // Alternative Connection string using Windows Integrated security
    // SqlConnection SqlConn =
    //    new SqlConnection("Initial Catalog=StockDB;" +
    //         "Data Source=(local);Integrated Security=SSPI");

    string SqlStr =
        "SELECT symbol, price, change, bid, ask, volume " +
        "FROM tbl_stocks WHERE symbol='" + stockSymbol + "'";

    SqlCommand SqlCmd = new SqlCommand(SqlStr, SqlConn);

    try
    {
        SqlCmd.Connection.Open();
        int Records = 0;
        StringBuilder TempString = new StringBuilder();

        SqlDataReader sqlDataRd = SqlCmd.ExecuteReader();

        while(sqlDataRd.Read())
        {
            for(int FieldCount = 0; FieldCount <= 5; FieldCount++)
            {
                TempString.Append(
                    sqlDataRd.GetValue(FieldCount).ToString() + ",");
                Records += 1;
            }
        }
        if(Records == 0)
        {
            sender.send("-1#");
        }
        else
        {
            TempString.Replace(",", "#", TempString.Length - 1, 1);
            sender.send(TempString.ToString());
        }
    }
    catch(SqlException sqlEx)
    {
        object [] Message = {sqlEx.ToString()};
        Invoke(new InvokeStatus(this.AddStatus), Message);
    }
    catch(Exception ex )
```

```
    {
        object [] Message =
            {"Unable to retrieve quote information from the Database."};
        Invoke(new InvokeStatus(this.AddStatus), Message);
    }
    finally
    {
        // Close the Connection and the Data Reader
        if(SqlConn.State != ConnectionState.Closed)
            SqlConn.Close();
        sqlDataRd.Close();
    }

    }
}
```

We also need a SQL query to return all six fields of the table for the individual stock the client has requested:

```
string SqlStr =
            "SELECT symbol, price, change, bid, ask, volume " +
            "FROM tbl_stocks WHERE symbol='" + stockSymbol + "'";
```

Now that we have the necessary SQL string and connection, we can instantiate the SqlCommand and SqlDataReader objects to read the data from the database server.

Finally, we execute the query by creating a new SqlDataReader class instance, and setting it to the result of the ExecuteReader() method of the SqlCommand object. After that, we iterate through each of the columns of returned data and append the values into a StringBuilder object, with a comma in between each value. If ExecuteReader() does not return any rows of data, then we have to send a string with a value of -1 back to the user to notify them of the non-existence of the requested data. Otherwise, we replace the last comma in the string with a # (to indicate the end of string) and send it back to the client using the Send() method. Lastly, we must ensure that the database connection is closed once we're finished with it. As you can see, the code in the Finally clause checks to see if the connection to the database is still open. If so, it will close it.

The Send() method of the server application resides in the QuoteClient class and requires slightly different code from the same method in the client application. The main difference is that we now are going to send the message asynchronously back to the client:

```
public void send(string sendData)
{
    byte [] Buffer =
        System.Text.ASCIIEncoding.ASCII.GetBytes(sendData);
    lock(MyClient.GetStream())
```

```
    {
        MyClient.GetStream().BeginWrite(Buffer, 0, Buffer.Length,
            null, null);
    }
}
```

The `BeginWrite()` method is quite similar to the `BeginRead()` method in terms of interface. We first have to convert the string message to a byte array, which can be easily accomplished by using the ASCII class in the `System.Text` namespace. Once again, we have to lock the stream to ensure that other threads are not writing to it as well. That's all that is required to asynchronously write the data to the client.

Running the Applications

Build each project in its own instance of Visual Studio .NET and don't forget to include the configuration files that we created earlier in the same directory as the application executables.

OK, let's now run the compiled applications. We need to run the `StockServer.exe` first so that it will start listening for clients:

Now run an instance of the client application. As you probably recall, we had disabled all the UI controls on the form until the user successfully connected to the server. So, let's go ahead and click on the Connect item of the menu:

253

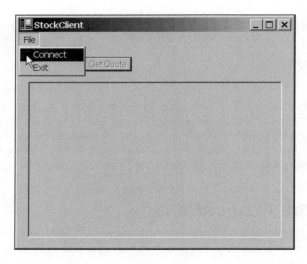

All the controls (except the Connect option of the menu) are now enabled and the ListView control has been instantiated with all the right columns. Enter a valid stock symbol from tbl_stocks table. Let's try CSCO, for example:

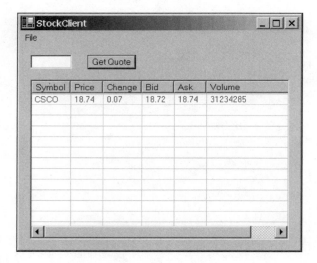

The Stock Server successfully returned a quote and, since the change amount is positive, the entire row appears in the color green. Let's go ahead and create a few other instances of the StockClient class and see if they all function correctly:

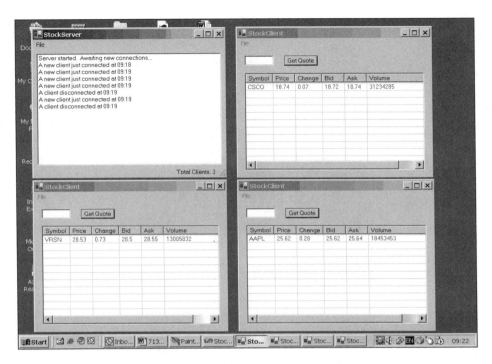

As you can see, the StockClient and the StockServer applications work very well with each other. The server keeps tracks of how many clients connect and disconnect and displays it in the ListBox. In addition, the multithreaded server is very easily able to handle numerous connections, as well as send and receive data in an asynchronous fashion. You can step through the code for both the client and the server application and get a better feel for the application workflow.

Summary

As we have demonstrated, it is straightforward to develop multithreaded network applications with the .NET Framework. Much of the plumbing and infrastructure has already been abstracted away in the form of a comprehensive and object-oriented set of classes. For even greater control over the network sockets, the System.Net.Socket class offers plenty of rich functionality. We also experienced how simple it is to use .NET's intrinsic support for asynchronous operations that run in the background worker thread without much code.

We hope that you found this book both helpful and enjoyable. The features in .NET give the C# developer more power than they have ever had – threading being just one of them.

C#

Threading

Handbook

Appendix

Support, Errata, and Code Download

We always value hearing from our readers, and we want to know what you think about this book and series: what you liked, what you didn't like, and what you think we can do better next time. You can send us your comments either by returning the reply card in the back of the book, or by e-mailing us at feedback@wrox.com. Please be sure to mention the book title in your message.

How to Download the Sample Code for the Book

When you log on to the Wrox site, http://www.wrox.com/, simply locate the title through our Search facility or by using one of the title lists. Click on Download Code on the book's detail page.

The files that are available for download from our site have been archived using WinZip. When you have saved the attachments to a folder on your hard drive, you will need to extract the files using WinZip, or a compatible tool. Inside the Zip file will be a folder structure and an HTML file that explains the structure and gives you further information, including links to e-mail support, and suggested further reading.

Errata

We've made every effort to ensure that there are no errors in the text or in the code. However, no one is perfect and mistakes can occur. If you find an error in this book, like a spelling mistake or a faulty piece of code, we would be very grateful for feedback. By sending in errata, you may save another reader hours of frustration, and of course, you will be helping us to provide even higher quality information. Simply e-mail the information to support@wrox.com; your information will be checked and if correct, posted to the Errata page for that title.

To find errata, locate this book on the Wrox web site (http://www.wrox.com/books/1861008295.htm), and click on the View Errata link on the book's detail page.

E-Mail Support

If you wish to query a problem in the book with an expert who knows the book in detail then e-mail support@wrox.com, with the title of the book, and the last four numbers of the ISBN in the subject field of the e-mail. A typical e-mail should include the following:

❑ The name, last four digits of the ISBN (8295), and page number of the problem, in the Subject field

❑ Your name, contact information, and the problem, in the body of the message

We won't send you junk mail. We need the details to save your time and ours. When you send an e-mail message, it will go through the following chain of support:

❑ **Customer Support**

Your message is delivered to our customer support staff. They have files on most frequently asked questions and will answer anything general about the book or the web site immediately.

❑ **Editorial**

More in-depth queries are forwarded to the technical editor responsible for that book. They have experience with the programming language or particular product, and are able to answer detailed technical questions on the subject. Once an issue has been resolved, the editor can post errata to the web site.

❑ **The Authors**

Finally, in the unlikely event that the editor cannot answer your problem, they will forward the request to the author. We do try to protect the author from any distractions to their writing (or programming); but we are quite happy to forward specific requests to them. All Wrox authors help with the support on their books. They will e-mail the customer and the editor with their response, and again all readers should benefit.

The Wrox support process can only offer support for issues that are directly pertinent to the content of our published title. Support for questions that fall outside the scope of normal book support is provided via our P2P community lists – http://p2p.wrox.com/forum.

p2p.wrox.com

For author and peer discussion, join the P2P mailing lists. Our unique system provides Programmer to Programmer™ contact on mailing lists, forums, and newsgroups, all in addition to our one-to-one e-mail support system. Be confident that the many Wrox authors and other industry experts who are present on our mailing lists are examining any queries posted. At http://p2p.wrox.com/, you will find a number of different lists that will help you, not only while you read this book, but also as you develop your own applications.

To subscribe to a mailing list follow this these steps:

❑   Go to http://p2p.wrox.com/

❑   Choose the appropriate category from the left menu bar

❑   Click on the mailing list you wish to join

❑   Follow the instructions to subscribe and fill in your e-mail address and password

❑   Reply to the confirmation e-mail you receive

❑   Use the subscription manager to join more lists and set your mail preferences

C#

Threading

Handbook

Index

Index

A Guide to the Index

The index is arranged hierarchically, in alphabetical order, with symbols preceding the letter A. Most second-level entries and many third-level entries also occur as first-level entries. This is to ensure that users will find the information they require however they choose to search for it.

G

H

I

J

L

S

T

C# Today

The daily knowledge site for professional C# programmers

C#Today provides you with a weekly in-depth case study, giving you solutions to real-world problems that are relevant to your career. Each one is written by a leading professional, meaning that you benefit from their expertise and get the skills that you need to thrive in the C# world. As well as a weekly case study, we also offer you access to our huge archive of quality articles, which cover every aspect of the C# language. www.csharptoday.com

C#Today has built up an archive of over 170 articles, in which top authors like Kaushal Sanghavi, Matthew Reynolds and Richard Conway have tackled topics ranging from thread pooling and .Net serialization to multi-threaded search engines, UDDI, and advanced techniques for inter-thread communication.

By joining the growing number of C#Today subscribers, you get access to:

- a weekly in-depth case study
- code heavy demonstration of real world applications
- access to an archive of over 170 articles
- C# reference material
- a fully searchable index

Visit C#Today at: www.csharptoday.com

WROX PRESS INC.

Wrox writes books for you. Any suggestions, or ideas about how you want information given in your ideal book will be studied by our team.

Your comments are always valued at Wrox.

Free phone in USA 800-USE-WROX
Fax (312) 893 8001

UK Tel. (0121) 687 4100 Fax (0121) 687 4101

NB. If you post the bounce back card below in the UK, please send it to:
Wrox Press Ltd., Arden House, 1102 Warwick Road, Acocks Green, Birmingham. B27 6BH. UK.

Registration Code : **82956B1Y5X2P8FP01**

C# Threading Handbook - Registration Card

Name _____

Address _____

_____

_____

City _____ State/Region _____

Country _____ Postcode/Zip _____

E-mail _____

Occupation _____

How did you hear about this book?

☐ Book review (name) _____

☐ Advertisement (name) _____

☐ Recommendation _____

☐ Catalog _____

☐ Other _____

Where did you buy this book?

☐ Bookstore (name) _____ City _____

☐ Computer Store (name) _____

☐ Mail Order _____

☐ Other _____

What influenced you in the purchase of this book?

☐ Cover Design
☐ Contents
☐ Other (please specify) _____

How did you rate the overall contents of this book?

☐ Excellent   ☐ Good
☐ Average   ☐ Poor

What did you find most useful about this book?

_____

What did you find least useful about this book?

_____

Please add any additional comments.

_____

What other subjects will you buy a computer book on soon?

_____

What is the best computer book you have used this year?

_____

Note: This information will only be used to keep you updated about new Wrox Press titles and will not be used for any other purpose or passed to any other third party.

Check here if you DO NOT want to receive further support for this book. ■

8295

8295

wrox
PROGRAMMER TO PROGRAMMER™